Seidlitz, Woldemar von

History of Japanese Colour-Prints

Seidlitz, Woldemar von

History of Japanese Colour-Prints

Inktank publishing, 2018

www.inktank-publishing.com

ISBN/EAN: 9783747711439

A HISTORY OF JAPANESE COLOUR-PRINTS

BY

W. von SEIDLITZ

WITH ILLUSTRATIONS IN COLOUR AND BLACK AND WHITE

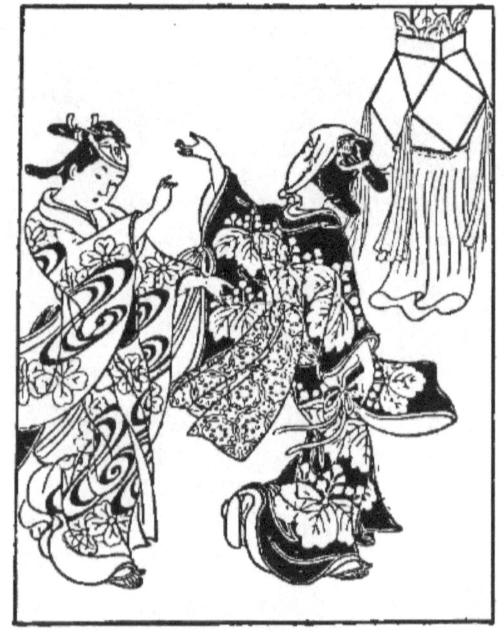

Translated by Anne Heard Dyer and Grace Tripler

LONDON
WILLIAM HEINEMANN
MCMX

PREFACE

THE first comprehensive survey of Japanese Wood-Engraving, Anderson's monograph in the *Portfolio*, appeared in 1895. The first attempt to write a history of this art was Strange's totally inadequate Japanese Illustration of 1897. Unfortunately, Strange had published before he was able to take advantage of the new light thrown upon his subject by Fenollosa, in his illuminating Catalogue of 1896, *The Masters of Ukiyoye*. The only remaining sources of information for the student were a number of scattered articles, monographs, exhibition catalogues, and sale catalogues, and it seemed to me that I might do a useful work by gathering together all this disjointed learning into a coherent whole. Japanese art has become an element in our European culture; it supplies certain needs of our age, and makes distinctly for its progress. But in order to appreciate Japanese Wood-Engraving to the full, we must know the interrelation between the various artists, and the successive stages of development in their art; we also require a criterion by which to test individual essays, that we may not rest content with weak and imitative work when the best is within reach. A survey of Japanese Wood-Engraving which would serve these ends was the task I accordingly set before me.

In any appreciation of Japanese art, everything depends on the standpoint adopted by the critic. If, as the majority of writers on this subject have been wont to do, we apply the European standard, we shall be led to hail the impressionistic artists of the nineteenth century, and notably Hokusai, as the protagonists of Japanese Wood-Engraving, for we are naturally affected by the affinities we discern between our own ideals and those of these artists, in whom the European leaven had begun to work. If, however, we try, like Fenollosa, to take the Japanese point of view, we shall recognise that Hokusai's real greatness lies in those very elements of his art which are most alien to us; and we shall see, further, that among the innumerable masters of the eighteenth century, there were many who were greatly superior to him. The art of the nineteenth century, with which alone the general public is to some extent familiar, has been given an importance far in excess of its deserts. It was at best an aftermath, and in some respects a decadence. I have therefore dealt with it somewhat summarily, whereas I have traced the developments of the eighteenth century, constituting a rich, a steady and a varied evolution, with all possible care and elaboration. My book is a provisional essay in the synthetic presentment of our knowledge of Japanese Colour-Printing, and a guide for those who require some direction in this, as yet by no means familiar field. I have made no attempt at exhaustive treatment, for any such a scheme would be impossible of execution, in the face of the contradictions which abound in the literature bearing on my subject in different countries. The collector must not look here for a treatise which will relieve him from the necessity of independent research or verification. Certain inequalities of the work may be explained by its genesis. Where the material on which I had to work was better prepared, as, for instance, in the case of Utamaro and Hokusai by the Goncourts, I was of course able to offer more. I have not shrunk from repetition on occasion, when it seemed necessary to emphasise notable facts or to impress important views on the reader. With few exceptions, I have relied upon Fenollosa's Catalogue in describing the development of Japanese Colour-Printing, and the characteristics of the individual artists. I trust I have in every instance rightly interpreted the opinions of this distinguished expert. Though it has been my earnest endeavour to keep the Japanese ideal in view, many may still object that the criticisms of artists such as Kiyonaga, Sharaku, and Hokusai are over-European in sentiment. In cases where there were materials for comparative judgment, and where it seemed likely to be fruitful of results, I have not hesitated to apply our own divergent standard occasionally.

My thanks are due to all who have helped me either in practical matters or with their advice, and in the first place to Messrs. Vever, Koechlin, Bing, and Gillot of Paris, Koepping, Liebermann, and Pächter of Berlin, and Oeder of Düsseldorf, who most kindly gave me leave to reproduce prints in their collections. Others to whom I am indebted are Messrs. Migeon of Paris, and Brinckmann of Hamburg, who supplied me with many valuable notes; and last, but not least, Mr. Shinkichi Hara, who was good enough to read through my text, to give me many precious hints and explanations relating to the prints, and briefly, to make this edition, imperfect though it may be, both more correct and more informing than its predecessor. The publishers of the English version of this work also owe acknowledgments to Mr. J. V. Scholderer of the British Museum for revision of the translation, and to Mr. Laurence Binyon for helpful suggestions in connection therewith.

CONTENTS

LIST OF ILLUSTRATIONS

IN COLOUR

BLACK AND WHITE

ERRATA

On plate facing p. 9 for Kujomitsu *read* Kiyomitsu
„ „ p. 22 for Shunti *read* Shunki
„ „ p. 68 for Byun *read* Bijin.

CHAPTER I

GENERAL CONSIDERATIONS

1. Character of Japanese Painting—2. Technique—3. The Opening Up of Japan

1. CHARACTER OF JAPANESE PAINTING.—Japanese painting, like its parent art, Chinese painting, differs from modern European painting in this, that it deliberately foregoes all means of producing an immediate illusion. It knows nothing of the third dimension, but confines itself to decorative effects in one plane; at the same time the extraordinarily developed powers of observation in the Japanese enable it to convey an unusual amount of life and spirit.[1]

With the Japanese space is not indicated by receding degrees of depth, and if represented at all, at least in the best period of their art, is not subject to the laws of a strict perspective, being merely indicated by a series of scenes, as on the stage. Men and objects in space are not rounded, and cast no shadows; shadows so cast being, according to the Chinese doctrine, something accidental and not worthy of representation at all. Objects do not throw back the sunlight in the form of high lights, nor do they reflect other objects in their neighbourhood; this is most conspicuous in the case of water, which shows neither reflections nor high lights. Hence anything in the nature of chiaroscuro, a homogeneous scheme of light altering

[1] See Madsen, p. 12 ff.; Brinckmann, i. 174–81.

A

all the colour-values in a certain direction, is out of the question, whether in representations of interiors or the open air. Moreover, the proportions of the figures are usually quite arbitrary, partly because of insufficient attention to this point, partly from deliberate purpose.

The immobility of the features is to be explained by the peculiar Japanese notion of decorum, which insists on a constantly equable seriousness of expression, one result being that the women have their eyebrows shaved off, their lips painted blue-red (with *beni*), and their faces thickly covered with powder—as is not unknown in Europe. But the bodies also generally appear in a state of repose bordering on rigidity; a slight flexure—to which the loosely flowing robes yield without effort—a scarcely noticeable inclination must suffice to express the character and psychology of the person represented: even in daily life the exchange of emotions leads to no bodily contact; hand-shaking is entirely unknown, kissing is not customary, any more than walking arm-in-arm. Even the dances of the Japanese offer few occasions for livelier movement; in general they are confined to pantomime, suggesting the emotions to be conveyed by the posture of the body, the movement of legs and hands, and especially by the expression of the eye. Hence there are few opportunities for foreshortening and overlapping.

To be sure, since the end of the eighteenth century some artists had begun to break through these rules, and endeavoured to apply the notions of perspective which they learnt from Europe, to give greater depth and unity to the landscape and greater expressiveness to the figures, and indeed certain masters of earlier periods, the book-illustrators Moronobu, Sukenobu, Shigemasa, had produced designs remarkable for movement and animation. But all of them adhered to certain significant characteristics, notably the absence of shadows and modelling, so that the

Gillot Collection, Paris

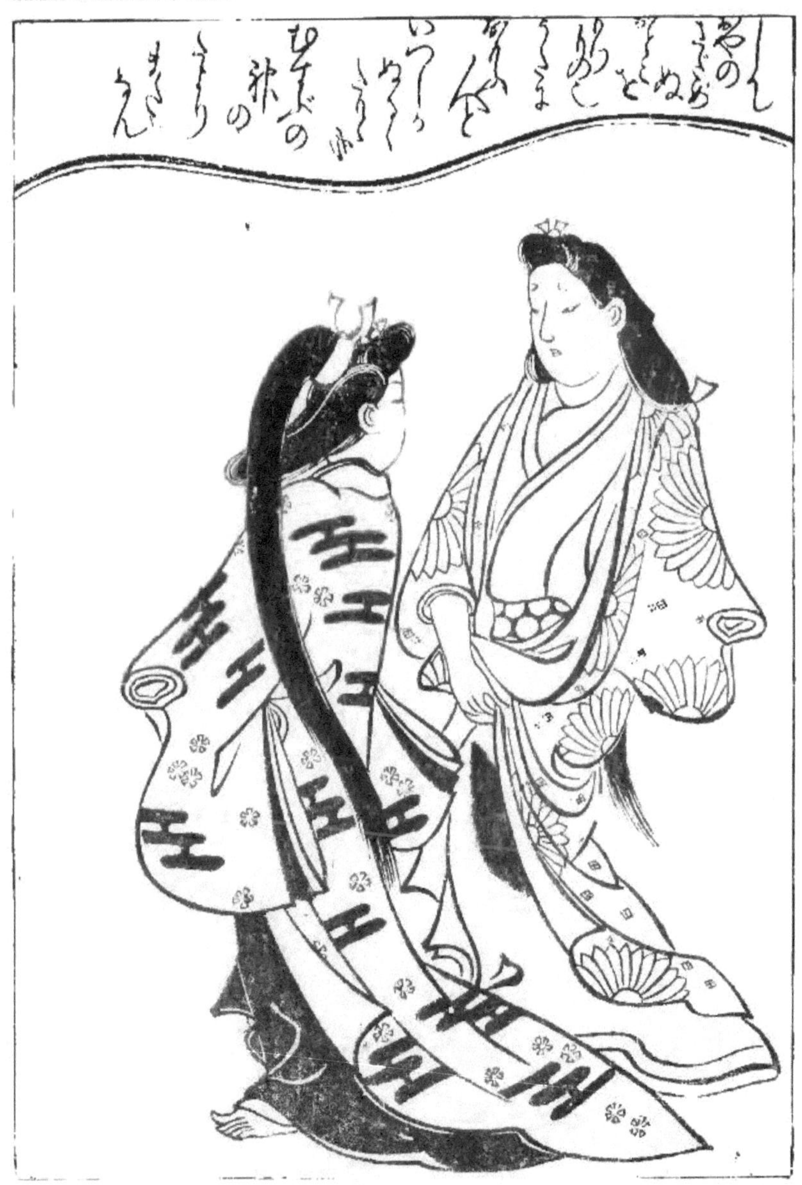

Moronobu: Two Court Ladies, an old one to the Right, a young one to the Left. *Book illustration.*

whole of Japanese art, even down to its most recent past, remains in its principles fundamentally opposed to modern European art.

In order to do justice to this peculiarity of Eastern Asiatic art, we must mentally revert to the point of view of such periods as have pursued similar decorative aims in contrast to the naturalistic aims predominating to-day. In the art of Egypt and of Greece up to Alexandrine times, in the Roman and Gothic periods up to the discovery of perspective in Italy and the invention of oil-painting in Flanders at the beginning of the fifteenth century, we meet with very similar endeavours. During all these periods the art of painting was absolutely conventional, and contented itself with certain more or less fixed types that altered only very gradually; yet by the aid of a careful and precise contour, nicely calculated masses of light and shade, and a harmonious colour-scheme, it succeeded in achieving effects at once decorative and monumental, and at the same time in imparting to the representation a varying content of strength, grace, or sublimity, according to the character of the subject. By this method no imitation of nature, no complete deception or illusion is either endeavoured or attained; and yet such an art ranks at least as high in our estimation as that of the realistic period in which we ourselves are living; not only so, but we see that the greatest artists of this very period, a Raphael, a Michaelangelo, a Da Vinci, when they were brought face to face with the highest problems of decorative art, sacrificed a great part of the literal truth which they might have attained in order to augment the grandeur, intelligibility, and impressiveness of their creations, thus approaching once more the simpler ideal of the past, though unable to achieve quite the same effects as the ancients.

The attempt has been made to account for the idiosyncrasy of Eastern Asiatic art on technical grounds inherent in the nature of the country, such as the flimsy construction of the houses, which are small and offer no solid wall-space for truly monumental painting to develop on, or the exclusive use of such elementary media as water-colour and Indian ink—or the position in which the artist works, according to the custom of the country, squatting on the ground and having his painting surface spread out horizontally before him; the consequence being that he only gets, as it were, a bird's-eye view of his picture, and that in the case of the usual long rolls, he can never overlook it as a whole, any more than the spectator can, who inspects the pictures in the same attitude. Now it is quite true that oil-painting, which might easily have brought about a revolution, as it did in Europe, remained unknown to the Eastern Asiatics. Again, had not the volcanic soil, which a succession of earthquakes keeps constantly trembling, prevented the erection of solid masonry, Japanese painting would probably have witnessed a more varied development. But its general character, tendency, and aims would have remained the same; the similarity of earlier developments in Europe and the adjacent countries proves it. National peculiarities of soil and custom may give rise to local variations, but cannot determine an art in its essence; for its roots lie in the national character, which creates its means of representation and technique according to its innate ideals, but conversely will not allow the main tendencies of its art to be determined by external factors.

The imitation of Nature is for the Japanese only a means to an end, not an end in itself. Mere virtuosity in this line does not move them to admiration; were it otherwise, we need only consider their renderings of birds, fishes, insects, and flowers to be sure that, with their splendid powers of observation, they might have achieved far more than they actually have done in this direction. On the contrary, Nature in their eyes merely furnishes forth the material from which the artist draws whatever he may require for the embodiment of his personal ideals and individual tastes. On these elements he works quite arbitrarily and with absolute freedom; for painting, after the Chinese precedent, is not regarded as a technical accomplishment or a craft, but ranks on precisely the same level as calligraphy, which is a liberal art and a pastime for people of rank and culture, far more dependent upon purity of feeling, sublimity of conception, exquisiteness of taste, in short, on individual creative power, than on any mere technical dexterity or skill. This estimate of painting as the peer of calligraphy explains not only the decorative character of Japanese art, the strict formalism of its style, the great importance which it attaches to the balance of light and dark masses, the subordination of colour to purely decorative ends, but also the wonderful freedom which Japanese art has always managed to retain in spite of its tendency to formalism. For the essence of calligraphy consists, according to Chinese ideas, by no means in mere neatness and regularity of execution, which might easily lead to stiffness and frigidity, but primarily in the most perfect solution of the artistic problem consistent with the greatest economy of means. The fundamental idea, in fact, here as in all the rhythmic arts, poetry, music, architecture, is that of play. The Japanese deliberately refrains from saying all that he has to say, from giving full plasticity to his figures or depth and breadth to his spaces, from breaking up and balancing his masses by symmetrical division or repetition; all this would merely draw him away from his goal and fetter the free activity of his imagination. All his efforts are directed towards restricting himself to what is essential to his purpose, employing natural forms in the full freedom and variety of their organic growth, making his contour lines as simple and expressive as possible (Madsen thinks he recognises the Japanese norm of beauty in the S-line) and striking an individual note in his choice of colours. As the objects to be represented are simple and the deficiency in means of realistic representation is skilfully made good by specially calculated effects of colour and technique, the conventionalism of this art, which works by mere suggestion, is very much less noticeable than in the productions of other peoples that are still on a low level of development.

To what extent all this is the result of conscious intention and design is well shown by the utterances of two Japanese who express the national sentiments on this subject. The first, Shuzan, wrote as follows in the year 1777:[1] "Among the various kinds of painting there is one which is called the naturalistic, in which it is thought proper to represent flowers, grasses, fishes, insects, &c., exactly as they appear in Nature. This is a special style and certainly not one to be despised; but since it only aims at showing the forms of things, without regard for the canons of art, it is after all merely a commonplace and can lay no claim to good taste. In the works of former ages the study of the art of outline and of the laws of taste was held in honour, without any exact imitation of the forms of Nature." The other authority, Motoori, the most eminent scholar and writer of modern Japan, says:[2] "Many kinds of style are now in vogue which profess to be imitations of the Chinese, and the representatives of which make a point of painting every object in exact accordance with Nature. This I conceive to be the so-called 'realistic' art. Now I make no question but that this principle is in itself excellent; but at the same time there is bound to be a certain difference between real objects and their pictorial presentation." He then enters more minutely into the difference between the Chinese and the Japanese points of view, and proceeds to set forth how the Chinese are realistic and ugly, how their landscapes are ill designed, sketchy where minute

[1] See Anderson, *Pictorial Arts*. [2] *Transactions*, xii. 226 ff.

TOYONÓBU

BOY DANCING WITH A HOBBY-HORSE

(Two-colour print)

BRITISH MUSEUM

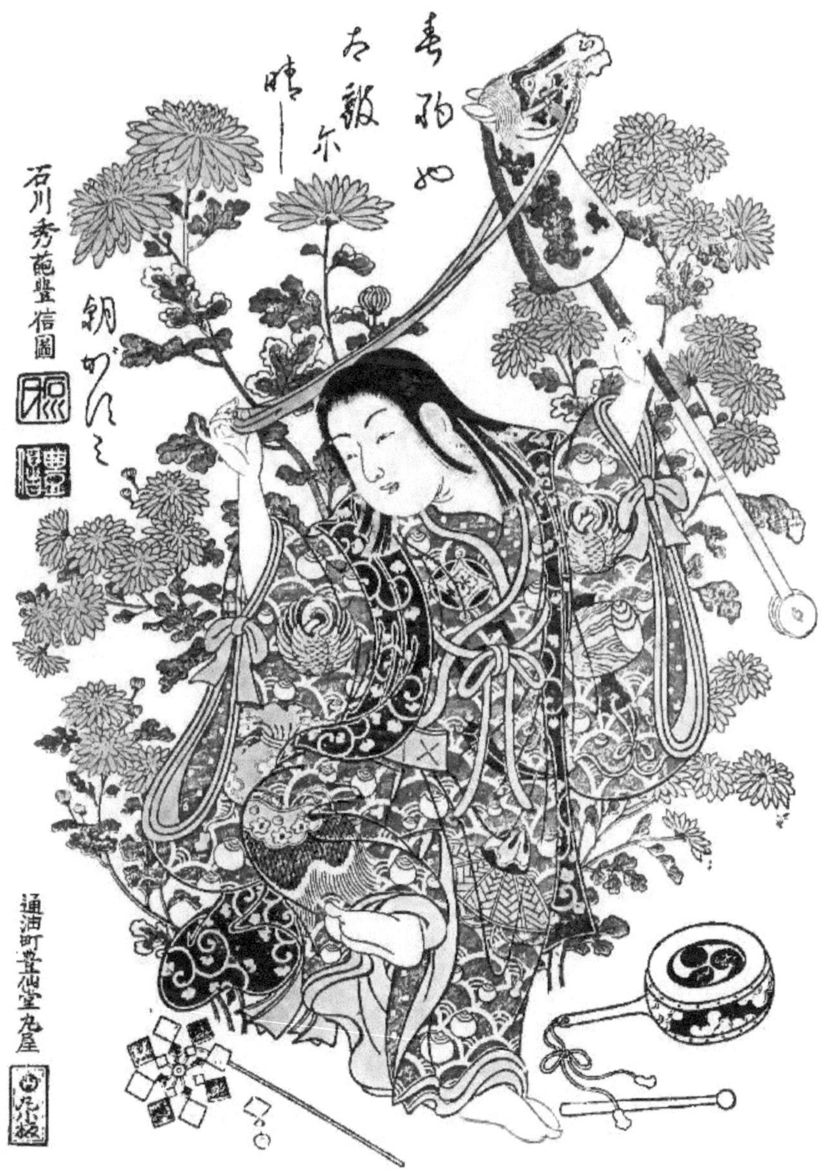
石川秀葩豊信圖
通油町豊仙堂丸屋

elaboration is called for, but overloaded with detail where a broad treatment would have been better—further, how their birds and insects do not look as though they flew or crawled, how their leaves and trees are not outlined—at least, since there exists no such dividing line between the object and its background in the real world he presumes that they will endeavour to imitate Nature by leaving out these lines. In conclusion he declares himself a strong supporter of Japanese conventionalism.

This is not the place to go into the exact nature of Japanese taste, for this only shows itself in its sharpest definition during the classic period of Japanese painting, which preceded the eighteenth century, the era of wood-engraving. It is the art of the nineteenth century alone which has influenced the most recent developments of European art and modified European taste, although for the Japanese it represents no more than a last phase, a second and less vigorous flowering, however new and subtle its manifestations. It will therefore be sufficient to confine our attention to its formal qualities—the decorative character of its design and its impressionistic point of view.

In these qualities lay predisposed the elements which Europe, during centuries of development along realistic lines, had almost entirely lost sight of. Only a return to the fresh and ever vivid hues of Nature could rescue us from the drab monotony of factitious monochrome; only a resumption of consciously decorative aims in design could rescue us from a method of figure-drawing whose results had as little distinction or individuality as a photographer's pose. Pioneers like Manet, Degas, Böcklin, and their followers were active in both directions. So long, however, as European art was still in the stage of preparation and apprenticeship, the Japanese wood-engravings could render but very limited services, nay, might even mislead into an entirely wrong track. To-day, on the other hand, as the goal of artistic endeavour grows gradually clearer, the time is at hand when they too may point the right way towards it, and are no longer in danger of being admired solely for their strange and exquisite subtlety—a subtlety eloquent of that wide-spreading deep-seated canker which afflicted eighteenth-century Japan just as it could have been observed to afflict contemporary Europe.

The differentia of Japanese art is just this, that into perfectly conventional forms is infused a content constantly fresh-drawn from Nature. The development of the European poster, which would be quite unthinkable without Japanese influence, is only the first step towards a renewal of European painting in all its branches, and especially of monumental painting. The solution after which we are reaching has been forming there for centuries. And, whatever the difference of circumstances, requirements, and race, the fact remains that Japanese art is far closer to us than the art of our own past, with which, however much we may admire its productions, we are completely out of touch. The transition to genuine Greek art, which after all is bound to remain our ideal, is easier by far to accomplish from Japanese art than from the romantic art which still endeavours to maintain its hegemony over us to-day.

2. Technique.—In considering the importance of the part which wood-engraving plays in the life of Japan, we must distinguish sharply between the productions of the decline, which began about 1840, and those of the preceding 150 years. The later productions, like our sheets of coloured illustrations, cater for the amusement of the masses: those of earlier periods, on the other hand, occupy a position midway between painted pictures and popular illustrations, much like the woodcuts and copper-plates of the European Renaissance. Here, as in Europe, the designs for the wood-engravings were supplied by professional painters, who either actually continued, or at any rate were fully competent, to follow concurrently their regular

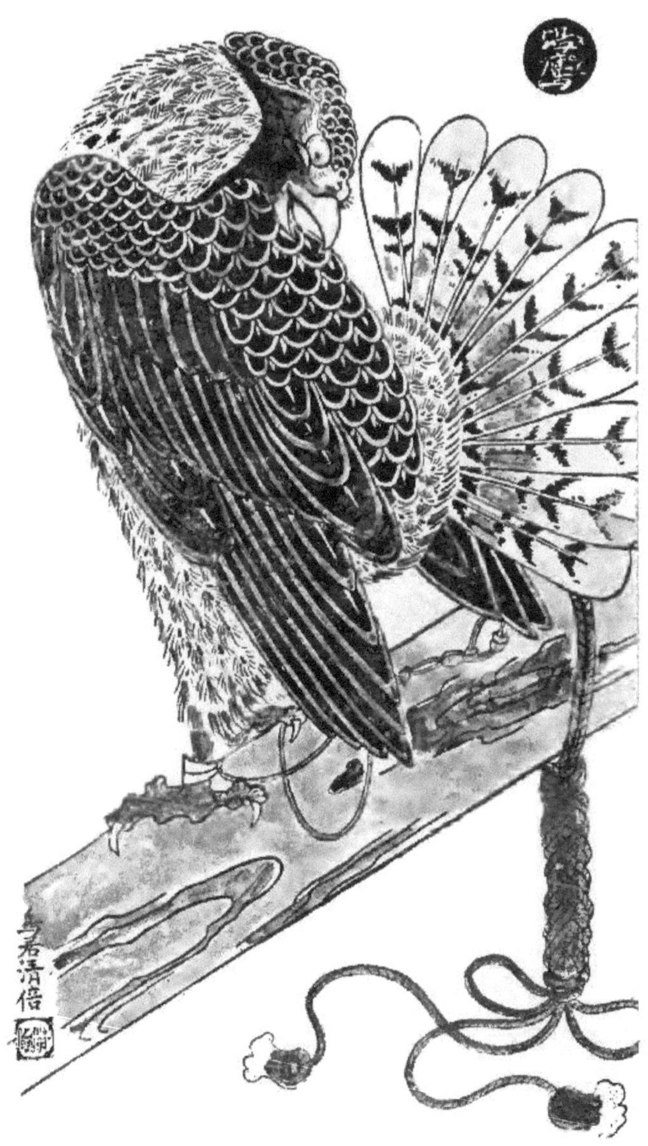

TORII KIYÓMASU : FALCON ON PERCH. A crested bird with outspread tail fastened to a bar by a cord, which terminates below in a heavy twist finished off by two tassels. Kakemono. Signed : Torii Kiyómasu. *Red and yellow predominate.*

avocation. But little trouble was commonly taken with the woodcuts intended for illustrative purposes, and the work was mostly ordinary black-and-white. But to colour-prints, whether published in book form or as single sheets, the artists devoted their utmost skill. Had not a considerable value attached to these productions even at their first appearance, comparatively large numbers of good copies would not have survived to the present day.

These woodcuts in fact were, just as in Europe, developed from the art of book-illustration and were not intended as a substitute for painted pictures; and to make this quite clear, it is necessary to indicate briefly the generically different shape in which Japanese woodcuts and Japanese pictures appear. Whereas the cuts of the good periods are as a rule approximately in large or small quarto, the pictures follow the Chinese model and are designed either (*a*) as kakemonos, long bands suspended vertically, or (*b*) as makimonos, rolls unwrapped horizontally. In the case of the kakemono, the true picture of the Far East, the painting itself is usually mounted on a frame of rich brocade. One, generally, or at most three, of these pictures are hung on the wall, invariably in the tokonoma or recess, where the censer, the flower-vase, and the candlestick are also to be found as a rule. The picture is changed from time to time, and on the occasion of a friend's visit or the reception of a distinguished stranger the most valuable and venerable piece in the collection is selected for exhibition. On the other hand, the long horizontal rolls called makimonos, which often measure fifteen yards or more, are usually spread out on the floor to be looked at. Originally they constituted the manuscript books of the Japanese and Chinese; then illustrations were added to the text, gradually encroached on it more and more, and finally ousted the letterpress altogether. The makimono was the favourite form of picture during the most brilliant period of the national art of Japan, when the ancient chivalry shone in full radiance and the Imperial court was at the height of its magnificence. All these paintings were executed in water-colours and were kept rolled up in a separate building (which was also the library), near the dwelling-house. Painting was also employed for the decoration of screens, fans, albums, and so forth.[1]

As to the Japanese book, it may be remarked that the extreme unpretentiousness of its exterior contrasts with that of the European book; it generally appears in the shape of a thin tract with a plain limp cover, either as an octavo approaching quarto size or else as a folio of medium dimensions. The sheets, which are ready cut to the size of the book, are folded only once, printed only on one side, and then sewn together with the fold outwards. The first page of the Japanese book is the last according to our method; the writing runs down the page in vertical lines, beginning in the right-hand top corner, and continuing towards the left margin. The pictures when in oblong form are continued across the pages of the book as it lies open; and although each half is enclosed in a border line, the careful adjustment of the sewing to the inner margin ensures continuity. Brinckmann points out that the Japanese, unlike many modern European printers, were never in the bad habit of inserting oblong pictures vertically in their books.[2]

The methods of producing the woodcuts are very similar to those formerly in vogue in Europe, the drawing in both cases remaining in high relief as the remainder of the block is cut away. Nowadays wood-engraving is usually treated like copper-engraving, and the lines of the drawing are incised. One essential difference, however, is this, that the Japanese never draw directly on the block itself, as was generally the case in Europe, but always make use of a sheet of thin or transparent paper,

[1] *Cf.* Madsen, p. 7 ff. [2] Brinckmann, i. 222–25.

which is then pasted face downwards on the block and furnishes the model for the wood-cutter to follow.

It has been much disputed whether the great European masters of wood-engraving, such as Dürer, Holbein, or Cranach, actually cut their own compositions; but there is now a general agreement that they did not do so as a general rule. It is true that a few later artists, *e.g.* Livens in the Netherlands, and Gubitz, who revived wood-engraving in Germany, practised the art of wood-cutting themselves—were in fact, to use the technical term, "peintres-graveurs"; but they were exceptions. In Japan not a single artist is known to have done his own cutting. They confined themselves to supervising and directing the wood-cutters, who in their turn carried out their employers' intentions so skilfully, readily, and intelligently that the technical part of the process could be entrusted to their hands with perfect security.

Something more must be said about the drawing, in view of its importance for the quality of the finished product. The artist conveys it to the paper, not by means of a pen or pencil as in Europe, but by means of a brush, either in outlines of the utmost delicacy and precision, to be filled in with colour where needed, or else in broad masses which receive no further contour, but on the contrary are the embodiment of the greatest imaginable freedom of artistic touch.[1] It is not necessary that the whole picture should be executed in either style throughout; the central portions may be precisely outlined, while other parts are broadly sketched in; indeed, this is more or less the general rule in the case of foliage, landscape background, and patterns on dresses. The style of precise contours is the traditional style, which was in vogue from the first beginnings of Japanese painting; the broader and sketchier manner is peculiar to the popular methods

[1] For drawing and writing the brush is held almost upright between the fore and second fingers: the whole arm moves, not the wrist. Since Indian ink cannot be erased, the artist is compelled to work with the utmost care and precision.

of representation which have developed since the sixteenth century. Although the Chinese method of Indian ink washing and shading has been taken up by many Japanese, even by whole schools in former centuries, it has very naturally received no recognition in wood-engraving, to which it is not applicable. Since the third dimension is never represented in Japanese pictures, no opportunity offered in xylographic drawings for rendering it with the brush, which is peculiarly well adapted to such work. Nor again is the Japanese artist under any temptation to represent relief by parallel or cross hatching—a process which, as Brinckmann rightly points out, is no less completely conventional than any other; only the reason lies not, as he supposes, in the use of the brush instead of a harder medium, for the Japanese with his brush can produce far finer and more uniform lines than the European draughtsman with his implements, as the absolute purity of Japanese outline conclusively proves. Rather is it the case that the Japanese has no occasion to employ strokes in this way. His attention being always concentrated on the decorative value of this design as a whole, what he principally aims at is, besides expressive contour, a suitable distribution and co-ordination of his colour-surfaces, more especially the proportion of dark, often unbroken black masses to lighter masses. Hatching, adds Brinckmann, is only found where the nature of the object to be rendered requires it, as in the case of a horse's mane, a tiger's skin, a peacock's tail, or the bark of a tree-trunk. To indicate modelling within the contour of an object treated as simply black, it is usual to leave white lines within the black mass.

When the drawing is thus completed on the paper, which is thin and of very hard surface, and if necessary may be rendered more transparent by a damp rub over or slight moistening with oil, it is pasted, as has been said, on the block.

The block generally consists of a species of very hard cherry-

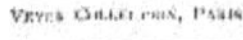

Vever Collection, Paris

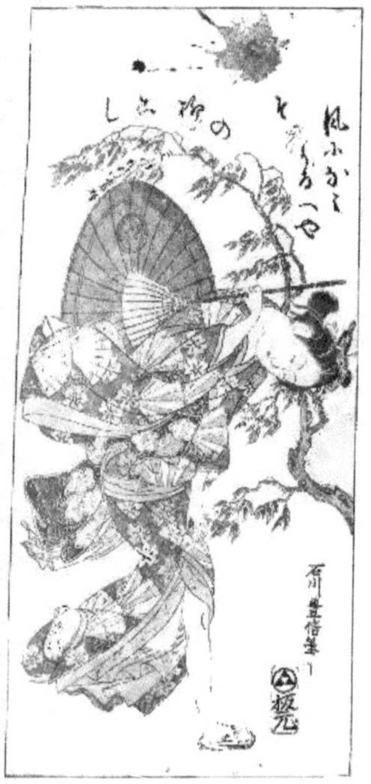

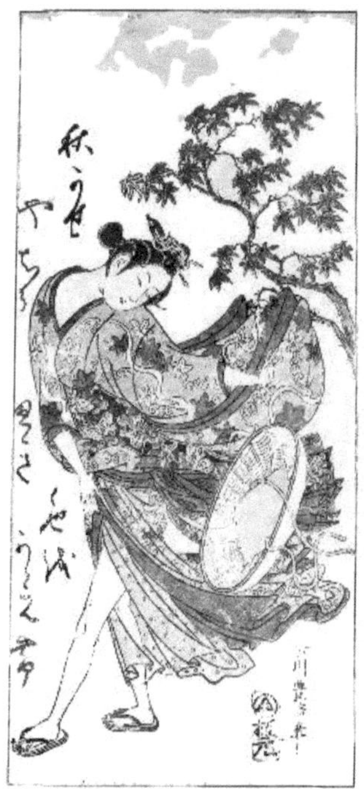

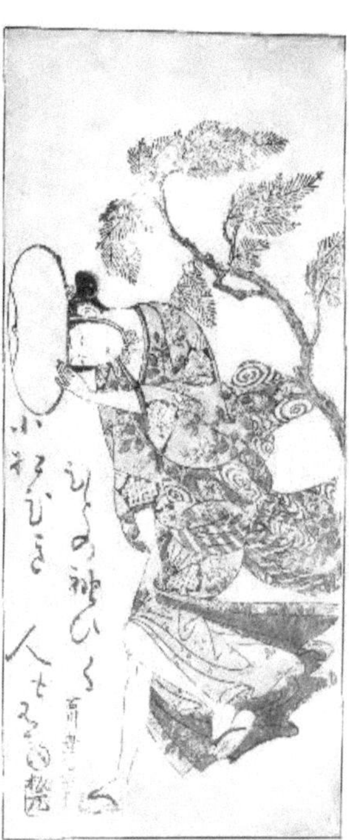

ISHIKAWA TOYONOBU: Three Geishas, representing the Spring Wind (on the right, with pine-branch), the Summer Wind (on the left, with willow-branch), and the Autumn Wind (centre, with maple-branch). Triptych. *Two colour print in pink and green*

wood or else box, and is always cut lengthwise, in the direction of the grain, and not across it, as in Europe. The cutting itself is done in this manner: first of all the two edges of the contour lines are cut along with a knife, and then the superfluous wood is removed with gouges of various shapes—formerly a knife was used for this too—so that nothing remains but the outlines of the drawing in relief. Finally, the fragments of paper still adhering to the wood are cleaned off and the plate is ready for printing. The impression itself is always taken off either with the hand, or else, as formerly in Europe, with a rubber. This is the secret of its clearness and beauty, as well as of the amazing fidelity with which it follows the artist's individual intentions. Special care is devoted to the selection of the paper, according to the quantity of colour which it is intended to absorb, and it is slightly damped before printing. In the case of some particularly fine old prints it is thick and of loose fibre, so that the design is deeply impressed on it; it has an ivory tone and a smooth surface. The colouring matter—always water-colour, not oil-colour—is mixed with a little rice-paste and carefully applied to the block with a brush; the paper is then laid upon the block and the back of it rubbed with the hand or the rubber. The most varied effects may be attained by varying the intensity of the colour, the proportion of water added to it, and the pressure applied to the print.[1]

In the case of colour-prints, the artist takes off as many copies of the outline-block as he intends to use colour-blocks, and then further outlines all the parts which are to be printed in the same colour on one of these copies in turn; these are then again cut on as many blocks as there are colours, one being generally put on each side of the same piece of wood,

[1] Tokuno, *Japanese Wood-Cutting*, 1894; Anderson, *Japanese Wood-Engraving*, p. 62 ff. (both with illustrations of the implements). See also Régamey, *Le Japon pratique* (1891).

and occasionally several side by side. The extraordinary development of this branch of the art is doubtless due to the fact that the cost of cutting rendered it essential to get the maximum of effect from a minimum number of blocks. This was more especially the case immediately after Harunobu in 1765 invented the colour-print proper with its unlimited number of blocks; and every artist was continually casting about for fresh expedients to reduce the number of his blocks, either by the partial superposition of different-coloured blocks in printing, or by special combinations of colours designed to modify the surrounding colours, and so forth. It is by no means always the case that a sheet is printed from just as many blocks as it has colours; for the printer has it in his power—indeed, this is the capital function of his art—to weaken his colours on any part of the block by rubbing off the pigment or to intensify them by adding more to it, so as to graduate his tones, or else to fuse one colour gradually into another and cover, whether simultaneously or successively, different parts of the block with quite different colours. The artists of the best period found five or seven colours sufficient for their needs; but in the case of the surimonos (see below), which were intended to be unusually sumptuous, especially at the beginning of the nineteenth century, the number often rises to twenty or even thirty.

Correct register of the various colour-blocks is secured by cutting an angle in the lower right-hand corner of the outline-block, and in the left-hand corner in the same straight line a slot. These two marks are cut in exactly the same place on all the other blocks, and in printing the sheets are imposed in such a way that their lower and right-hand edges fit exactly against these marks. By this simple device perfect adjustment of register is almost invariably secured.

Those of us who are only acquainted with modern prints, with their predominance of aniline red and blue, can form no conception of the colours of the fine old prints.[1] Chief among the reds are a bluish red made from vegetable juice, called *beni*, a brick-red oxide of lead, called *tan*, which has a slight tendency to become black, and the Chinese cochineal red. The yellow is generally a light ochre; red ochre was introduced later. The blue is either carbonate of copper or indigo; the green was originally light, dark green came in later. Intermediate colours such as grey, cold brown, and olive green were added in the course of time. Black has played an important part from the earliest period down to modern times; at first somewhat greyish, it afterwards gained full intensity and lustre, and was much employed in broad masses. Flesh tints are indicated almost imperceptibly, if at all; but in some prints *de luxe*, especially at the end of the eighteenth century, they are brought out by sprinkling the white ground that relieves them with finely powdered mother-of-pearl, called mica, which produces a soft sheen.

There is also a special class of colour-print in which the second block is employed merely to produce a grey intermediate tint, a third block being often added for flesh tints. These two-block and three-block prints, which are very delicate in effect, are used chiefly in facsimile reproductions of drawings, *e.g.* of Hokusai. Wash sketches in broad brushwork and few colours, like those of Korin, Masayoshi, &c., are reproduced in the same way, sometimes with blue and red from a second and third block.[2]

The effect of colour-prints may also be heightened by dry or blind impressions, which are cut on yet another block and render the patterns of dresses or stuffs, the details of distant landscapes, wave lines on water, occasionally the folds of light-coloured robes. They are seldom absent on carefully executed

[1] Tokuno, p. 226 ff.; Anderson, *Japanese Wood-Engraving*, p. 67 ff.

[2] Brinckmann, p. 229.

prints ; Shigenaga is said to have been the first to employ them, about 1730.

Colour-prints go by the name of nishikiye, *i.e.* brocade pictures; the general name for single-sheet prints is ichimaiye. Three further special kinds must be mentioned here. The first is the triptychs, consisting of a single design covering three folio leaves; pentaptychs are not unknown. The second is the long narrow strips which Fenollosa calls kakemonos. The best masters have been tempted to try their hand at this species, which at first sight would seem to give scope but for a single figure, and even that in none but quiet poses. Yet it has been employed with the happiest results for designs with two, three, or even more figures, side by side or one above the other, at rest or in active movement. Thirdly, there are the square surimonos, which art-lovers sent to each other as New Year's greetings, and which also served to convey congratulations or announcements on other occasions; their get-up was most luxurious, gold, silver, and various kinds of bronze toning, a profusion of colours and blind impression were lavished upon them.[1] Harunobu is said to have been the first to bring them into fashion, his prints dated 1765 being doubtless referred to; Hokusai and his pupil Hokkei produced a number of the very finest. A celebrated example of them is the series of seven designs by Shuntei, representing the seven Gods of Good Fortune in the shape of well-favoured and gorgeously robed ladies; these same seven gods entering harbour on their ship in the night between the second and third days of the New Year, is another favourite subject. Brinckmann has pointed out that two years, 1804 and 1823, are conspicuous for their large output of finely printed surimonos. The former was the first year of a cycle of sixty years, according to a system of computation borrowed from China, the seventy-fourth cycle, to

[1] Brinckmann, p. 291 ff.

VEVER COLLECTION, PARIS

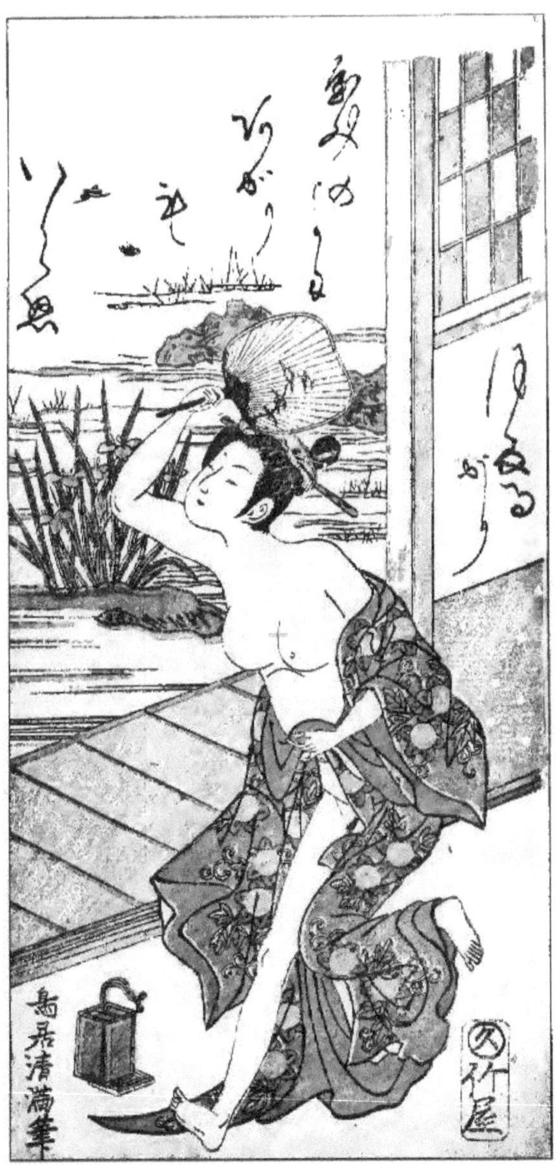

KIYÔMITSU: YOUNG GIRL CHASING FIREFLIES AFTER A BATH. An insect-trap on the floor. In the garden a pond with irises. *Three-colour print in grey, pink, and yellow.*

KOEPPING COLLECTION, BERLIN

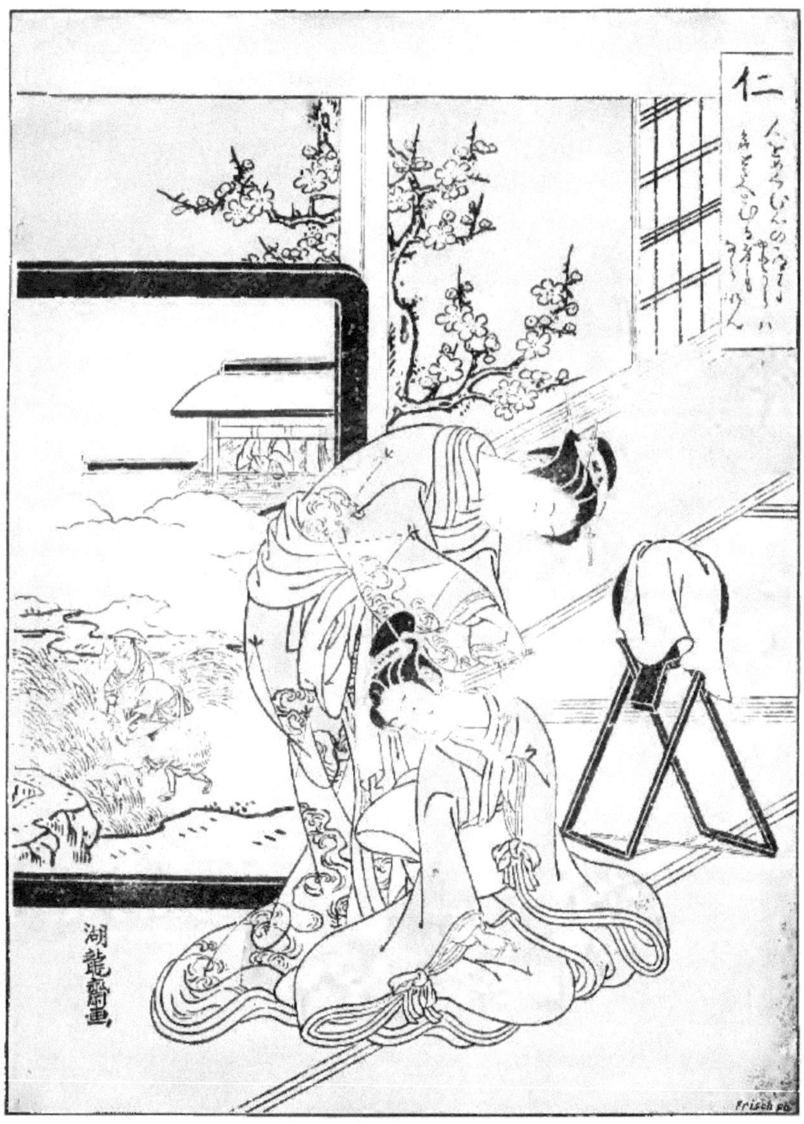

KORIUŠAI: A LADY CUTTING THE HAIR FROM THE NAPE OF HER YOUNGER SISTER'S NECK. On the screen a harvest scene, which a prince watches from his palace window. To the right a mirror on a stand; behind, a branch of blossom. The first of a series of five plates. *In grey and brown.*

be precise, and a year of the Rat, in terms of the short notation. The latter was the twentieth of the same cycle and a year of the Goat. "The year 1804, a time of general festivity and the development of Japanese social life in all its brilliance, witnessed the production of many surimonos, among them the most characteristic and elaborate of Hokusai. In 1823 competitions took place for the finest designs in New Year cards; art clubs and other societies, among them more especially the 'Society of Flower Hats,' vied with one another in the invention of original and elegant surimonos, and gave commissions to the artists."

3. The Opening Up of Japan.—Since the *coup d'état* of 1868 Japan is open to Europeans. Indeed, so great was the zeal of the Japanese to turn the achievements of European civilisation to their own profit, that at first they took over in indiscriminate haste good and bad alike, science and industries as well as the ugly and the "cheap and nasty," and were misled into despising their own best possessions—their national costume and their national art. It is true that they began remarkably soon to realise their folly in this respect; still, the interval was long enough to enable European and American dealers and collectors to get into their hands a considerable proportion of the national art-products, and among them particularly colour-prints. Our knowledge of this branch of art is based upon collections so formed. Since the Museum of Japanese Art was founded in Tokio, the ancient Yedo, in the seventies of last century, and retrospective exhibitions held there have once more opened the eyes of the Japanese to the merits of their indigenous art, prices have risen so enormously that scarcely anything of special value is likely henceforward to leave Japan.

From the time that a Portuguese mariner in 1542 first touched its shore, Dai Nippon, the "Empire of the Rising Sun," with its 3800 islands, which Columbus had set out to

B

seek and found America in its stead, has always been the object of European longing, cupidity, and admiration.[1] To this day the traveller returning from Japan is full of enthusiasm for the beauty of the landscape, the mildness of the climate—in the temperate tracts round Yedo there is scarcely a month of snow and ice—the skill and industry of the men, the charm and modesty of the women. To be sure, the first European settlers contrived to make themselves thoroughly detested. The Jesuits, who landed there in the sixteenth century, formed business connections, imported guns and tobacco, and made numerous proselytes. When their behaviour became too imperious, the natives rose against them; in 1638, 40,000 Christians of Japan are said to have suffered martyrdom. 1597 was the date of the first Dutch East India voyage, 1602 that of the foundation of the Dutch India Company. Relations between the Europeans and Japan were principally maintained from the island of Deshima; but soon after, feeling against the foreigners in the country began to run high. From 1641 onwards Japan remained accessible only to the Dutch and to the Chinese, and that only through the port of Nagasaki; from this port were shipped a special class of goods, notably porcelain, which was manufactured, specially for export, in immense quantities according to recognised patterns, particularly in the western province of Hizen, where Nagasaki is situated. 45,000 pieces of such porcelain were thus brought to Europe in 1664 on board of eleven Dutch vessels; and a large trade was similarly done in lacquered furniture during the seventeenth century. No European, however, was allowed to enter the country.[2]

The middle of the nineteenth century witnessed radical changes in this respect. In 1853 a commercial treaty was

[1] Madsen, pp. 1–6.

[2] O. Münsterberg, *Japans auswärtiger Handel von 1542–1854* (Stuttgart, 1896), ch. v.

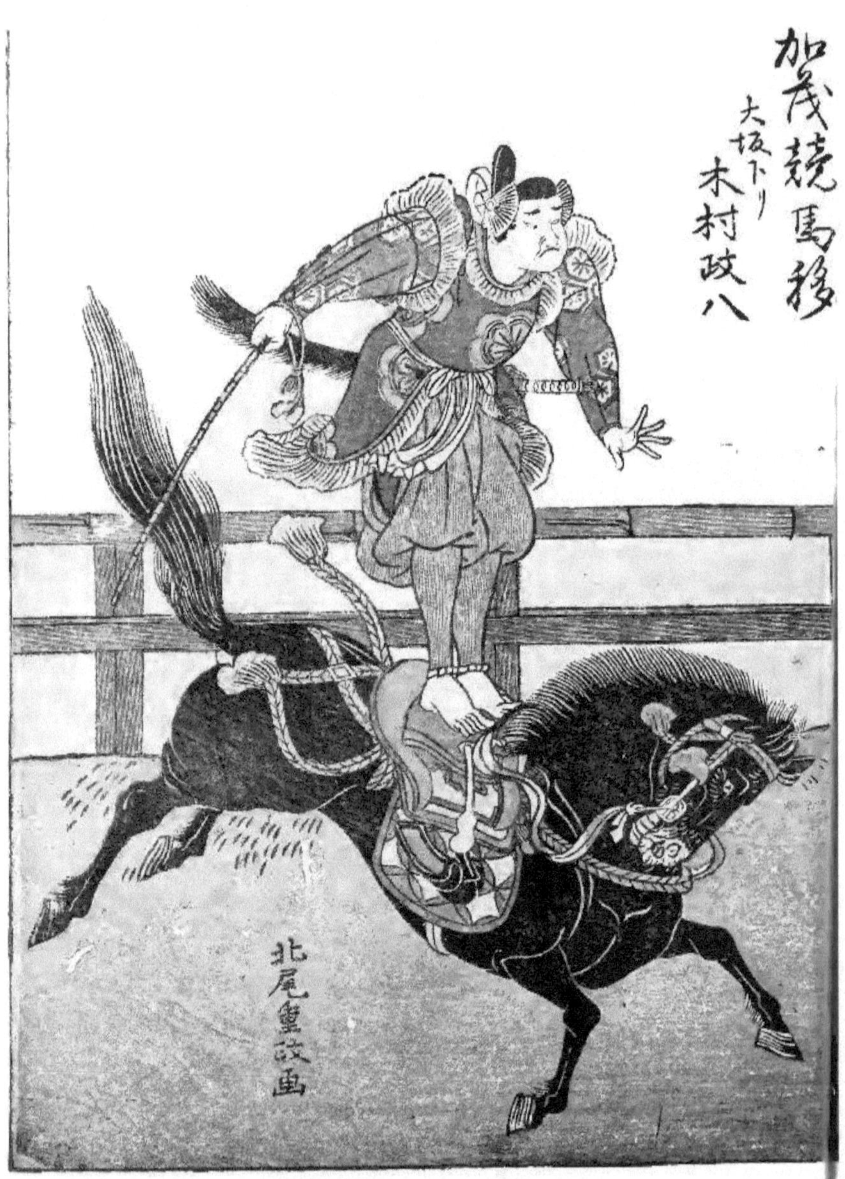

SHIGÉMASA: A CIRCUS SCENE IN THE OPEN AIR. A parody of the aristocratic races at Kamó (Kiotc
hence the court costumes and bearskin sword-sheaths. Dresses violet and pale pink. Diptych.

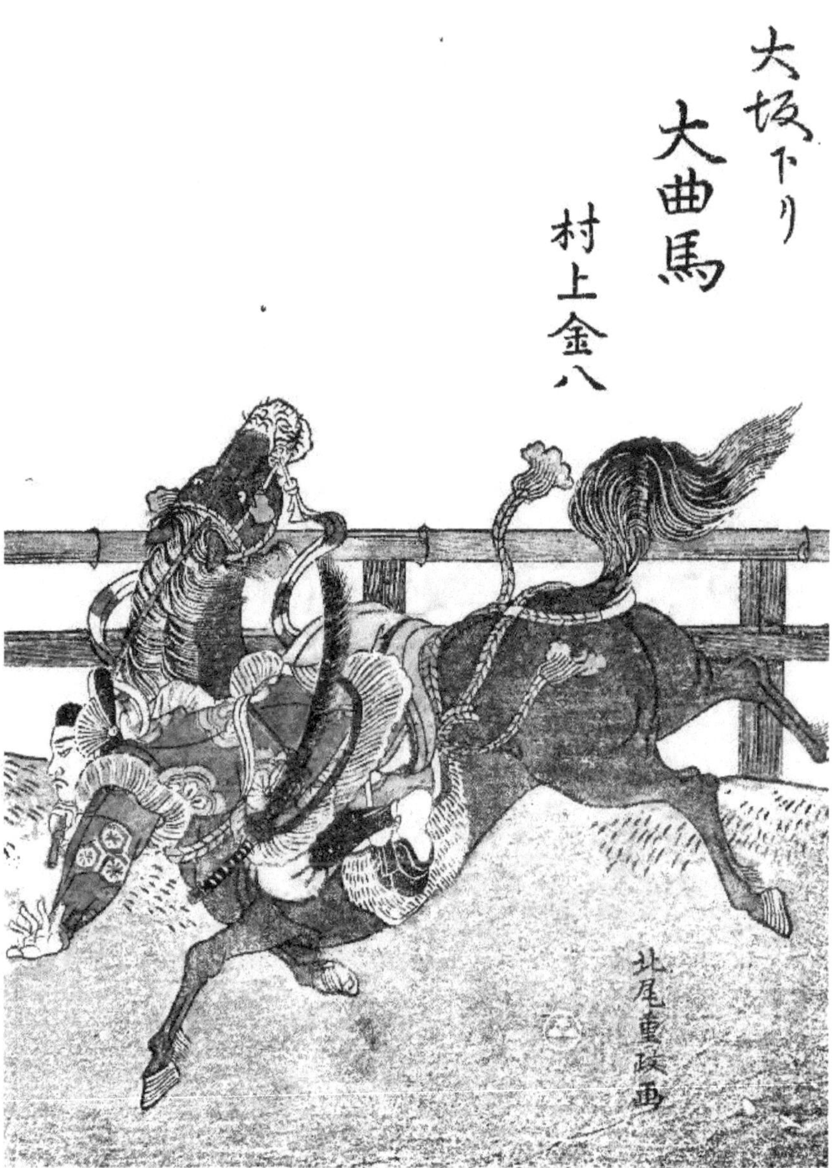
大坂下り
大曲馬
村上金八
北尾重政画

concluded with the United States of America, and was followed by similar treaties with England, France, and Russia. In 1860 the first Japanese embassy embarked for Europe. In 1890 a constitution was granted to the nation.

Japanese woodcuts first attained more general recognition at the Great Exhibition of 1862 in London; the first colour-prints reached Paris by way of Havre in the same year. Artists like Stevens, Whistler, Diaz, Fortuny, Legros, who were then living in Paris, gave them their immediate attention;[1] they were followed by Manet, Tissot, Fantin Latour, Degas, Carolus Duran, Monet, and people began collecting the prints. The etchers Bracquemond and Jacquemart, and Solon of the Sèvres porcelain works, became the most ardent champions of this latest discovery in art. Travellers like Cernuschi, Duret, Guimet, Régamey, returned from Japan and began to sing the praises of the country and the country's art. Writers like Goncourt, Champfleury, Burty, Zola; publishers like Charpentier; craftsmen like Barbedienne, Christofle, Falize, joined in the movement. Villot, the former keeper of the Louvre pictures, was one of the first to found a collection of Japanese woodcuts. The ground having been so thoroughly prepared, the Paris Exposition of 1867 became in due course the scene of a decisive triumph for the art of Japan. Soon afterwards the Parisian friends of Japan formed themselves into a Société du Jinglar, which met once a month at a dinner in Sèvres.

Since the revolution of 1868, by which the Mikado's residence was transferred from the old inland capital Kioto to Tokio, till then known as Yedo, on the south coast, formerly the seat of the Shoguns (the ruling military commanders), and the feudal lords were gradually abolished, Japan, and consequently Japanese art, has been entirely open to Europeans.

[1] E. Chesneau, "Le Japon à Paris" (*Gazette des Beaux Arts,* 2me pér., tom. xviii. (1878), pp. 385, 841 ff.).

The recognition of Japanese art was still further advanced by the Universal Exhibitions of 1873 at Vienna and of 1878 at Paris, which latter had been organised by Wakaí, a man with a thorough knowledge of his country's art.

It was not until the middle of the seventies that a museum was founded in Japan itself, at Tokio, for collecting the productions of the ancient art. The first director was Yamataka. When a second museum was founded in the middle of the eighties at Nara, Yamataka exchanged his position for the directorship of Nara, the Tokio Museum being allotted to the former Director-General of Art and Science, who subsequently became Viscount Kuki. And when the year 1895 saw the foundation of a museum in the old imperial city of Kioto, near Nara, Yamataka took over the superintendence of both together.

The most important collections formed in Europe are as follows:[1] Siebold brought home in 1830 his collection of some 800 paintings (kakemonos), which is now preserved at Leyden. Sir Rutherford Alcock exhibited his collection of wood-engravings at the London Exhibition of 1862, and John Leighton delivered an address upon it in the Royal Institution on May 1, 1863; it seems, however, to have consisted principally of works of the nineteenth century. In 1882 Professor Gierke, of Breslau, exhibited his collection of paintings, some 200 pieces, in the Kunstgewerbemuseum at Berlin; this collection was acquired for the Prussian State, which already possessed, in the Berlin Print-Room, a small collection of illustrated works formed by an earlier owner. Professor Gierke was prevented by his death, which took place in the eighties, from taking in hand the history of Japanese painting which he had planned. In the same year (1882) the British Museum acquired, for £3000,[2] a collection

[1] *Cf.* Madsen, pp. 9–11. Ph. Fr. von Siebold was surgeon to the Dutch Indian army in Japan from 1823–30.

[2] Anderson had had the assistance of Satow, the Japanese secretary of the English embassy at Yedo, in the formation of his collection.

KIYÓNOBU

KUMAGAI NO JIRO AT THE BATTLE OF ICHINOTAMI
(TAN-YÉ)

BRITISH MUSEUM

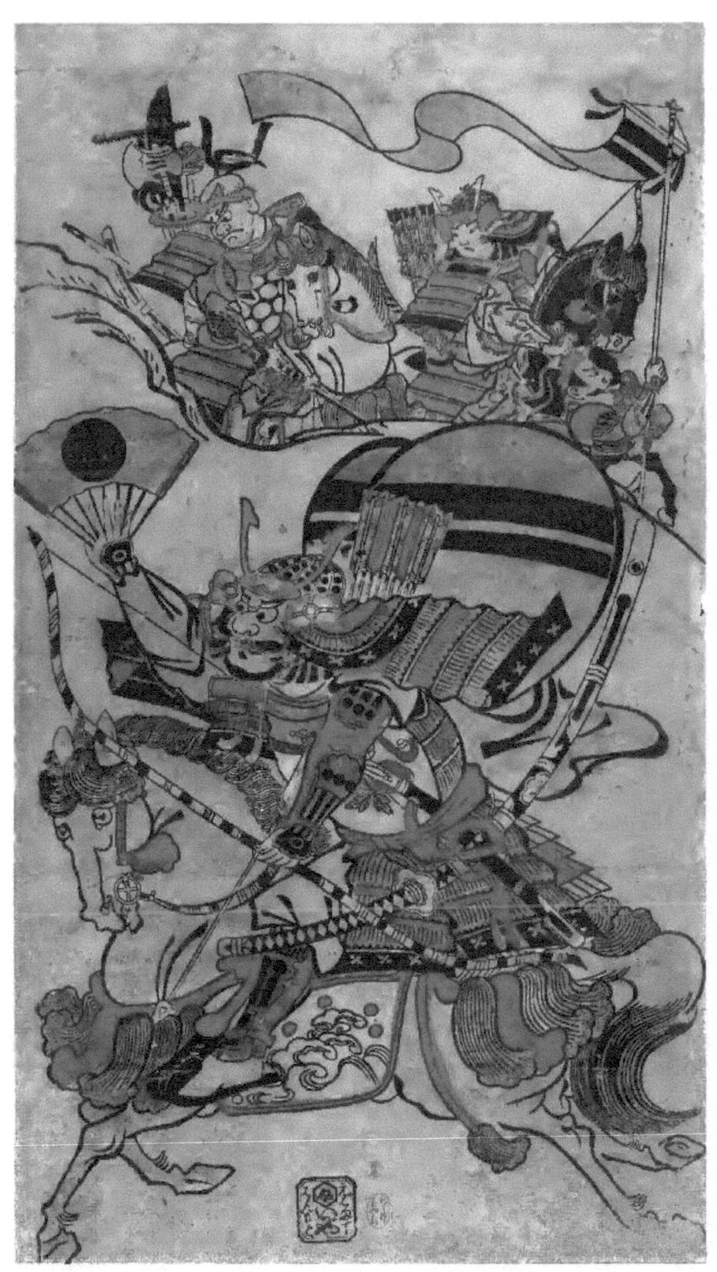

of about 2000 Japanese and Chinese paintings and prints from Dr. William Anderson, who had been Professor of the Medical Academy in Tokio. In Paris, where many private collections of Japanese woodcuts came into being—those of Gonse, Bing, Vever, Gillot, Manzy, Rouart, Galimart, and latterly of Koechlin and Count Camondo, deserve special mention—a retrospective exhibition of Japanese art was organised as early as 1883, and was followed by a special exhibition of Japanese wood-engravings in 1890. At the beginning of 1893 a select exhibition of Hiroshige's landscapes took place in Durand Ruel's rooms. The Oriental department of the Louvre possesses a small collection of wood-engravings, and so do the Musée Guimet and the Bibliothèque Nationale (the Duret Collection of illustrated books). A society of Japanophiles (Japonisants), consisting of about fifteen members, holds monthly meetings in Paris. In February 1909 the first exhibition of Japanese wood-engravings in private possession was held in the Musée des Arts Décoratifs, and was to be followed by a series of others. In 1888 the Burlington Fine Arts Club organised an exhibition of Japanese wood-engravings; a Japan Society was founded; among English private collections that of Edgar Wilson is specially highly praised. The largest collection, however, is in the possession of the Museum of Fine Arts in Boston, viz. some 400 screens, 4000 paintings and 10,000 prints, which were brought together by Professor Ernest Francisco Fenollosa, who stayed twelve years in Japan as Imperial Japanese Fine Arts Commissioner, and many years of whose life were spent in describing and classifying these treasures. He also possessed a noteworthy collection of his own. Among other American collections, those of Charles J. Morse and Fred. W. Gookin in Chicago and of George W. Vanderbilt in New York may be mentioned. Mr. Francis Lathrop, of New York, possesses about 170 Kiyonagas. Dr. Bigelow had exhibited a rich collection of Hokusais in Boston. In Germany there are the collections of Koepping and Liebermann in Berlin, Stadler in Munich, Frau Straus-Negbaur in Frankfort-on-the-Main, Jaekel in Greifswald, Moslé in Leipzig, Oeder in Düsseldorf, Grosse in Freiburg (Breisgau), and others. The Berlin Print-Room has already been mentioned; the library of the Berlin Kunstgewerbe-museum has since then tended more and more to become the central repository of State collections; the Museum für Kunst und Gewerbe at Hamburg possesses a number of prints, &c.; and in the Print-Room at Dresden the foundations of a collection have been laid.

Hand in hand with this increased interest in and comprehension of Japanese wood-engraving has gone the development of the literature on this subject (see the bibliography at the end). The first detailed and trustworthy information about the history of Japanese painting, as well as some notes on the history of the wood-engraving, was supplied by Anderson in his pioneer work, *A History of Japanese Art*, published in the *Transactions of the Asiatic Society of Japan*, vol. vii. (1879); his work *de luxe*, *The Pictorial Arts of Japan*, in two volumes (1886), and the Catalogue of his Japanese and Chinese paintings acquired by the British Museum, which appeared at the same time, further elaborate the same material, while his *Japanese Wood-Engraving*, published in the May number of the *Portfolio* of 1895, condense it into a short, popular outline of the history of Japanese wood-engraving. Professor Gierke followed Anderson in 1882 with the Catalogue of the exhibition of his collection in the Berlin Kunstgewerbemuseum, which contained a short but comprehensive and exhaustive and quite independent survey of the history of Japanese painting; and in the following year came Gonse's *L'Art Japonais*, a monumental work in two volumes, the first comprising painting and wood-engraving, in which a first and not unsuccessful attempt was made to comprehend

Koechlin Collection, Paris

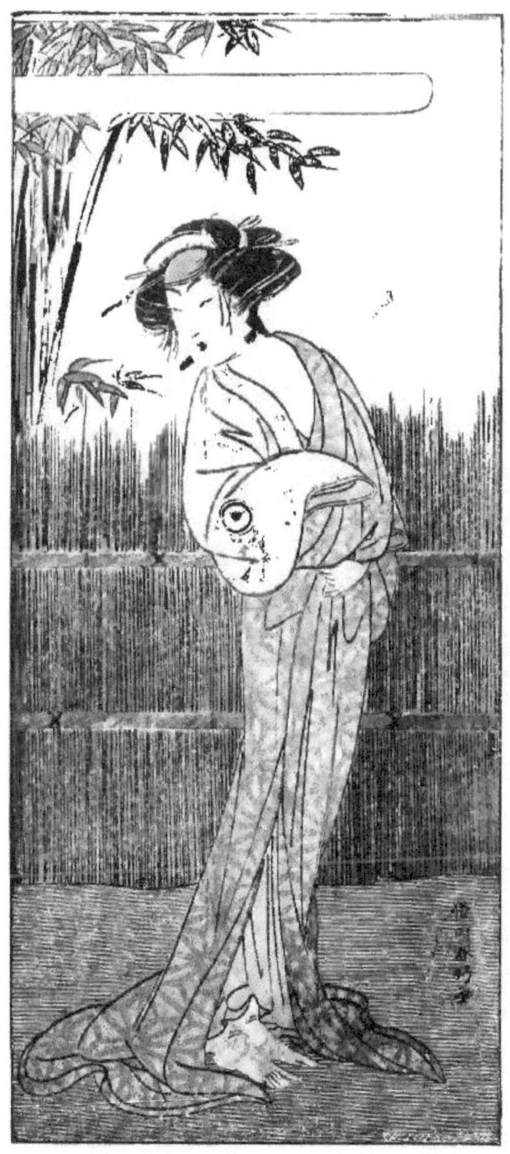

SHUNTI: An Actor in a Female Part.
Bamboos behind the rice-straw fence.

Japanese art from the artistic point of view. Gonse's work was criticised by Fenollosa in his *Review of the Chapter on Painting in Gonse's "L'Art Japonais"* (published first at Yokohama, then at Boston in 1885), and his energetic repudiation of Gonse's (the current) gross over-estimate of Hokusai's importance in Japanese art was doubtless very well justified; at the same time Fenollosa was bound to admit that Gonse had succeeded admirably in making clear to his readers the genius of Korin, an artist whose qualities are by no means obvious to Western appreciation. Incidentally Fenollosa's far wider and deeper knowledge of both the pictures and the authorities enabled him to contribute a most stimulating survey of the chief points of view from which the development of Japanese painting is to be judged. In 1885 appeared a little book, entitled *Japansk Malerkunst*, by the Danish artist Madsen (pronounced Massen). The language in which it is written has unfortunately prevented it from attaining anything approaching the publicity which it deserves for its thoroughness, its *esprit*, its genuinely artistic feeling, and its fascinating style. Even now a translation of it would constitute the best possible introduction to the genius of Japanese art.

In 1889 a new generation appeared on the scene, which began to extend the province thus lately thrown open by painstaking researches on single points. Brinckmann in Hamburg published the first volume of his work on the Arts and Crafts of Japan, in which he offered a complete survey of the history of Japanese painting and wood-engraving, but still evinced a tendency to take his stand beside Gonse rather than Fenollosa, particularly in his over-estimate of Hokusai. Bing in Paris laboured zealously to familiarise the widest circles with Japanese art through his *Japon Artistique*, a splendidly got-up production, which appeared in three languages, French, German, and English, and by its excellent illustrations made possible a profound insight into the Japanese point of view. The series of reproductions entitled *Kokkwa*, which has been publishing at Tokio since 1890, attains a much smaller circulation, in spite of being far more magnificent still. The catalogues of the Paris Loan-Exhibition in the École des Beaux-Arts, 1890 (with an introduction by Bing), and of the Burty Collection, 1891 (with an introduction by Leroux), competently initiated the collectors of Paris into the province of the wood-engravings, hitherto unknown to all but a few. In 1891 Goncourt published his book on Utamaro, the first monograph devoted to a Japanese artist, and followed it up in 1896 by his book on Hokusai, which provoked a good deal of recrimination, as it was based on materials which a Japanese had originally collected on commission for Bing, but fraudulently disposed of a second time, whereby Bing was anticipated by Goncourt and prevented from carrying out his plan of publishing a monograph on Hokusai. Muther's widely read *Geschichte der Malerei im XIX. Jahrhundert* contributed its share to popularising the Japanese wood-engraving in Germany, but, owing to the shortness of the chapter in question and the smallness of the reproductions, could convey no more than a very general notion of the subject. A better result was achieved by Anderson's popular work on *Japanese Wood-Engraving* (*Portfolio*, 1895), with its very serviceable illustrations.

Finally, the beginning of the year 1896 saw the knowledge of Japanese wood-engraving enter on a fresh and presumably final phase by the publication of Fenollosa's exhaustive Catalogue of the "Masters of Ukiyoye" Exhibition in New York, a work which combines full mastery of the materials with artistic freedom, vigour of style, and the minutest penetration into every detail. This catalogue, which expressly excludes all historical information, comprises a description of some 400 selected wood-engravings, arranged in their presumable chrono-

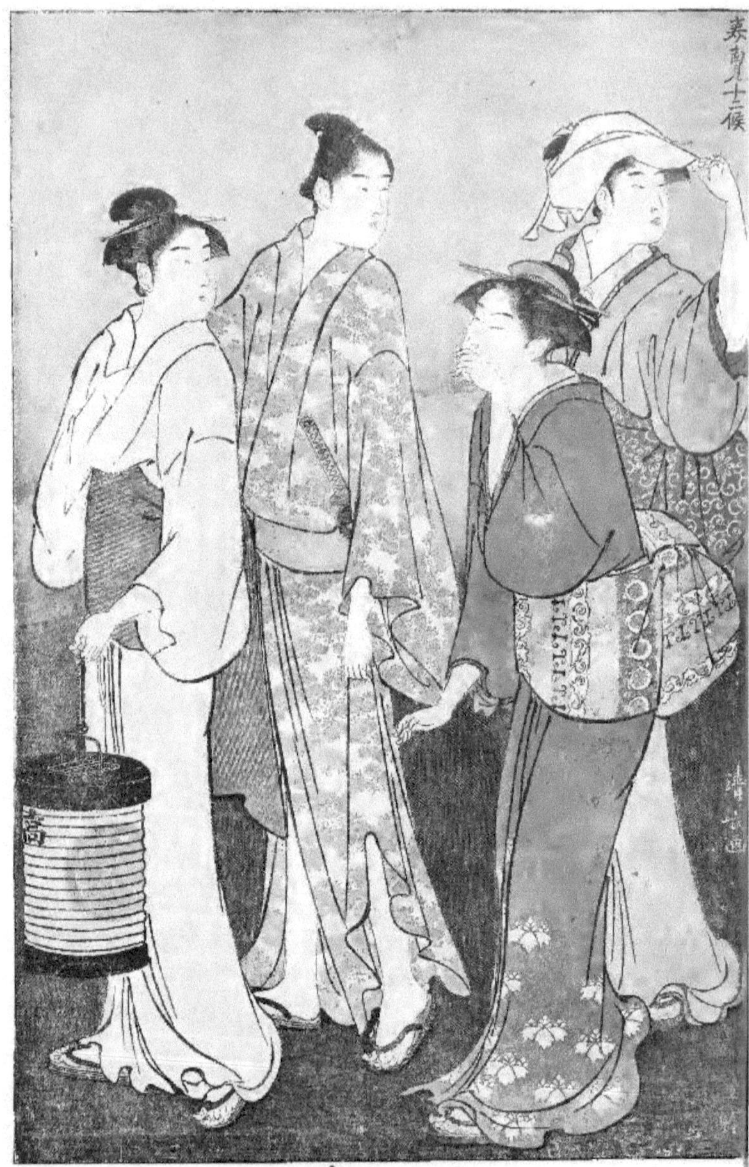

KIYÓNAGA: A STREET SCENE AT NIGHT. On the left a young man is conducted from the tea-house to the *oira* house. On the right a singer and an attendant carrying her *shamisen*. Part of a triptych, the right side of which is missing.

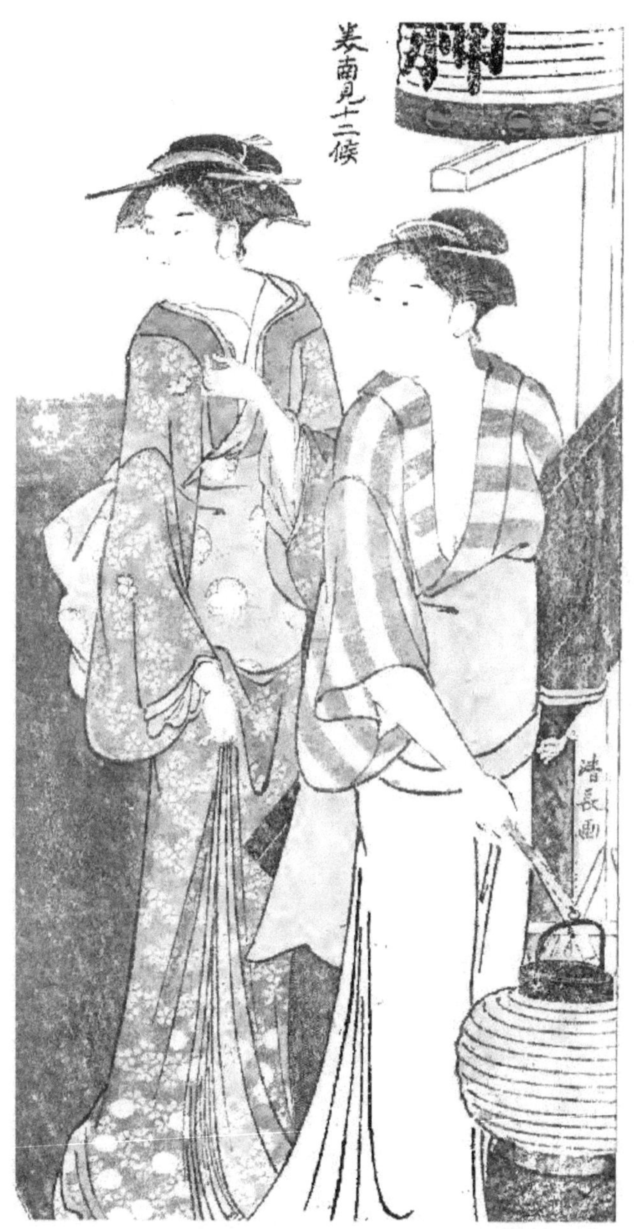
美南見十二候
清長画

logical order, together with some fifty paintings by the same artists, which are inserted in this scheme of development; it determines in effect—what no one had hitherto succeeded in doing—the time-limits within which each artist worked, the changes which the style of each underwent, and lastly, based on these special investigations, the main periods in the development of Japanese wood-engraving as a whole from about 1675 to 1850. All this is set down with such convincing lucidity that for the future nothing more than corrections of minor detail need be looked for; the history of Japanese wood-engraving in all its ramifications stands so compactly built up that we might think ourselves fortunate if we had an equally good foundation for even a single period of European art-history—in which connection it must be remembered that Fenollosa deals not with a small group of artists, but with hundreds, even ignoring as he does the multitude of quite insignificant wood-engravers who flourished in the nineteenth century. All this mass is here, as all competent art-history requires, already so sifted and arranged that only the comparatively small band of choice and leading spirits stand out above the rank and file. The confidence with which Fenollosa dates each sheet in his catalogue within the limits of a single year may seem surprising; but we must take into consideration—as he himself remarks and is bound to remark as an experienced investigator—that the date in each case is only approximate, since there is no such thing as absolute certainty in things artistic, however fully a man may be convinced that his opinion is correct. Moreover, these exact dates have not been arrived at, as might at first appear to be the case, simply by comparing the styles of the various sheets; Fenollosa must surely have taken the traditional dates of the various artists into consideration—no small assistance, as it happens, since fortunately most Japanese woodcuts are signed with the artist's name, while the certainly dated sheets are too few in number—in the eighteenth century, the best period, *e.g.*, some of the years 1743 (Shigenaga), 1765 (Harunobu), 1783 (Kiyonaga), 1795 (Utamaro)—to give us a precise chronology by their help alone. It is true that the styles of coiffure, to which Fenollosa rightly attaches great weight, constitute a very material aid to the exact dating of individual prints; but how, we may ask, can he know what the fashion of any particular year may have been, for purely stylistic considerations cannot, as has been shown, have given him the required information? We know of no such thing in Japan as a fashion paper, no chronicle of the yearly changes of taste such as we have in Europe. There does, however, exist one source of information, a source from which Fenollosa, as he himself states, has drawn lavishly, by which all mutations of dress and especially of coiffure can be followed up as accurately as need be. This source is the illustrated books, which are in the majority of cases dated. They are the basis of Fenollosa's powers and the key to the astonishing results of his researches. If he had included these illustrated books, as he did the paintings, in the New York Exhibition and his catalogue, their relation to his whole work would have immediately appeared, and his results would have become still more instructive and convincing, since they enable us to trace the changes not merely of fashions but of style in the individual artists, who as we know were frequently the same as those who produced the single sheets.

Fenollosa, unhappily, succumbed to heart-disease in London on the 21st September 1908, without having had time to write the exhaustive history of Japanese painting and wood-engraving which he projected. Besides the works already mentioned he edited the small but important Catalogue of the exhibition at Tokio (1898) and published the splendidly got-up work, *The Masters of Ukiyoye.*

In 1897 there at last appeared a compendious *History of Japanese Wood-Engraving*, by Edward F. Strange, of the staff of the South Kensington Museum. Although not altogether devoid of a sense of artistic values, it yet devotes far too much time to all sorts of unessentials, such as the life-history, the surnames and the residences of the artists, while in most cases dismissing their artistic activity with a few general phrases. Its greatest shortcoming, however, is that it gives a totally false impression of the development of Japanese wood-engraving, that it discusses the art of the nineteenth century, of which alone the author appears to have had an adequate and first-hand knowledge, in altogether disproportionate detail, to the neglect of the eighteenth century, which is historically the most important, while in the nineteenth century there are, except Hokusai and Hiroshige, very few names that count. The author has herein shown that he has not approached his task with the necessary seriousness and love of his subject, so that there is a suggestion of commercialism about the whole book which is likely to do the study of Japanese art more harm than good. Strange had, however, not yet been able to make use of Fenollosa's fundamental catalogue of 1896. He further published a book, *Japanese Colour-Prints*, in 1904.

In the same year (1897) the first edition of the present work was published. In 1900 Duret published a list of illustrated books which had been acquired for the Print-Room of the Bibliothèque Nationale. Several sale catalogues which have appeared since 1902 have advanced our knowledge of the subject. Since 1904 Perzinski has published several short but discriminating essays on Japanese wood-engravings. In 1907 Kurth published a comprehensive work on Utamaro.

Japanese notices about artists of the older period are contained in the following works mentioned by Anderson (Catalogue, p. vii.) :—

Honcho-gwashi, 6 vols. 1693.
Mampo-zensho, 14 vols. 1694.
Gwako-seuran, 6 vols. 1740. With a genealogical table of the artists of the Kano school and reproductions of famous pictures.

Nineteenth-century Works.

Kun in hosho. 1810.
Kocho meigwashiu, 5 vols. 1818.
Shogwa shuran. 1836.
Gwajo yoriaku, 2 vols. 1850.
Shogwa zensho, 10 vols. About 1862.
Grajin-riaku-nempio. 1882.
Shogwa Kaisui, 3 vols. 1883.

One chief source of information is the *Ukiyoye ruiko*, which exists in the British Museum (in a MS. of 1844) and elsewhere, and which is said to have been afterwards printed as well. The original draft is said to date from the year 1800, and to have been gradually supplemented, among others by the painter Keisai Yeisen, in 1830. The Musée Guimet in Paris intended to publish, in 1893, a French translation by Kawamura (see Deshayes, *Considérations*), but so far nothing seems to have come of it. It appears from Kurth's *Utamaro* that three Japanese sources, which have been made use of for Barboutau's Catalogue, are of special importance, viz.: (*a*) *Mon cho gwa ka jin mei ji sho*, by Kano Hisanobu, 1894, 2 vols.; (*b*) *Nihon bijutsu gwaka jin meisho den*, by Kigushi Bunzan, 1892, 2 vols.; (*c*) *Yoho ukiyoye ruiko:* Tokio, 1889 (new edition, 1901).

CHAPTER II

A SURVEY OF THE HISTORY OF JAPANESE PAINTING

SINCE Japanese wood-engraving grew out of Japanese painting and represents no more than one stage, though a peculiar stage, of development of this branch of art, it is necessary to give a short survey of the history of Japanese painting.

The art of painting, like all the other arts, poetry and science, found its way to Japan from China, the mother-country of East-Asiatic culture, through Korea, about the fifth century after Christ. Until then Japan had been sunk in deep barbarism, but being a powerful and advancing State she had, in the third century A.D., exacted tribute from Korea, which was saturated with Chinese culture. The Japanese received from Korea, along with other accomplishments and handicrafts, the art of painting. In the second half of the fifth century there came to the court of Japan a Chinese painter of imperial birth, by name Nanriu, who took up his abode there permanently. We also know of Korean painters of the sixth and seventh centuries who were employed at the Japanese court.[1]

These Korean painters introduced not only the Chinese tradition, but also another, destined to have an equally lasting influence upon the formation of Japanese painting—namely, the Buddhistic. This latter, as it seems, originated under late Greek influences in the north-west of India, and had found its

[1] Gierke, p. 11; Anderson, *Transact.*, p. 339 ff.

way to Korea through Central Asia and China. Gonse had already pointed out that the earliest productions of this Buddhistic art in Japan are surprisingly like such works as the ruins of Borobudhur in Java, and especially those of Angkor in Kambodia, and are accordingly much more Indian than Chinese in character.[1] Friedrich Hirth has since then traced for us the probable path which this art-tradition took. The painter Wai-tschi I-song, whose works served the Koreans as models for their Buddhistic paintings, came from Khoten in Central Asia, where the princely court was noted for its love of art. Presumably the art which had been brought thither from India he transported to Tschang-an-fu, the capital of the seventh century, and from there it was propagated farther to Korea.[2] Buddhism was introduced into Japan in 552 and became the religion of the establishment in 624. Under the Emperor Kotoku (645–654) Japan received a constitution after the Chinese model.

To this Buddhistic, stiffly hieratic painting, there stood opposed from the start the vivacious, purely secular painting of the Chinese; but each had its own peculiar justification. Buddhistic painting, mindful of the mysteries it represented, always remained solemn and dignified, and occupied itself with the minutest elaboration and the richest ornamentation, heightened by the use of gold and brilliant colour. Chinese painting, on the contrary, being the fashionable pastime of the cultivated, followed the varying tendencies of the time and adapted itself to the tastes of different countries, preserving, however, its fundamental principle, namely, to strive for a bold, light, sure, and as far as possible individual touch. This affinity with calligraphy had the effect, not indeed of banishing colour altogether, but of making its interest for the most part

[1] Gonse, i. 166.

[2] F. Hirth, *Über fremde Einflüsse in der chinesischen Kunst*, p. 46.

Koechlin Collection, Paris

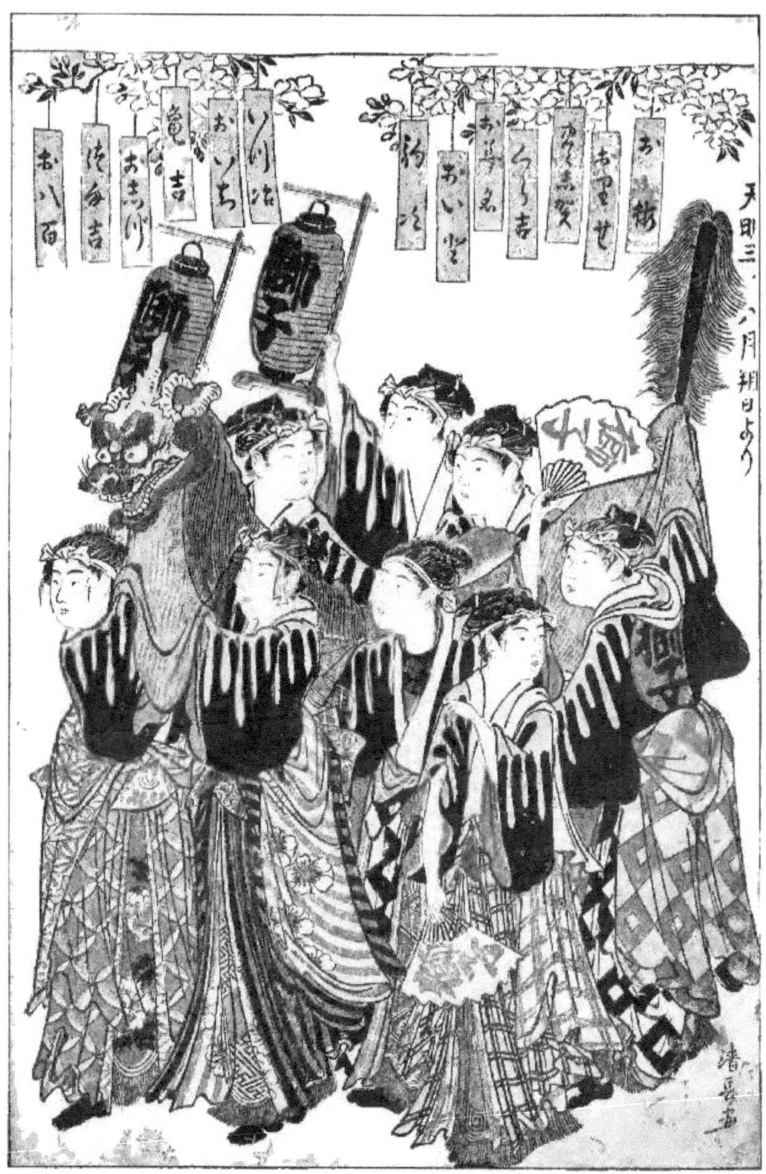

KIYÓNAGA: A Temple Festival. Eight female singers, wearing black sleeves with a yellow pattern, and a peculiar headdress, are carrying a lion. Dated 1783. *Yellow and pink predominate.*

subordinate, and of laying all the emphasis upon skill in giving as perfect a picture as possible with a few bold powerful strokes, that is to say, in getting the utmost effect out of the contrast of black and white. This economy of means has always remained the characteristic of Chinese painting.[1]

Although the first Japanese painter of whom we have actual knowledge, Kanaoka, does not appear until the end of the ninth century, everything points to the fact that he represents the culmination of the first great epoch of Japanese art, and not, as one might suppose, the beginning of real Japanese painting. For the little that we know of his work and of Japanese art of the preceding seventh and eighth centuries, especially of sculpture, bronze and wood-carving, suggests the conclusion that this young and vigorous nation had rapidly built up an art of its own, full of power and expression. Although, to begin with, the forms represented in painting remained at first foreign —Korean, Chinese, and Buddhistic—the contents of the representation must have been purely Japanese, corresponding to the high standard of culture that the country had achieved. Otherwise, Kanaoka would not have been able to preserve through all the succeeding ages the fame of having been the greatest Japanese painter; for it is not possible to attain to such a height by mere imitation of a foreign art. At the beginning of the ninth century, Buddhism had already been completely absorbed into the national point of view, and so was reconciled to the dominant creed of Shintoism.

To this early period, comprising the seventh and eighth centuries, which is known as the Nara period (so called after Nara, then the capital city, with its new High Street and new gates), belong the following works among others: the well-known full-length portrait of Prince Shotoku with two boys (*Kokkwa*, 78),

[1] Bing in the *Revue blanche* (1896), p. 164. Binyon, *Painting in the Far East* (1908).

which is now, however, supposed to be appreciably later; a fresco of Indian character in the Horiuji Temple; six paintings on a folding-screen, representing the "Beauties under Trees," which are Chinese in style, but already Japanese in feeling. A portrait of Kobo Daishi, a saint of the early ninth century, by the priest Gonzo, is also mentioned.

Kose no Kanaoka, as a son of that ninth century which the powerful China of the Tang dynasty influenced so profoundly, worked entirely under the spell of the Chinese, and especially of the Buddhist school. He lived from about 850–890. His teacher had been a Chinese emigrant named Gokioshi. As Kanaoka's chief work are mentioned the pictures of the Chinese sages, which he copied in 888 from Chinese originals in the palace of Kioto (whither the capital had been transferred from Nara in 794). Besides pictures of deities according to Buddhistic rules, he also painted representations from life, or from history and tradition, as well as landscapes and animals; it is reckoned as his principal merit that he enlarged the traditional scope of representation by including scenes taken from Japanese history, from heroic legend, and from the lives of celebrated priests. Gonse had alleged that only four paintings of Kanaoka's could still be traced; one of these, a kakemono belonging to the dealer Wakaï of Tokio, which represents the Buddhist saint Jizo, is reproduced in his *l'Art Japonais* (i. 169). Fenollosa, however, considered two of these pictures to be certainly of later origin, and the remaining two doubtful; but he names three others in their stead, which in his view are to be reckoned among the very grandest creations of Japanese art, and on the basis of these he defines Kanaoka's position by a comparison with that of Phidias in Greek art.[1] In the Boston Museum are four paintings which are

[1] Anderson, *Transact.*, p. 342 f.; the same, Cat., p. xv.; Gierke, p. 12; Gonse in Cat. of Jap. Ex. at Paris, 1883; Fenollosa, *Review* (1885), p. 9 ff.

R. WAGNER, BERLIN

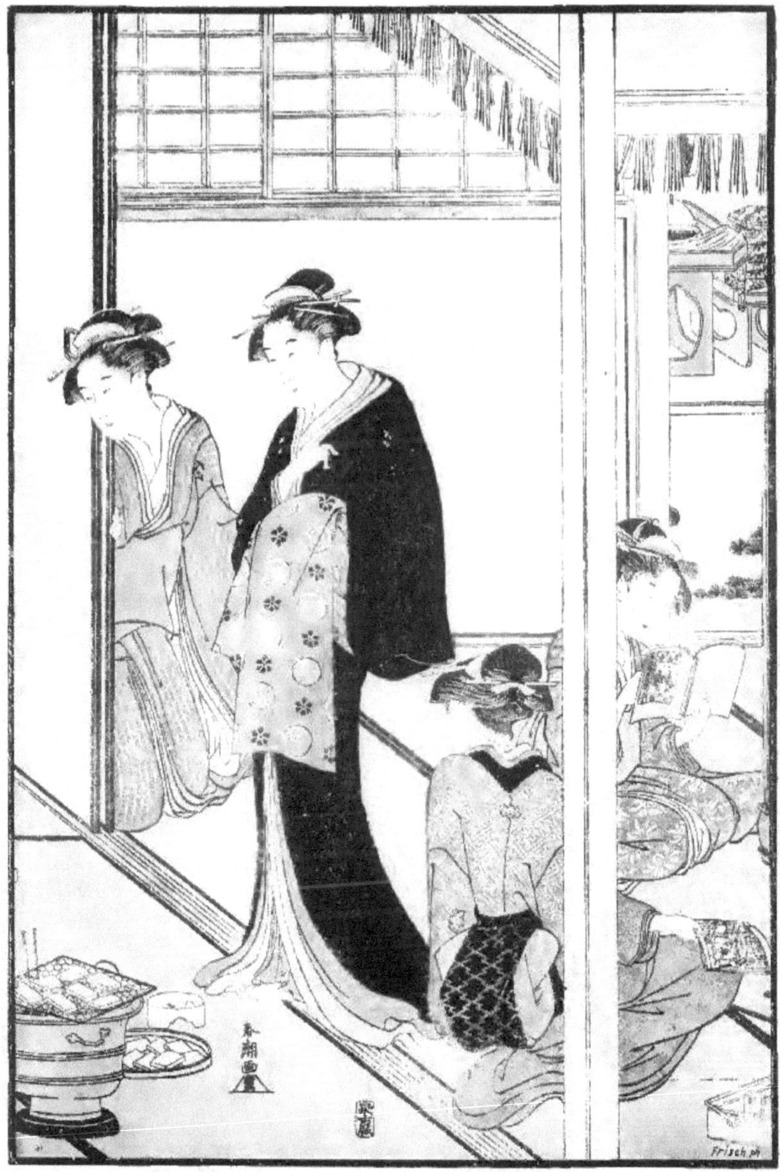

SCHUNCHŌ: WOMEN ON NEW YEAR'S DAY. A lattice of straw and paper on the porch. In the foreground a brazier, and on it rice-cakes on a wire griddle. From a polyptych.

probably the work of "Shi Ten O" himself, also the copy of the portrait of a young prince by Kanaoka. The Hayashi collection (sold by auction in Paris in 1902) contained the seated figure of the Bodhisattva Jizo, probably that reproduced by Gonse (*v. supra*). Binyon[1] reproduces the beautiful full-length portrait of the minister Sugawara Michizane, which is pronouncedly Chinese in character.

But still greater renown than his paintings ever brought him accrued to Kanaoka as the founder of the first national school of Japanese painting, the Kose-riu, so called from his family name. In Japanese a sharp distinction is made between schools (*riu*) and styles (*ye*, sometimes erroneously written *e* or *we*). Schools (*riu*) arise through the propagation of definite methods of painting within certain families, which are further strengthened by the adoption of strangers who assume the name of the clan; in several cases (dealt with below) they have prolonged their activity through a series of centuries. *Ye* (community in style) is, on the contrary, a quite loose and external connection, corresponding exactly to our idea of style. Until Kanaoka's time there were, as has been said, three styles of painting—the Chinese (Kara-ye), the Korean (Korai-ye), both of which may be grouped together, and the Buddhistic (Butsu-ye). Painting was a refined pastime, indulged in by priestly and noble amateurs.[2] Kanaoka was the first, in the year 880, to found a school of professional painters which was at the same time a national school of painting; its basis was principally Buddhistic, and it stood under the influence of the Chinese Tang school. As he himself belonged to the highest nobility, so the aristocratic character was always preserved in the school or clan of painters that he founded, the Kose-riu. This holds good for all painters and schools that arose subsequently until the sixteenth century. It was not till then that one of the *bourgeois* succeeded in

[1] *Painting in the Far East*, frontispiece.

[2] Gierke, p. 23.

C

winning a name for himself; and it was not until the seventeenth century that a really popular, or, according to the Japanese ideas, plebeian school arose, of which the maturest fruit is that colour-printing to which we are about to give our attention. Kanaoka's clan was continued in his son Aimi, whose son again was Kintada; Hirotaka, Kanaoka's grandson, continued the school in the tenth century. To him is ascribed "The Death of Buddha," in the British Museum,[1] which is akin to the style of the Chinese painter Wu Tao Tze, and is remarkable for its expressiveness.

Although Chinese influence subsequently continued even down to our own century, at times in fact grew in strength, still Japanese painting must have retained its independence, as otherwise it would be inexplicable that at the end of the tenth century Japanese paintings were presented as a gift to the Chinese court, where the most exacting standards of taste had always obtained.[2] The difference between Japanese and Chinese art methods is brought out by the discerning Le Blanc du Vernet, in a small work that appeared anonymously, *Le Japon artistique et littéraire* (p. 11), where he remarks that, while the art of the cool and sceptical Chinese was usually methodical, exact, dainty, and "precious," that of the Japanese, corresponding to their character, had become in all respects free, lively, cheerful, and full of variety. We must emphasise, he says, the fact that Japanese art did not fall into slavish imitation, but that it took over from the art of the Celestial empire only experience, method, and technique, and by applying these to national subjects, developed an independent style that possessed more elegance, creative power, mobility, and pliancy than did that of the "Celestials." Yeshin Sozu, who died in 1017 at the age of seventy-six, is mentioned as one of the most remarkable Buddhistic painters of this period.

[1] Binyon, pl. 5. [2] Hirth, *Fremde Einflüsse*, p. 73.

KIYÓMITSU

THE ACTOR KIKUGORO HOLDING A MIRROR

(Three-colour print)

BRITISH MUSEUM

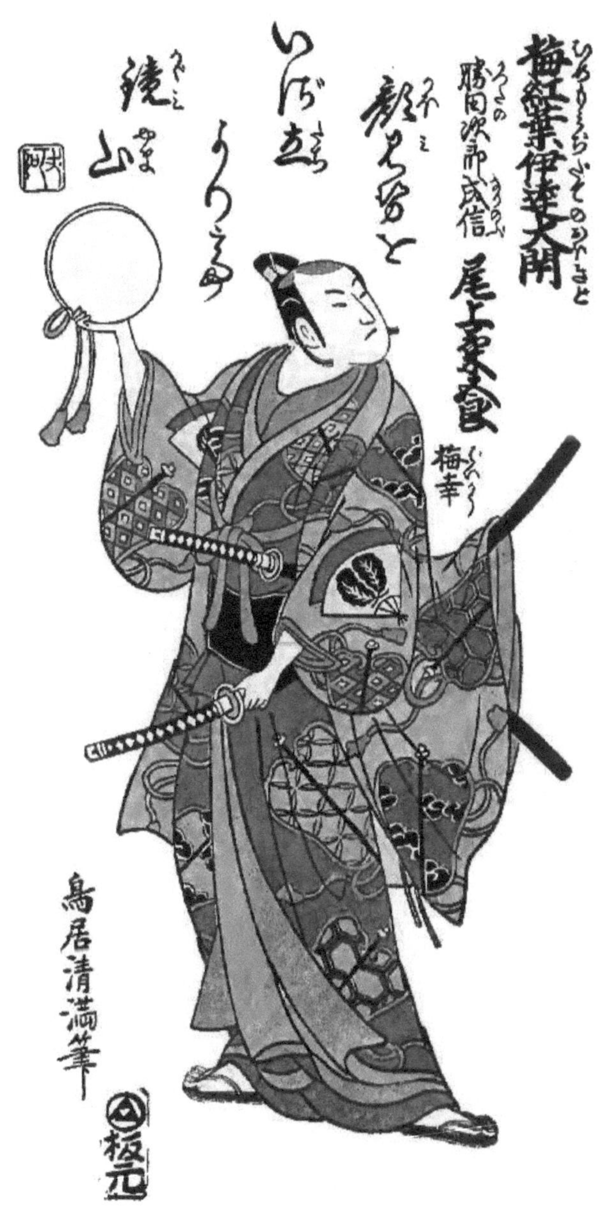

梅紅葉伊達大關
梅幸
鳥居清満筆
板元

But it was not until the beginning of the eleventh century, when Japan was beginning to seclude itself from the foreigner, that the Japanese method of painting seems to have freed itself definitely from the Chinese. For the Kasuga school, which now succeeded the moribund Kose school, is also noticed as the founder of the Yamato-ye, or Japanese style, which then found its most conspicuous propagator in the great Tosa school, which flourished in the twelfth century. This style received its name, Yamato, from the contemporary name of Japan. In those days, during the Haian period (794–1186), synchronising in essentials with the Fujiwara period (870–1130), which derives its name from the family which possessed the hereditary monarchy since 669, the Japanese gave themselves up unrestrainedly to the pleasures of life, and their morals suffered grievously in consequence.

The founder of the Kasuga school at the time mentioned was the painter Motomitsu, a pupil of Kose Kimmochi, one of the last representatives of the Kose school. Burty traces back the designation "Kasuga school" to the temple of the same name at Nara, which temple, it is said, was from the eleventh to the fifteenth centuries furnished with paintings by Takachika and his successors.[1] Burty mentions the Takuma school as another fairly contemporaneous school, which flourished from the eleventh to the fourteenth century.

Not indeed a school, but a particular branch of painting, that called Toba-ye, or the Comic, was founded in the twelfth century by a Buddhist priest of high mark, Ko Kuyu, called Toba Sojo, who died in 1140, and is supposed to have been the first to draw caricatures. Bing praises their liveliness and modern spirit. Fenollosa observes, however, that these humorous sketches are not necessarily to be considered as his pre-eminent

[1] Cat. Burty, p. xvi.; not so Gierke, p. 23; *cf.* Anderson, *Transact.*, p. 344.

work, for he is said to have painted some very beautiful things in the Buddhistic style.[1]

The fierce contests which were fought out during the twelfth century between the noble families of Minamoto (Genji) and Taira (Heike), and which ended in its concluding years with the elevation of Minamoto no Yoritomo to the Shogunate (Generalissimoship), brought about a noteworthy change in art: the Kasuga school was succeeded, in the beginning of the thirteenth century, by the Tosa school, which was destined to long activity and profound influence, and whose significance, as chief representative of the national Japanese style, the Yamato-ye, became especially conspicuous when, in the fifteenth century, the influence of Chinese style reasserted itself with renewed strength, and led to the founding of the Kano school, equally eminent, but pursuing other aims. The Tosa school represented courtly art, which had its centre in the imperial residence at Kioto, in the middle of Japan, whereas the Shogun, who at the end of the civil war had achieved independence, had set up his residence first in Kamakura in the Kuanto, then in Yedo, the present Tokio, on the south-east coast. The period is thence known as the Kamakura period (1181–1333). During it feudalism developed itself, the Samurai, hitherto the warrior caste, rising to be the caste of nobility. It was particularly on the makimonos, long horizontal rolls with many figures, as also on screens and in gift-books, that this school depicted, with the delicacy and minuteness of a miniature, those historical scenes from the battles of the Fujiwara, Minamoto, and Taira, from court festivals and the life of chivalry, which may be taken as the faithful expression of national Japanese feeling. Such pictures, with their brilliant colouring of vermilion, blue, and green, standing out from a background of gold, give an

[1] Bing, in the *Revue blanche* (1896), p. 166; Fenollosa, *Review*, p. 13; Anderson, *Transact.*, p. 345.

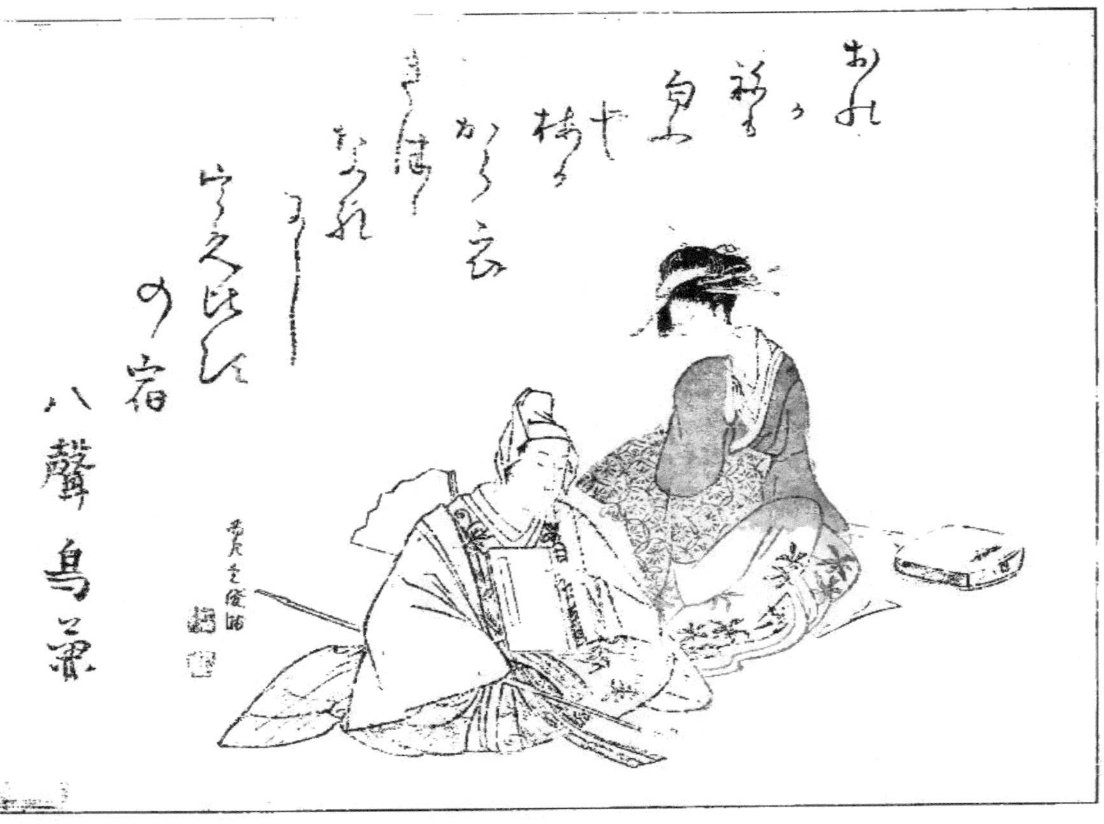

SHUMMAN: A YOUNG MAN AS NARIHIRA AND A GEISHA. *Granulated background.* Surimono in delicate lilac tones.

opulent representation of the life of that time. Especial weight was given to the true and accurate rendering of the court ceremonial costumes; but, although the motions of the persons portrayed, as the refined etiquette of the court required, were represented as serious, grave, and dignified, this art never degenerated into pettiness, but always maintained its broad decorative character. The fact that the vertical picture, or kakemono, which makes a more independent appeal, was more rarely used in this period would seem to indicate the beginning of a decline, and accordingly Fenollosa conceives of the whole Tosa school as a revolt from the robuster style of Kanaoka.

The founder of the school, at the beginning of the thirteenth century, was Fujiwara no Tsunetaka, who as Director of Fine Arts bore the title Tosagon no Kami.[1] Other artists of this school are Fujiwara Mitsunaga, whose makimonos are full of movement; also Fujiwara Takanobu, and his son, Nobuzane (1177–1265), who in 1221 painted the picture of the poet Hitomaro, and one of whose pictures, a beautiful study of the saint Kobo Daishi as a boy, is reproduced by Binyon (pl. 6). Keion is mentioned as the founder of a special school, the Sumiyoshi-riu, which lasted into the eighteenth century. In consequence of renewed civil wars, a certain decline seems to have taken place in the second half of the thirteenth century; this decline continued into the fifteenth century, though there still remain for the fourteenth century a number of eminent names, especially Tosa Yoshimitsu. In 1274 came the invasion of the Mongols under Khubla Khan; in 1334 the Hodjo were overthrown by the Ashikaga, and the Ashikaga Shoguns ruled from that date until 1573.

In the beginning of the fifteenth century came the revival

[1] Thence Le Blanc du Vernet (*Le Japon artistique et littéraire*, p. 28) deduces the name of the school; otherwise Gierke, p. 14 f.; *cf.* Anderson, *Transact.*, p. 346; Fenollosa, *Review*, pp. 9, 13 f.; Cat. Burty, p. 3; Appert, p. 142.

of Japanese art by the influence of China. The Buddhist priest, Chodensu, who in 1409 painted his famous picture of the death of Buddha, is by Anderson compared with his contemporary Angelico, but from Fenollosa's description he must have represented rather a revival of the powerful style of Kanaoka. He died in the year 1427, at the age of seventy-six. His masterpiece, the priest Shoichi Kokushi seated, is reproduced in Tajima's work, vol. vi.; a shoki as devil-queller in Binyon (pl. 13). His contemporary, Josetsu, according to some a Chinese priest, according to others at any rate educated in China, developed a still more enduring activity by establishing a school for painting in Kioto, by which the Chinese style was again brought into repute and from which proceeded a series of the most important painters, such as Soga Shubun, Sesshu, and Kano Masanobu. Josetsu himself painted principally landscapes of delicate execution, but not in accordance with the style then prevailing in China, which flourished afresh under the Ming dynasty (1368–1644), but in that of the remote Sung period (960–1278), the productions of which, even in China itself, are still counted as unsurpassable models. Nen Kawo, who worked about the middle of the fourteenth century, is mentioned as a predecessor of Chodensu and Josetsu.[1]

Josetsu's pupil, Soga Shubun, a Chinaman naturalised in Japan, painted landscapes, figures, birds, and flowers in the style of his master; as a painter he is perhaps more remarkable than Josetsu, and more especially in landscape painting, he occupies one of the first places in the history of Japanese art. His works are chiefly executed in Indian ink and lightly tinted. Anderson[2] gives a reproduction of one of his landscapes. Among his pupils we may mention Sotan. Of still greater importance

[1] Anderson, *Transact.*, p. 346 ff.; the same, Cat., pp. 21, 263, 274; Fenollosa, *Review*, p. 16 ff.; Gierke, p. 15 f.; Cat. Burty, p. 15.

[2] *Pictorial Arts*, pl. 14.

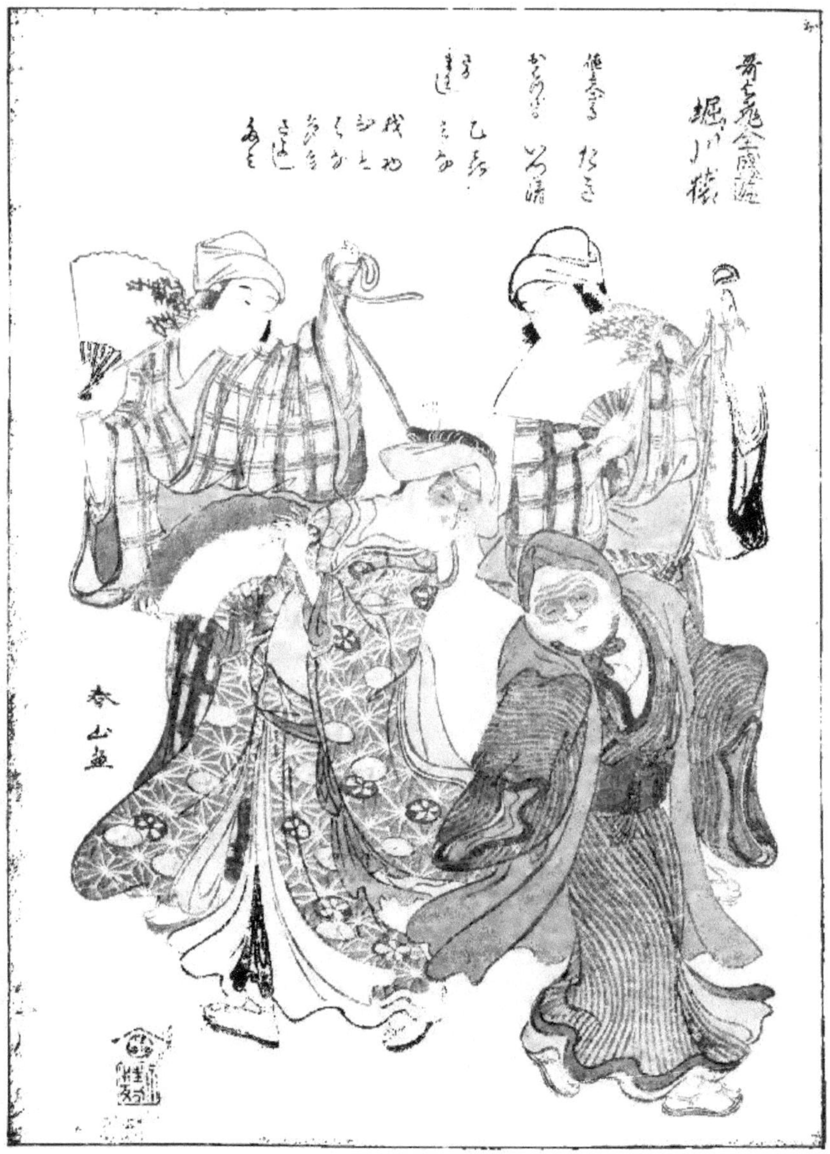

SHUNZAN: DANCE OF FOUR GEISHAS, TWO DISGUISED AS MONKEYS. *Pink predominates.*

is Sesshu, very likely a pupil of Shubun. He lived from 1420 to 1507, acquired about 1460 the art of painting in China itself, and then established himself in 1469 in the temple Unkokuji. He is universally extolled as the greatest artist of Japanese antiquity. He also is distinguished for his landscapes, one of which Gonse (i. 194) has reproduced. Binyon (pl. 14) reproduces "Jurojin, the Genius of Old Age," by Sesshu, drawn in the manner of the classic period. According to Chinese custom, he used chiefly Indian ink which he laid on with a bold brush, and only occasionally enlivened his work by the addition of a little colour. However productive as a painter, he is chiefly distinguished for the number of pupils he trained, a number never equalled by any artist before or since. One of his pupils was Shugetsu, from whom Gonse (i. 194) has reproduced a crow, which, however, is, according to Fenollosa, hardly a hundred years old. Anderson (pl. 18) reproduces a picture of an Indian priest, which makes a very favourable impression. The third important painter of this Chinese school founded by Josetsu, is Kano Masanobu (1453–1490), a scion of the Fujiwara stock; he was especially influenced by Sesshu, but did not equal his master in originality; on the other hand, he made an extensive reputation for himself by the foundation of the Kano school, which was destined to a long period of activity. One of his landscapes is reproduced by Anderson.[1] Mention must be made of Sesson as an admirable landscape-painter of the period, in the Chinese impressionist style. Binyon (pl. 15) reproduces one of his landscapes, executed in Indian ink.

The foundation of the Kano school, upholding the Chinese style, in the second half of the fifteenth century, was an event closely connected with the political development of the country. Whereas the court of the Mikado in Kioto, and with it the courtly and national Tosa school, was gradually being thrust

[1] *Pictorial Arts*, pl. 19. See also Binyon, pl. 16.

into the background, the reputation of the Shoguns was continually in the ascendant, they being in very close touch with China, then flourishing anew under the Ming dynasty. It was, therefore, quite natural that the school which was principally influenced by the Chinese should have its stronghold and support near the seat of the Shoguns in Yedo. This statement holds especially for the Kano school, which, as the acknowledged representative of the art favoured by the Shoguns, stood in opposition to the Tosa school, which was favoured by the imperial court, an opposition by no means hostile indeed, but sharp enough to stir the keenest rivalry on both sides. In contrast with the subtler method of the older school, which laid special stress on splendour of colouring, the newly arisen Kano school gave eloquent expression to the daring spirit of youth that reigned in the entourage of the Shoguns by the force and sublimity of its style, qualities to which its calligraphic black-and-white technique after the Chinese model naturally tended. Although there existed, as Duret well expresses it, the same reverential admiration in Japan toward the Chinese as was formerly shown by the Romans for the Greeks, yet the Japanese painters descended to no slavish dependence upon China, but constantly renewed, out of their lively love of Nature, their powers of new and original creation.

It is accounted the especial merit of Kano Motonobu, the second great master of this school, and the eldest son of Masanobu, that he not only represented scenes of court and heroic life, but also characters from daily life. He lived from 1476 to 1559. Although not quite the equal of his father, he attained lasting fame by giving to the Kano school a coherent academic organisation. Indeed, he is recognised as the true classic of the school, and when he received the honourable title of Ko-Hogen in his old age, was regarded with almost idolatrous reverence. The means he employed

Vever Collection, Paris

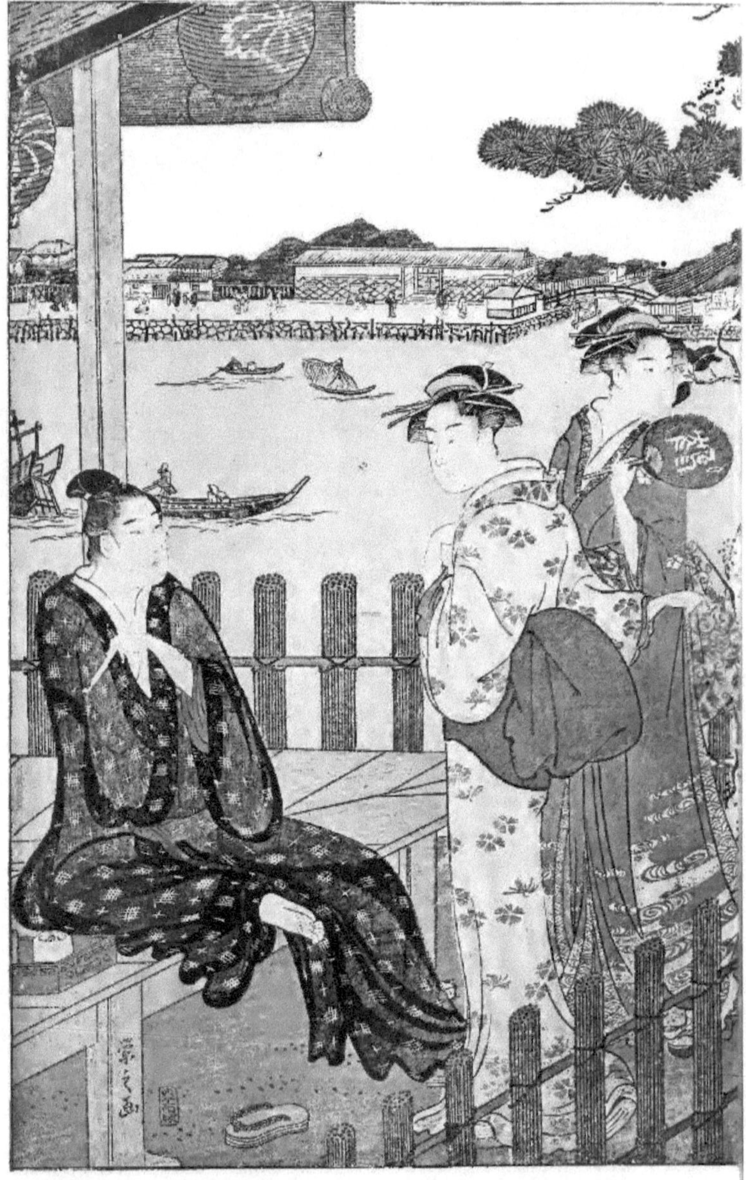

YEISHI : A Tea-house by a River. A young man seated ; a singer with long sleeves ; three attendants, one of whom is catching fish under the *mon* (gate). Part of a triptych.

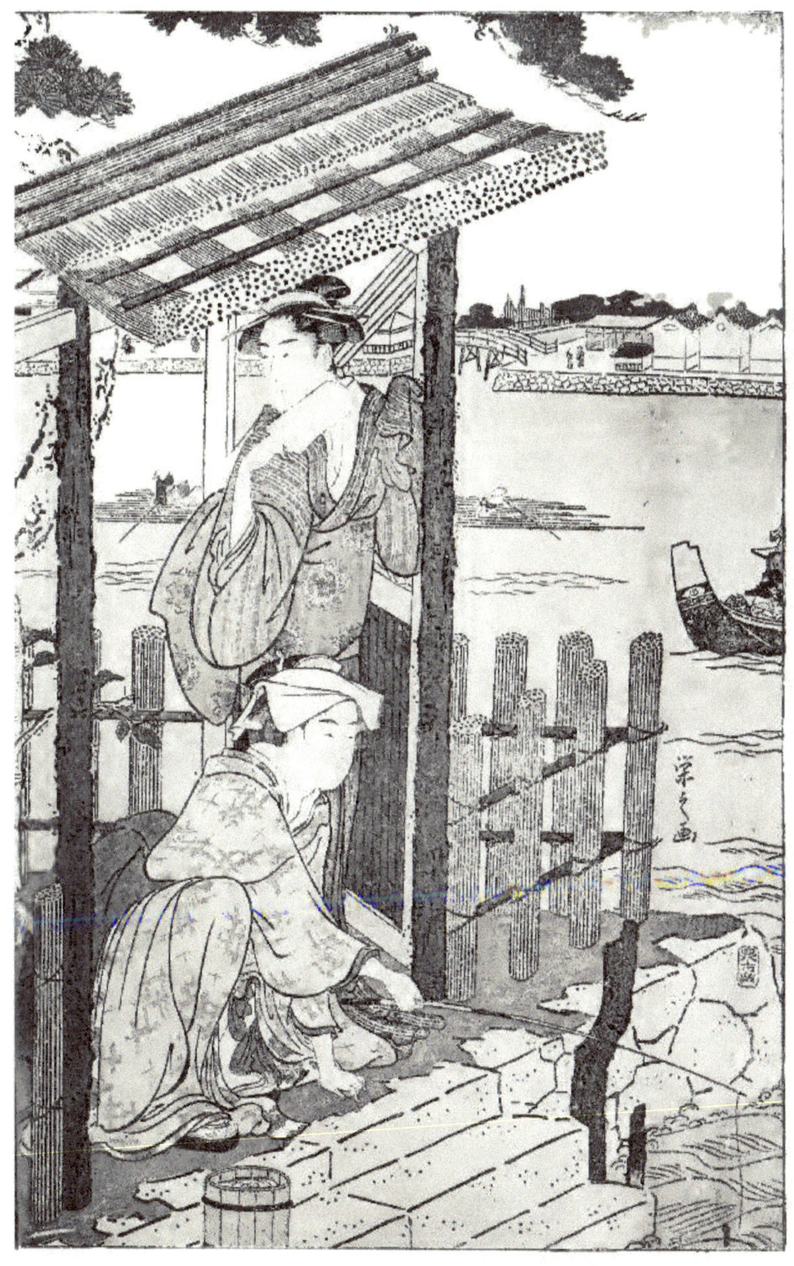

were extremely simple and the treatment of his subject not very elaborate, but along with all his swift and bold sketchiness his work remained always powerful and stimulating. It was not so much his peculiar manner, which was no more than the ancient Chinese manner in general, as the individuality and distinction of his creations, that secured him his position in the school. Although he was esteemed perfect in all branches of pictorial representation, yet it was his landscapes that enjoyed the highest renown. Anderson[1] reproduces one of his "Eight Immortals" as well as "Tieh Kwai." Masanobu's brother, Utanosuke, was one of the greatest bird and flower painters.[2]

Through his alliance with a daughter of Mitsushige, at that time head of the Tosa school, Motonobu established a connection between the two rival schools, but with no new result. Each of the two schools maintained its individual character. This competition with the newly flourishing Chinese school had a good effect upon the Tosa school, which had been merely marking time. It was especially through Mitsunobu, the father of the above-mentioned Mitsushige, that new life was given to this school in the second half of the fifteenth century. His delicately outlined drawings enabled him to take up the challenge of the Kano school successfully.

From this Tosa school, towards the end of the sixteenth century, issued the artist who was the true founder of the popular genre-pictures which hitherto had been only occasionally cultivated—Iwasa Matahei, who lived from 1578 to 1650. He was the father of that national school which later found its chief expression in wood-engraving, and brought this form of art to full development and general diffusion. He began by being a pupil of Tosa Mitsunori, but later went over to the Kano school, and created for himself, about the year 1620 (according to Fenollosa), an individual style marked by expressive design

[1] *Pictorial Arts*, pls. 20 and 43.

[2] Binyon, pl. 17.

and lofty grace; finally, in 1630, he entered upon a thoroughly realistic phase, which, by the force of its decorative effect and the careful elaboration of details, established a model never again attained in later years. From the popular or worldly nature of his subjects he received the epithet, Ukiyo (painter of the fleeting world), which was then transferred to this entire class of work as the popular style, the Ukiyo-ye, under which the whole school of wood-engraving is usually comprehended. Though Matahei himself was the first Japanese painter of non-noble descent, his creations were by no means of a common kind; on the contrary, that which made him celebrated was not so much the subjects that he chose, but rather, as in the case of the other eminent artists of his time, his creative gifts, the power, the individuality, the elevation, and the finish of his style.[1] It is true that no paintings exist which can with certainty be assigned to him: Professor Oeder possesses a very beautiful representation of a dancing girl; Binyon (pl. 24) reproduces another dancing girl, but this seems very doubtful. Fenollosa[2] reproduces a dancing and singing old man, painted about 1640–50, after Masatoshi, the son of Matahei.

Another incentive to progress was applied to the Kano school in the second half of the sixteenth century under the great Shogun, Hideyoshi (the Taigo), whose work was completed by his successor, Iyeyasu, the victor in the battle of Sekigahara, in 1600, and the founder of the Tokugawa dynasty. Nobunaga had overthrown the Ashikaga in 1574. On his death in 1582 he was succeeded by Hideyoshi, under whom the invasion of Korea by the Japanese took place (1592–98). In 1604 Iyeyasu followed him in the shogunate. We owe it to the influence of these two men that the ancient works of art were

[1] Fenollosa, *Review*, p. 30 ff.; the same, Cat., No. 1; Anderson Cat., p. 328; Binyon also spells his name Matabei, to distinguish him from another, lesser, Matahei.

[2] *Outline*, pl. 1.

ROYAL PRINT ROOM, DRESDEN

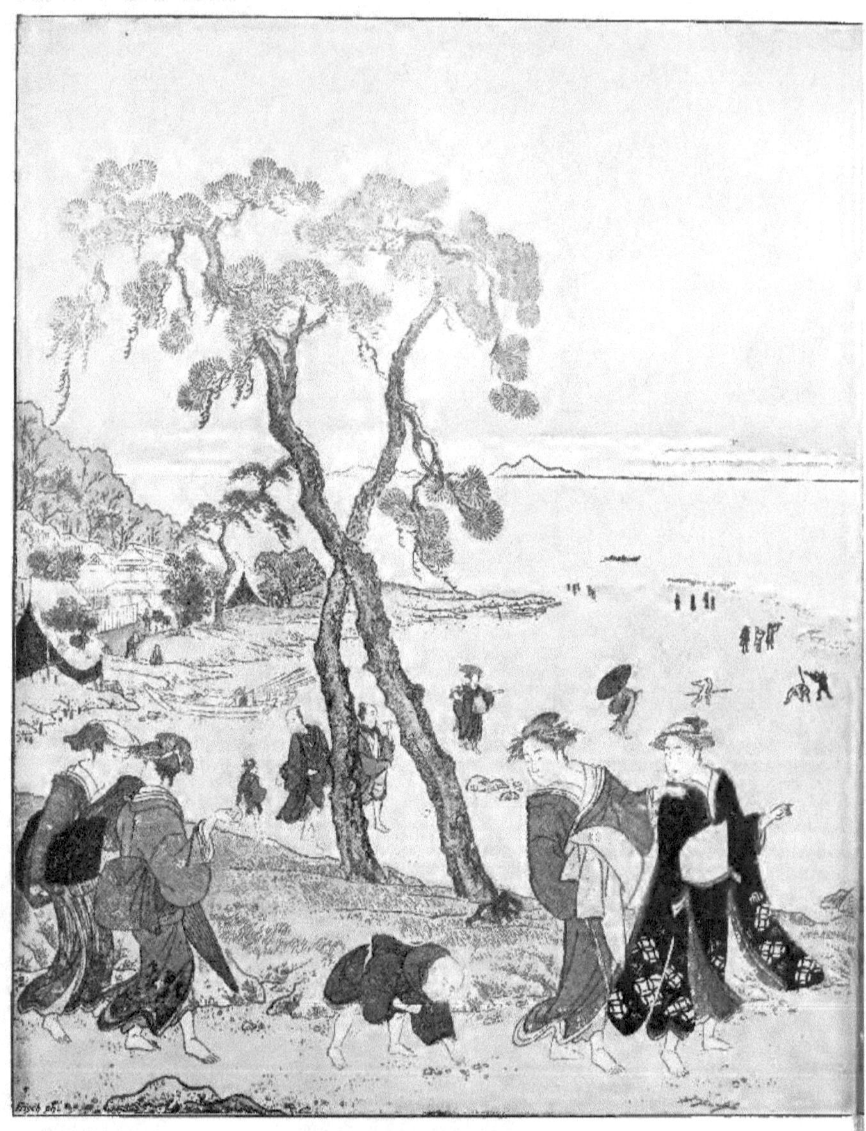

UTÁMARO: A WALK AT LOW TIDE. From the "Shell Book." Diptych. *Vivid colours.*

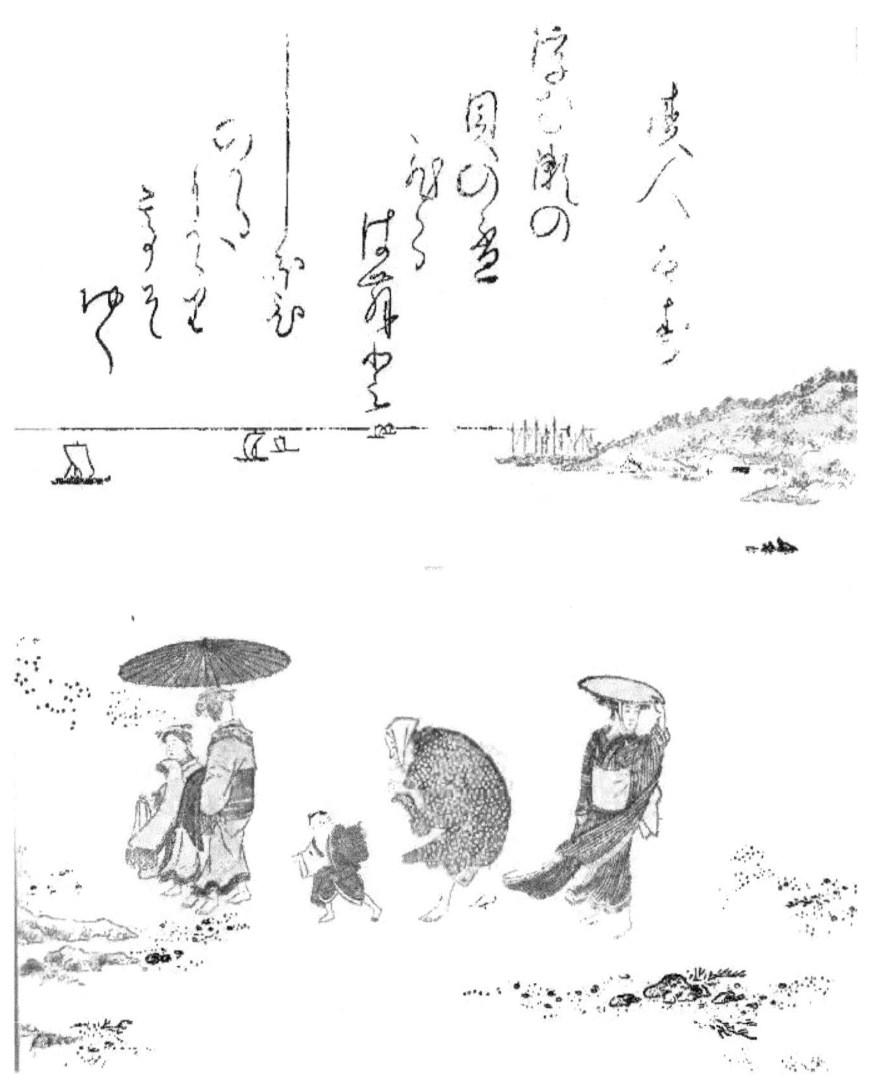

collected, that Japanese ceramic attained its culmination, and that the castles of the gentlefolk were ornamented with rich mural decoration. Kano Yeitoku, the grandson of Motonobu, who died at the age of forty-eight, towards the end of the sixteenth century, deserves especial mention. He was the creator of a great decorative style, and was the first to use gold-leaf in large quantity for backgrounds, especially in his folding screens; he ranks, according to Fenollosa, as the last great representative of the Kano school, being hardly inferior to Motonobu, and indeed almost the greatest of Japanese painters. Binyon (pl. 21) reproduces a winter landscape by him. His method was carried on by his son-in-law, Kano Senraku, as also by his sons, Mitsunobu and Takanobu. Binyon (pl. 22) gives a wash-landscape in the Chinese style by a pupil of Senraku, Sansetsu (died 1652). Takanobu had three sons distinguished as painters —Morinobu, also called Tanyu, Naonobu, and Yasunobu.[1]

Tanyu, who lived from 1601 to 1675, and is regarded as the founder of a special branch of the school, tried to unify the endeavours of the ancients and to quicken them into new life. More notable for the originality of his creations than for careful execution, he painted in a style which stands midway between that of Sesshu and Motonobu, seldom using colours; but he was lacking in the power and originality necessary to create a new style. His representation of Fuji, in which only small quantities of green and blue were made use of, was particularly famous. Prints after his drawings were published in the collection *Gwako senran*. Binyon (pl. 23) reproduces one of his pictures. Gonse (i. 213) gives a sketch by him, and Anderson[2] a print. From Naonobu, the younger brother of Tanyu, Gonse reproduces a hare (i. 234). A landscape by Yasunobu, the third of the brothers, is reproduced by Anderson.[3] Tsunenobu, the son of Naonobu, Fenollosa calls

[1] Anderson, *Transact.*, p. 353 ff.; Fenollosa, *Review*, p. 25 ff.; Gierke, p. 17 ff.
[2] *Japanese Wood-Engraving*, No. 17. [3] *Pictorial Arts*, pl. 24.

a tolerable imitator of Tanyu. The Tosa school, for its part, produced in the seventeenth century, as its last representative worth mentioning, Mitsuoki, the grandson of Mitsunobu, whom Fenollosa considers a fair but rather feeble painter, and whose best work is in his flower-pieces. Mitsuoki's great-grandson, Mitsuyoshi, continued his manner in the eighteenth century.

This entire art of the seventeenth century is characterised by Fenollosa as the art of a period of decadence. Only four great artists, like oases, appear conspicuous—Sansetsu, Sotatsu, Itcho, and Korin. We will quote in his own words his description of the spiritual conditions then obtaining:—

"On the other hand, in the seventeenth century, the Japanese mind fell largely into indolence and triviality. There was no healthy outlet for greatness under the crushing despotic political system. Society was occupied with innumerable formalisms and petty conceits. What had once been the living rules and ideals of living heroes dwindled away into romantic traditions and unreal affectations. It was then that the Japanese learned to be dissipated and deceitful. Puppet-shows and cock-fights and courtesans and midnight escapades now absorbed the energies of the young bloods whose grandfathers had conquered Corea. The art of this period reflects truly the character of the times. The greater part of it is taken up with representations of the famous public women of the day, of actors and jugglers and drunken gentlemen and beastly obscenities; with irreverent caricatures of gods, the gloss and glitter of fine garments, trivial half-minute sketches which drove wild the shallow-pated bibbers of tea, and old Chinese designs in their twentieth dilution to suit the *delicate* taste of the age. No doubt the Yedo despots were well pleased to see the dear people so happy and contented with their innocent amusements. There are, of course, many delightful and some new characteristics of the art of this epoch;

Vever Collection, Paris

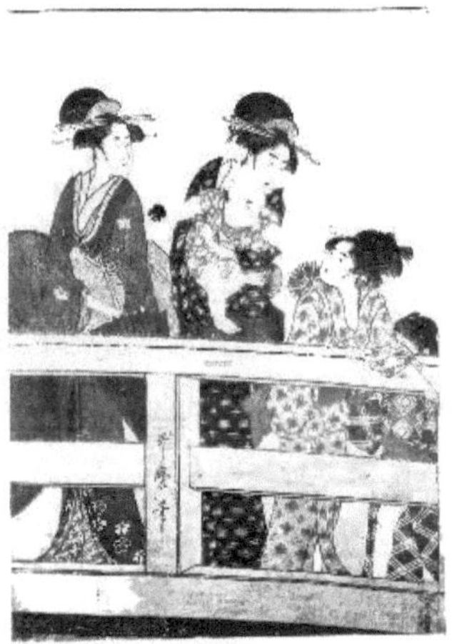

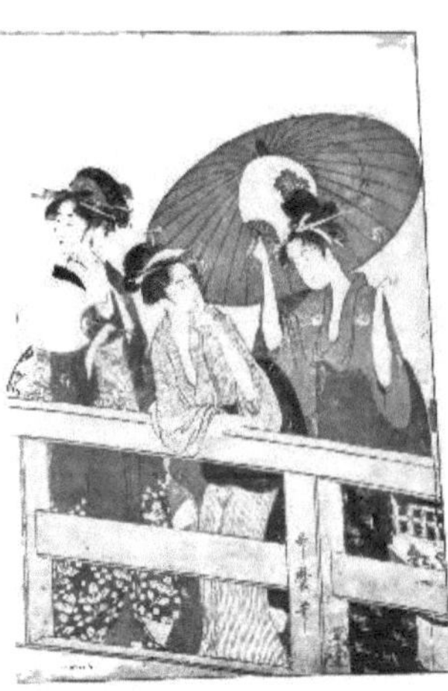

UTAMARO: WOMEN ON A BRIDGE ON A SUMMER EVENING. To the left two ladies of rank with an attendant.
Triptych in colour: black, yellow, and green, with a little red.

but it has a decided childishness and insincerity about it. The spiritual element has all fled; and the materialistic gaiety which remains can never be mistaken for true artistic inspiration."[1]

Of the four artists who constitute exceptions, Sansetsu (see above) is the last representative of the old Kano school, according to Fenollosa really an anachronism in the seventeenth century, as his style belongs wholly to the sixteenth. Sotatsu, who, after Utanosuke, is the greatest flower-painter of Japan and one of the greatest colourists of his country, was Korin's teacher and even more gifted than he. He is already breaking with the linear style, and inclines to renderings by pure brush-work. A picture of a group of chrysanthemums may be found in Binyon (pl. 25). Hanabusa Itcho, of Yedo (1651–1724), a pupil of Kano Yasunobu, was also one of the greatest colourists of this school, and distinguished himself, as Tanyu did, by his original representations of scenes from popular life; a list of reproductions after his drawings will be given in the next chapter. Anderson gives a reproduction after him in his *Japanese Wood-Engraving*, No. 9. Lastly, Korin, the celebrated lacquer-painter, who lived from 1660 to 1716, came of a middle-class family, by name Ogata, in Kioto, spent a part of his life in Yedo, and then returned to his native town, where he remained till his death. He was a pupil of Sotatsu, but Tsunenobu and Yasunobu are also mentioned as having been his teachers. Thanks to the largeness and originality of his style, he has become the best known among Japanese painters, and fully deserves his high repute by virtue of the force of his creations, which stamp themselves ineffaceably upon the memory and remind us of the works of the remote primitives, though without ever imitating them. The peculiar position that he occupies, as the

[1] Fenollosa, *Review*, p. 28. For the following, see the same, pp. 29, 33 ff.; Anderson, *Transact.*, p. 355 f.; Brinckmann, p. 192 ff.

greatest and boldest of the Japanese impressionists, has been excellently appreciated by Gonse in his *L'Art Japonais*. He may, indeed, not unreasonably be called the most peculiarly Japanese of all the painters; certainly he is excelled by none in expressiveness. A reproduction of one of his flower-pictures is given by Anderson,[1] and one of his bird-pictures in *Japanese Wood-Engraving*, No. 8. The screen representing a troubled sea, given by Binyon (pl. 26), seems too heavy and mechanically regular to be his work. His numerous sketches of plants and animals, treated quite broadly and for the most part relieved with very little colour, were admirably reproduced by Hoitsu in facsimile woodcuts at the beginning of the nineteenth century. A list of these reproductions will be given in the next chapter. One of his chief titles to fame is his lacquer-work inlaid with mother-of-pearl and lead. Korin's brother, Kenzan, made himself especially famous for original and highly artistic decorations of *faïence*. Another teacher of Korin, Koyetsu, the friend of Sotatsu, already forms a transition to those artists who drew directly for wood-prints; though Fenollosa appreciates his taste highly, still he does not reckon him among the great painters of Japan, esteeming him only a dilettante. The book, *Sanju rokkasen*, the Six-and-thirty Poets (Gillot Catalogue), is by him; his chief activity likewise lay in lacquer-work. The other painters who drew for wood-engraving, beginning with Hishikawa Moronobu, will be treated in connection with this particular technique.

These decorative artists, who, however, according to Japanese ideas, were by no means sharply distinguished from those that represented loftier subjects, are characteristic of a period in which luxury had attained its highest point. The women, for instance, did not shrink from the labour of changing their dresses several times a day. Similar conditions obtained with regard to objects used by the male population.

[1] *Pictorial Arts*, i. 67.

Vever Collection, Paris

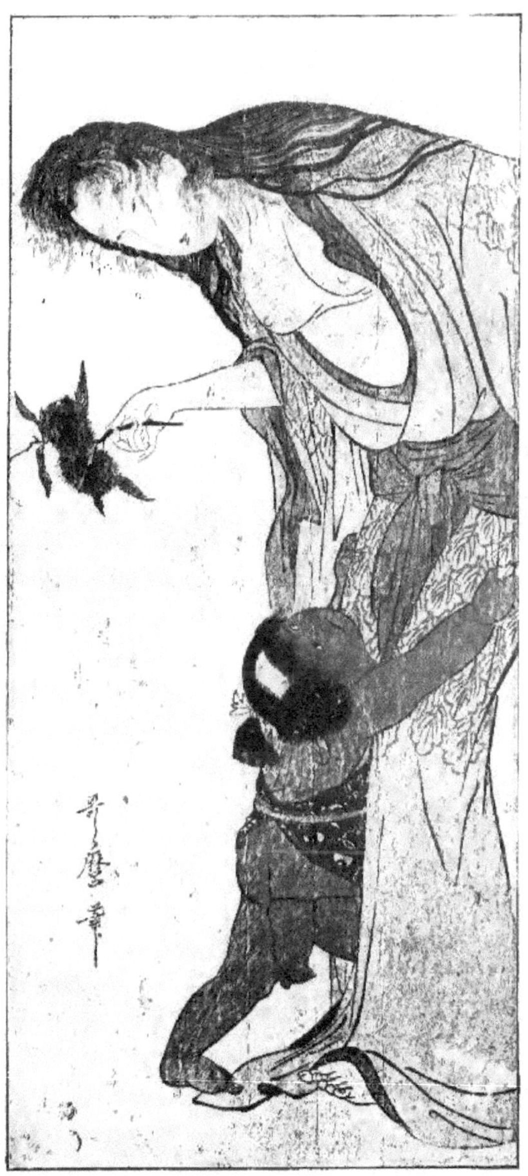

UTÁMARO: Kintoki with the Mountain-woman, Yamáuba, who offers him a Bunch of Chestnuts. *Yellowish background.* Large.

We must especially note, in the second half of the eighteenth century, the founding of the naturalistic Shijo school, whose name is derived from the fourth street of Kioto. Maruyama Okio (1733–1795), an artist who followed first the ancient Japanese, then the Chinese style, and who had settled at Kioto during the height of his fame (about 1772–1789), became its founder. He drew principally from nature. Some reproductions of animal paintings after him are given by Anderson.[1] He did not draw for wood-engraving, but copies of drawings by him appeared in 1837 in the *Eno* (?) *gwafu* and in 1851 in the *Okio gwafu*. Another notable representative of this tendency is Mori Sosen (1746–1821), who distinguished himself especially in his renderings of animals, and particularly monkeys. Some of these are reproduced by Anderson,[2] by Gonse,[3] and by Binyon (pl. 29). His work is already degenerating into excessive delicacy. A purely Chinese school was founded by Okio's most notable rival, Ganku (1749–1838), by basing his style upon that of the masters of the Sung dynasty. He was one of the best painters of modern times, and was noted for his delineations of tigers; an admirable example of these is to be found in Binyon (pl. 28). Lastly, Shirai Naokata was celebrated for his depiction of mice. With the end of the eighteenth century, however, about 1780, European influences began to make themselves felt here and there; and in connection with the increasing impotence of Japanese art, brought about its gradual decline in the nineteenth century. In the same century Yosai (1787–1878), who also worked as a wood-engraver, deserves passing mention.

[1] *Pictorial Arts*, pls. 29 and 30.
[2] *Ibid.*, pls. 31, 42, and 68.
[3] *L'Art Japonais*, i. 234, 242.

CHAPTER III

THE BEGINNING OF WOOD-ENGRAVING—BLACK AND WHITE (1582–1743)

1. General Considerations—2. Moronobu and his Contemporaries—3. The first Torii and Masanobu—4. Book-Illustration in the first half of the eighteenth century

1. General Considerations.—Those who are not well informed on the history of Japanese wood-engraving, and whose ideas are formed only from chance prints that they may have seen, will generally suppose that we are here speaking of an art which flourished especially in the nineteenth century, and that Hokusai, of whom most is heard, is its chief representative. But this point of view, which has prevailed quite long enough, and which has been encouraged by the over-estimation of Hokusai even on the part of the better informed, may now be considered as abandoned, thanks to the continued efforts of Fenollosa. As in so many other branches of the history of art, so also in the art of Japan, a theory is beginning to make headway to the effect that its heroic age was not merely a time of preparation, but rather the actual high-water mark of the whole movement, and that all subsequent to it constituted only the development of the original germs, without adding anything essentially new, without even attaining the power of those first periods. In a history of the Japanese woodcut, accordingly, the chief centre of interest is the development of the eighteenth century; and this period must in turn

R. WAGNER, BERLIN

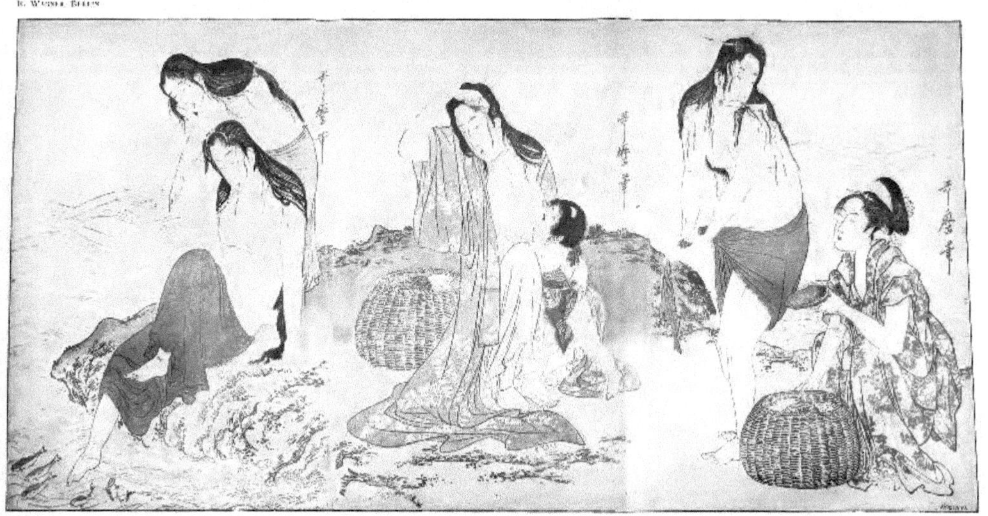

UTAMARO: FISHERWOMEN ON THE SEA-SHORE. The one on the right holds an implement for opening shell-fish in her mouth; an attendant heeds her. Draperies red, ground green, waves blue. The contours of the naked bodies reddish brown. Triptych.

be considered as the outcome of that great art which had been created in the seventeenth century by the painters of the popular school. Therefore, we are not to regard as its highest achievements those products of wood-engraving which most resemble European art, which challenge comparison with European productions, and hence are easiest for us to understand, but those which by virtue of their calligraphic and decorative character approach most nearly to the Japanese ideal of artistic greatness, dignity, and elegance, and at the same time attest the greatest individuality and creative power. This holds good especially of the work of two artists: Moronobu, the founder of the genus at the end of the seventeenth century, and Kiyonaga, the consummate master thereof, who at the end of the eighteenth century concentrated all the aims of this art up to that time into a carefully considered and in its kind perfect whole, not only as regards composition and colour, but also drawing and expression. These two will form the cardinal points of the following history. For it is due to their activity that this whole species of art, which, owing to its easy production and reproduction, was especially fitted to bring the sense for artistic enjoyment into the poorest homes, did not, on the other hand, succumb to the obvious perils of its familiarity with actors, courtesans, and low society, and degenerate into the farcical and vulgar, but remained worthy of the attention of intellectual and artistically cultivated circles.

Before outlining here the main features of the development of the Japanese woodcut, it is necessary to glance at the development of wood-engraving before it attained to actual independence. Wood-blocks for printing off written characters were used as early as the eighth century, but for pictorial representations not until the twelfth century, while no such prints earlier than the fourteenth century are actually traceable. A series signed with the name of the priest Riokin, for instance, bears a

D

date of the year 1325;[1] a denjio daishi (figure of Buddha), which, according to the inscription, was cut about the year 1400, reproduces a painting of the founders of the monastery of Heiyan (about 800 A.D.)—the Buddha stands on a lotus flower over a rock, and his outlines are well executed (Jaekel Collection in Greifswald, black and white). Indeed many of these monastic woodcuts are notable for their delicacy of contour. This industry was intended for the edification of pious pilgrims, by turning out cheap copies of famous temple pictures.

The beginnings of wood-engraving proper, which took the shape of book-illustrations, are connected, like the revival of painting and the rise of the popular Ukiyoye school towards the end of the sixteenth century, with the revolution caused by the rise of the Shogunate at this time. The more elevated standard of popular education, combined with the enforced leisure to which the nobles saw themselves reduced after they had lost their political power to the Shoguns, created a large demand for entertainment by romances of chivalry and stage plays, which was assiduously catered for by the popular authors; and the popular draughtsmen were not slow to decorate such productions with illustrations, which were multiplied in simple outline by means of wood-engraving.

The earliest known illustrated book is the *Butsu y wo kyo* (the book of the Buddhist Canon or the Ten Kings of Hell), published in 1582, which is an exact reprint of a Chinese work.[2] Here, therefore, as elsewhere, China supplied the model for the new branch of art. It is embellished with rather coarse woodcuts.[3] Another work which goes back to the sixteenth century, *Tengu dairi* (the World of Tengus, *i.e.* monsters), in three

[1] Reduced reproduction in Anderson, *Japanese Wood-Engraving*, No. 4.

[2] Duret Cat., No. 1; also in the Vever Collection, Paris.

[3] The assertion in the first edition that woodcut illustrations only began in the year 1608 must therefore be corrected in accordance with these facts.

Koechlin Collection, Paris

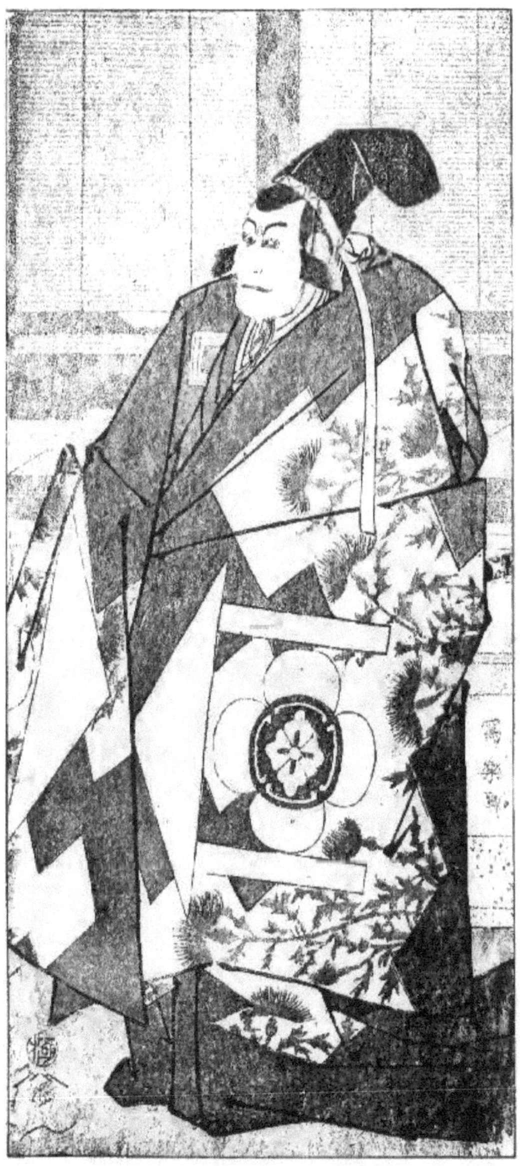

SHARÁKU : An Actor in the Costume of a Noble. (*Yebóshi*, a cap with a band across the forehead; *nagabákama*, a long underdress, enveloping the feet.) Medium size.

volumes, contains thirteen simple outline illustrations (Gillot Catalogue).

Next, in 1608, appeared a collection of romances of love and chivalry, composed in the tenth century, known by the title of *Ise Monogatari*, and now first embellished with woodcut illustrations, forty-eight in number.[1] So early as 1610 a second edition of this work appeared. The pictures, in the style of the Tosa school, are still quite conventional, and display but slight effort at individualisation; the cutting imitates the Chinese method and is handled with but moderate care.[2] In 1626 appeared the *Hogen Monogatari*, with still cruder woodcuts. Neither is the *Jokio Hiden* of 1629, a school book for girls, any better. Another book to appear in 1626 was the *Maiji Monogatari*, two volumes, in the manner of the Tosa school, coloured (Duret Catalogue, as also the following). *Takatachi* appeared about 1630, and *Nichiren shonin chugwasan*, stories from the life of the priest Nichiren, with eighty-nine pictures, in 1632 (Gillot Catalogue).

The following may be mentioned as belonging to the end of the seventeenth century: the illustrations by Hasegawa Toun in the *Yehon Hokan*, a collection of legends of the year 1688; those by Ishikawa Riusen in the *Yamato Kosaku gwasho*, an annual of Japanese customs, about the same time; collections of views, as for example of Itsukushima and environs, in 1689; *Tokiwagi*, a collection of cloth patterns, in 1700; also works on the arrangement of flowers, on uniforms, on sword-blades, all illustrated. In all these books the text, as well as the illustrations, is cut on the block. In fact, printing with movable characters can be shown to have existed in Japan only for a short time, from the end of the sixteenth century to about 1629, and even then only as an exception, probably to be traced to the immediate

[1] Duret, p. 33; Douglas, *Japanese Illustrated Books*, No. 2.

[2] Anderson, *Japanese Wood-Engraving*, No. 5.

initiative of the contemporary Shoguns, who were interested in all artistic progress. It was not until the nineteenth century that the custom of printing books with movable characters was revived.[1]

Side by side with these we find, at an early date, the illustrated sheets (broadsides), which merely catered for a popular demand, and must not be brought into immediate connection with the later artistic wood-engravings. The Jaekel Collection in Greifswald contains a single-sheet print in large folio of the year 1615, in black and white, representing the overthrow of Hideyori and the burning of his castle in Osaka, with small but well-drawn and spirited figures. In the same collection is a battle-picture with the names of the commanders, &c., intended for a fan. Somewhat later court scenes were represented in a style which already marks the transition to that of Moronobu and which are coloured, especially the faces, with body-colour, quite after the manner of the contemporary miniatures, being thus meant as substitutes for these miniatures, as they were easier, and therefore cheaper, to produce. Specimens are to be found in the Jaekel Collection. To this style also belongs a large broadside folio sheet by Baisetsudo (Jaekel Collection), done soon after 1700, a very spirited rendering of the eight views of Nara.

The illustrated books, whose first appearance dates from the sixties of the seventeenth century, already show greater powers of representation, and prepare us for the development which was brought about by the activity of Moronobu and which elevated the Japanese woodcut to the level of a true work of art. As specimens of this transition period we may, following Duret, instance: *Soga monogatari*, 1663, twelve volumes with 102 pictures (a new edition in 1704); *Eiri valkakusa monogatari* (Yedo, 1667), three volumes. With the creation at

[1] Brinckmann, p. 217 ff.

ROYAL PRINT ROOM, DRESDEN

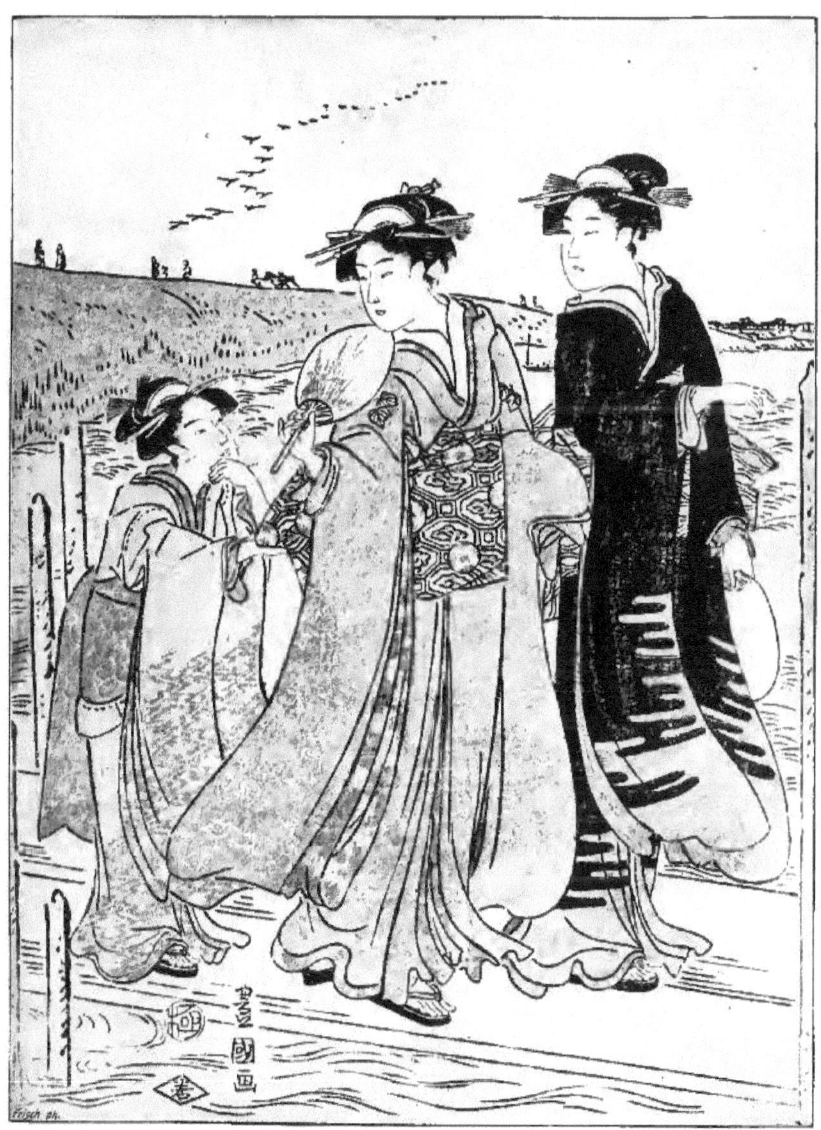

TOYÔKUNI: A YOUNG LADY WITH HER LITTLE SISTER AND A FRIEND WALKING ON A BRIDGE LATE ON A SUMMER EVENING. Wild geese on the wing.

this time of a true theatre, which had developed from the old puppet-shows, is connected the fact that since 1677 little plays were being printed, which in turn soon attracted illustrators. Fenollosa[1] draws attention to the otsuyé, slight sketches produced in great quantities for popular consumption, as being precursors of the artistic single-sheet print which began to be developed in the last decades of the seventeenth century. The otsuyé came into special vogue about the years 1630–40 and continued to be popular until about 1730. This popular art of Ukiyoye had first developed on Matahei's initiative in the Shijo school of Kioto, where it continued to be a living art far into the nineteenth century; but it had been transferred to the new capital city of Yedo as well, since the last decades of the seventeenth century, and it was there that it actually attained its greatest perfection.

Japanese wood-engraving owes its rise to truly artistic heights to the influence of Moronobu, whose most important work was done between 1675 and 1695, and whose numerous illustrations, composed after the style of the Tosa school, but freshly and vividly conceived, set an example which exerted an influence as late as the middle of the eighteenth century. Among his numerous followers, who cultivated more and more the artistic single-sheet print, was Masanobu, who lived until the middle of the eighteenth century, and distinguished himself as the first to imbue his designs with a gentle and delicate charm which may be best compared with the spirit of the rococo style then prevailing in Europe, and which continued to be a characteristic feature of Japanese style. Torii Kiyonobu, however, is noted for his foundation of the Torii school, which lasted through the eighteenth century, and the achievements of which in effective drawing and decorative balancing of black and white masses remained unequalled. Occasional sheets by

[1] Tokio Cat., p. 11.

Moronobu show an as yet monotonous and heavy hand-colouring, which became the rule for single-sheet prints from about the year 1715 onwards, increasing in variety until about 1743, when Shigenaga and Masanobu, and then gradually all other artists, began to apply themselves to the production of colour-prints, which consisted at first of only two blocks, usually of green and red. At length, towards the end of the fifties, this same Shigenaga, and along with him especially Torii Kiyomitsu, added a third block for blue or grey. Shigenaga's pupil, however, the inventive and graceful Harunobu, introduced, about 1765, the principle of printing colour-blocks over each other; henceforward colour-printing was freed from all restrictions whether as to the number of the blocks or possible colour effects, and the road that was destined to lead to the highest triumphs of the colour-printing art was clear of every obstacle. The right moment had now come for Shunsho with his numerous school, for Kiyonaga and for Utamaro, who in the closing third of the eighteenth century brought Japanese wood-engraving to its full development. Hokusai, at the beginning of the nineteenth century, was the last of the great artists of this line. Out of the multitude of the artists who follow, still for the most part admirably trained but lacking in dignity and precision, Hiroshige, with his subtly subjective landscapes, alone stands out conspicuously.[1]

A comparison of the development of wood-engraving in Europe will show that events took a very similar course in the East and the West. In Europe wood-engraving was invented towards the end of the fourteenth century. For more than fifty years its use remained confined to single sheets, principally pictures, with the occasional addition of a name or a few lines of text engraved on the same block. Soon after the invention of printing with type, about the middle of the fifteenth century,

[1] Fenollosa Cat., p. 114.

HARUNÓBU

THE BOWL OF GOLD-FISH

BRITISH MUSEUM

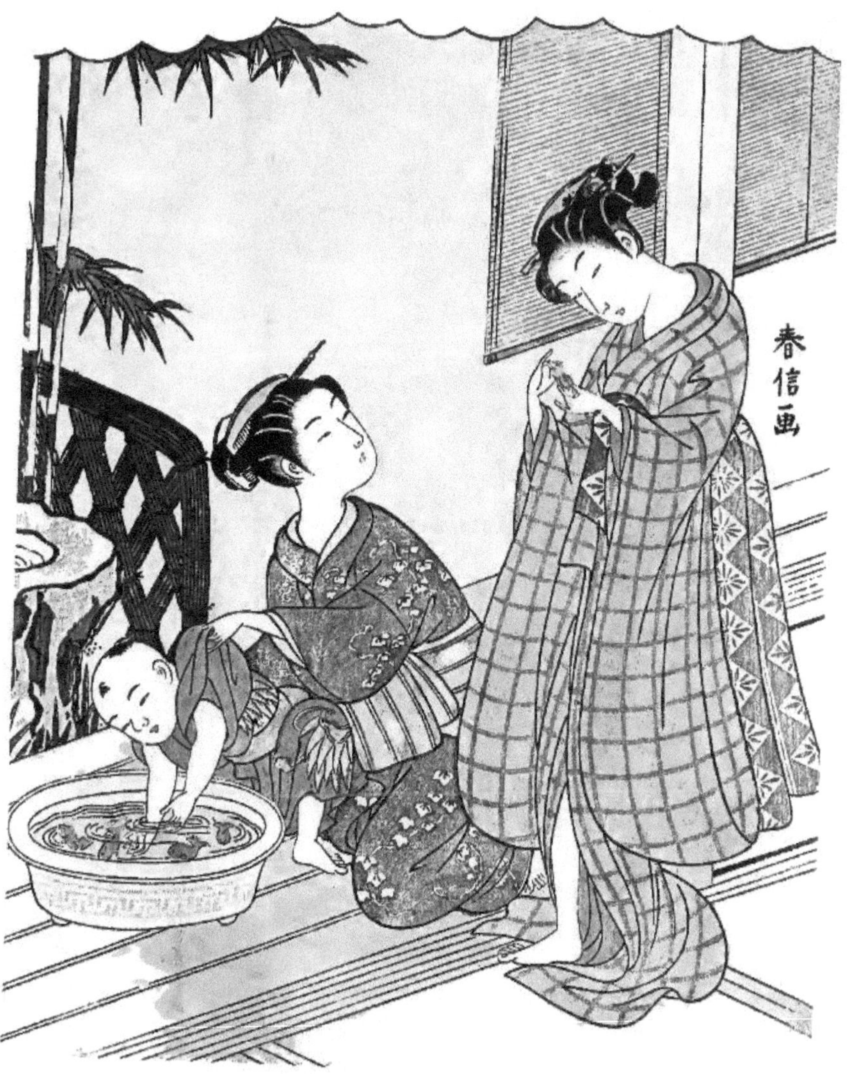
春信画

the first wood-block prints (block-books) appeared, which united both text and pictures, in imitation of the popular illustrated manuscripts. In the beginning of the seventh decade of the same century, separate woodcuts were inserted as illustrations in books printed with movable types. From these unpretentious outline-drawings, serving chiefly as a basis for colouring, there were gradually evolved by the efforts of independent artists, especially Dürer, compositions completely elaborated in light and shade, and therefore able to dispense with colour. Wood-engraving was now ready to take the field, like copper-engraving, in the shape of single-sheet prints, and to make its way into the ranks of the people; nevertheless, some time elapsed before any one ventured on the production of coloured plates. It was not until 1506 that Cranach's "Venus" appeared; in 1508 Burgkmair produced his equestrian figures of St. George and the Emperor Maximilian; Ugo da Carpi soon followed in Venice with his chiaroscuro prints. But this method did not go beyond tinted sheets, and it was only occasionally employed. True polychrome woodcuts were first produced as late as the end of the eighteenth century by Gubitz, but found no wide or permanent circulation.

In both cases, therefore, the technique of wood-engraving grew out of the necessity of producing, in large quantity and with little effort, devotional pictures for the pious pilgrims to holy shrines; was then applied to the illustration of books; gradually won for itself an independent position by the side of the productions of the painting art; and finally, since the invention of colour-printing, even entered into a kind of competition with painting. While, then, in both countries, about the same space of time (somewhat more than a century) was required for wood-engraving to pass through the various stages of evolution during which it served mainly as a basis for subsequent colouring by hand, the polychrome print, in its final development, attained in Japan a far greater significance than ever fell to its lot in Europe. It is in the high perfection of just this branch of artistic reproduction, attained in no other land and no other period, that the chief value of Japanese wood-engraving lies.

Before we enter in detail upon the history of this development, it will be well to say what there is to say of that special group of wood-engravings which were not produced from drawings especially made for them, but reproduce the designs of celebrated artists, whether in facsimile or in simple outline, and which were generally executed long after the death of the artists themselves.

There are in this class, first of all, a series of collections of faithful copies after celebrated paintings of antiquity, which appeared in the course of the seventeenth century. These are:[1]—

Gwashi kwaiyo, 6 vols. 1707, then 1754.
Yehon tekagami, 6 vols. 1720.
Gako senran, 6 vols., octavo. Osaka, 1740. With a genealogical table of the Kano school. A very beautifully executed work.
Wakan meigwayen, 6 vols. 1749.

Anderson, in *Japanese Wood-Engraving*, p. 40, traces the reproductions of the above works to Ooka Shunboku, a member of the Kano school. He died about 1760, at the age of eighty-four. *Gwahin*, three volumes of reproductions of old pictures (1760), and the *Gwahon hiroika*, signed Seshosai (Osaka, 1751), are also the work of Ooka Shunboku.

This undertaking was continued by Sakurai Shuzan in the following works:—

Wakan meihitsu gwayei. 1750.
Gwaho. 1764.
Wakan meihitsu kingioku gwafu. 1771.
Gwasoku. 1777.

---

[1] Anderson Cat., p. 341.

VEVER COLLECTION, PARIS

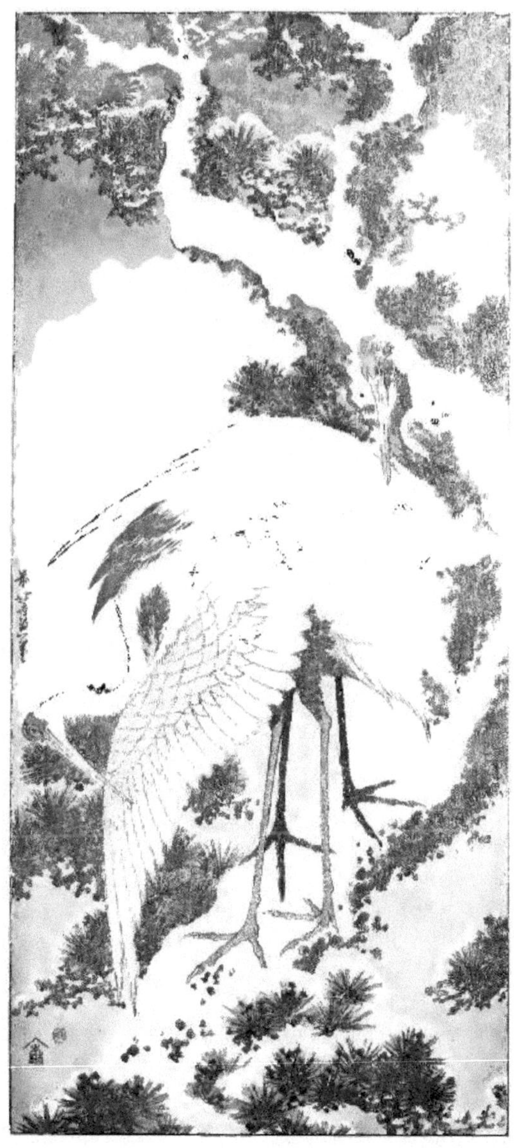

HÓKUSAI: CRANES IN THE SNOW ON A PINE-TREE.
Large. Signed: Saki no Hókusai Iitsu.

After copies of Kano Tanyu, who died in 1674, the following very beautiful work was produced by his friends:—

Shinchin gwacho, 3 vols., small quarto. Yedo, 1803. Pictures partly in black and white, partly delicately tinted.

Reproductions after drawings by Hanabusa Itcho (1651–1724) are to be found in the following works:[1]—

Hanabusa uji gwahon, 3 vols. Osaka, 1751.
Hanabusa Itcho hiakugwa, 5 vols. *Circa* 1760.
Itcho gwafu, 3 vols. 1770. Another series of the same work in one vol. 1773.
Guncho gwayei, 3 vols. 1772.
Gwato setsumiyo, 3 vols. 1774. New ed., 1821.
Gunto setsumiyo, 3 vols. 1779.
Hanabusa Itcho kiogwa. In colours, 1 vol. Nineteenth century.

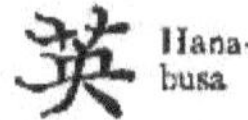
英 Hana-busa
一 Itsu
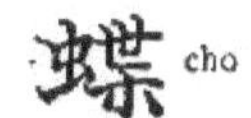
蝶 cho

In the Burty Collection[2] there existed an album in square quarto with twenty coloured double sheets of beautiful design and peculiar colour, representing bath-house scenes, theatre, dance, and street scenes, tea-drinkers, and celebrated poets, along with the picture of a ford in three sections.

The artist is said to have been banished to the island Hachijo owing to the boldness of his caricatures.

Although he had been trained in the Kano school he put himself under the influence of Moronobu. Only the works of his later style, done in the first decades of the eighteenth century, after his return to Yedo, are met with as a rule.[3]

Of the drawings of the celebrated lacquer-painter Korin (1660–1716), mostly representations of plants and animals, sketched with a few strokes and broad washes of colour, only a few were reproduced during his lifetime. His works are noted for extraordinary keenness of observation, sureness and delicacy of touch, and refinement of taste. In the collection *Gwashi*

光 Ko-
琳 rin

[1] Anderson Cat., p. 337. [2] Cat., No. 175. [3] Cat. Tokio, p. 15.

kwaiyo, of 1707, we find a picture in black and white, representing four birds asleep on a branch of a tree with the moon in the background, which Anderson reproduces in *Japanese Wood-Engraving*, No. 8.

In 1735 Nonomura Chubei published three volumes of reproductions after Korin with the title *Michi shirube* (sixty-five leaves). The pictures in the *Korin mangwa* (see below) are taken from this work. There appeared besides, in the eighteenth century, his designs for dress materials: [1]—

Hinagata someiro no yama, several vols., 8vo. 1732.
Hinagata mamiga no yama, 3 vols., 8vo. Osaka, 1754.

The majority of reproductions of his drawings, however, did not appear until the nineteenth century:—

Korin gwafu, 25 sheets, 2 vols., small folio. Kioto, 1802. Sketches of flowers in rapid brushwork; in light tones of blue, green, and red. Reproductions by Yoshinaka.

The same, 50 coloured sheets, 8vo. Containing plants, animals, landscapes, and figures.

Korin gwashiki, 56 sheets. Kioto, 1818. Large double sheets of very delicately coloured reproductions. These slight and rapid animal sketches, which contain the three puppies reproduced by Bing in his *Japon Artistique*, count among the most original, lively, and delicate work of this master.

Korin hiakuzu, 2 vols., 8vo. Yedo, 1815. Reproductions in black and white, by Hoitsu (born 1763, son of a daimio, became high priest in a temple at Kioto, died 1828); the first pulls bear his stamp. 100 drawings of miscellaneous content, kakemonos, fans, screens, landscapes, birds, and flowers. They were collected by a group of his admirers on the occasion of the centenary celebration of Korin's death, each member contributing one or more drawings. A second series, in two volumes, appeared in 1826. Finally, in 1864, a third, also in two volumes, was issued.

---

[1] Anderson Cat., p. 405; Cat. Burty, No. 87 f.

The two first series were edited by Hoitsu, the third by Keda Koson, Hoitsu's pupil.

Oson gwafu, 8vo. 1817. Coloured reproductions by Hoitsu. Executed with great care.

Original work by Hoitsu is to be found in the *Oson Gwafu* of 1817 (Hamburg). He also published reproductions after Kenzan, the brother of Korin, with the title, *Kenzan iboku*, Yedo, 1823, 23 sheets.

Korin mangwa, 60 sheets, 8vo. Yedo, 1819. Plants and flowers.

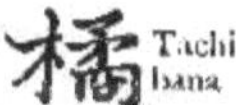
Tachi-bana

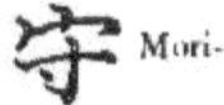
Mori-

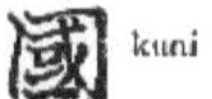
kuni

Here we must mention Tachibana Morikuni (1670–1784), a fertile illustrator during the first half of the eighteenth century, not on account of his own illustrations, of which we shall speak later, but on account of the excellent facsimiles of the sketches he dashed off in bold liquid colours, which appeared directly after his death :—

Umpitsu sogwa, "Brush-strokes," 3 vols., fol. 1749. In black and white. Especially animals. Reproduction in Bing, *Japon Artistique*, No. X., pl. ABG.

Riakugwa, 3 vols. 1750.

We have further the following reproductions from drawings by Maruyama Okio (1733–1795), the founder of the Shijo school :[1]—

Yenno gwafu, 2 vols., 8vo. Kioto, 1837. Coloured. Historical scenes, deities, flowers, and landscapes.

Okio gwafu, small folio. Kioto, 1850. Tinted. Illustrated books after Soken, one of the ten great pupils of Okio, appeared in Kioto in 1802 and 1806. Nishimura Nantei, another pupil of Okio, is the artist of the *Nansei gwafu*, humorous pictures, two vols., 1812, a continuation of which appeared in Kioto in 1821.

Lastly, Kitao Masayoshi, also called Kitao Keisai (died 1824), a pupil of Shigemasa, deserves mention here. He himself, it is true, had his drawings reproduced in wood-engraving,

[1] Cat. Burty, No. 131 f.

but did not execute them in the usual xylographic manner, with sharp outlines, but as hasty brush-sketches with rich liquid colouring, of which he simply had facsimiles made. Thus he became the originator of those numerous reproductions of sketches which, like those of Hokusai's *Mangwa*, appeared in the nineteenth century.

Of his works, we may name the following:[1]—

Yehon kwacho kagami. 1789. Coloured reproductions after flowers and birds, which are copied from the drawings of a Chinese artist (Siebold Collection).

Shoshoku yekagami. 1794. Model sketches for artists. Later editions are less valuable.

Jimbutsu riakugwashiki. Various sketches. First series 1795, second 1799. Coloured.

Shuki Ichi futsu. Sketches. 1800. Coloured.

Sansui riakuzushiki. 1800.

Giobai riakugwashiki. Fish and shells. Small fol. 1802. 30 coloured double sheets of rich colouring. A marvel of art, grand in style, and of delicate rich tone; printed with great care. New edition, 1860.

Riakugwayen. Slight sketches. 1809. Coloured.

Kwa riakugwashiki. Quarto. Yedo, 1813. Flowers and shrubs. 27 double sheets, coloured.

Landscapes, 3 vols., containing 20 sheets. Of no special interest.

Shoshoku gwakio. Yedo, 1794. Black and white.

Gengwa yen. Yedo, 1808. Coloured figure pieces.

Keisai gwafu. 60 coloured compositions.

Most of these works are executed in a few bold colours, broadly laid on, often without any sort of contour. The artist, of whom we shall have more to say at the end of the chapter on Kiyonaga, is in this line of work the continuer of Morikuni.

We have similar sketches in rapid brushwork dating from the end of the eighteenth century by Gokan (1784),[2] Hasegawa

[1] Anderson Cat., p. 347; Cat. Burty, No. 204 ff.

[2] See Cat. Burty, No. 215.

HARUNÓBU

VASE OF FLOWERS, AND RISING MOON

MONSIEUR J. PEYTEL, PARIS

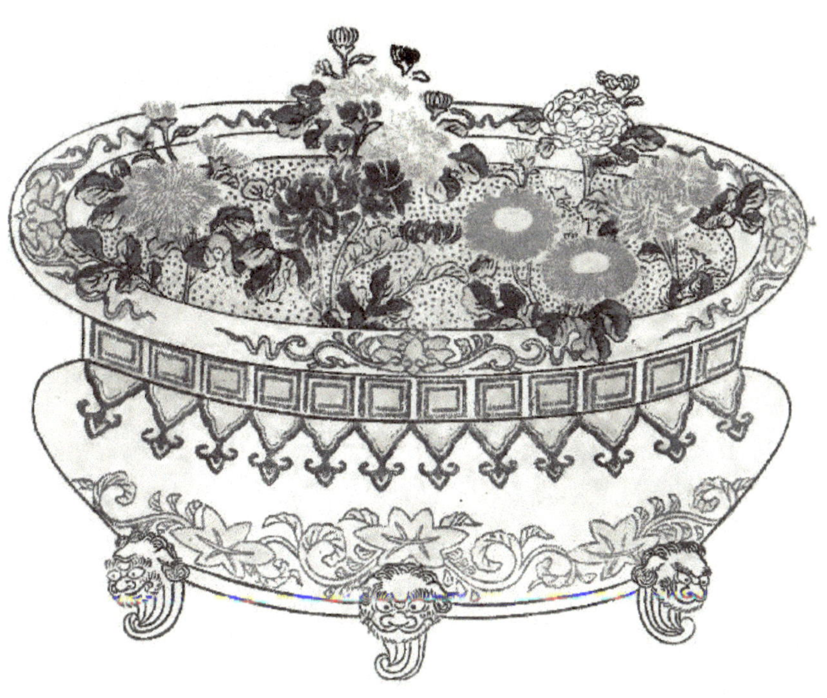

Mitsunobu[1] and many others. Illustrated books by Mitsunobu appeared in Osaka, 1724, in Kioto, 1750, and a book with scenes of war in 1756.

2. MORONOBU AND HIS CONTEMPORARIES.—The real history of Japanese wood-engraving does not begin until the seventies of the seventeenth century. As so often happens in the history of art, a single richly gifted man, appearing at the right time, suddenly elevated the art to its fullest height. In this case Moronobu was the elect of Providence. At the beginning of his activity there was no such thing as colour-printing. His own sheets are still without exception done in black and white, and only occasionally relieved with a little colour applied by hand; and another fifty years were destined to pass after his death before a series of the most various experiments, at first in hand-colouring, then in two-block, and lastly in three-block printing, culminated in the perfect polychrome print, untrammelled in its choice of means. But with this last, world-famous phase of Japanese wood-engraving the work of Moronobu had no immediate connection. Even if the subsequent development had not reached this point, he would still have maintained the place he holds in the history of Japanese wood-engraving, for his significance lies not only in the fact that he was a forerunner and a pioneer, but in the eminence to which he advanced in his own individual achievement.

It was, to be sure, a great step forward when the ordinary illustrations, intended only to entertain the general public and turned out ever since the beginning of the seventeenth century in the traditional style and with no special care, were suddenly replaced by pictures that were, alike in conception and execution, works of art. We must also count it an especial merit of Moronobu that he took up and awakened to new life the popular art created by Matahei in the first half of the

[1] Cat. Burty, No. 539.

seventeenth century, which in the subsequent era of universal stagnation had fallen into oblivion. His peculiar glory, however, consists in this, that he brought wood-engraving to such instant perfection that his influence remained predominant throughout the entire period that elapsed until the invention of tone polychrome-printing, the period, that is, of the "primitives," which lasted for two whole generations.

Such "primitives" are now held in far higher estimation than formerly. We recognise in them not only forerunners, but men of heroic race, who, without being able to claim the highest honours paid to the gods, still exhibit a power, a freshness, and a grace that are hardly met with in the same degree in later times. Despite the imperfections that necessarily attach to their works, despite their lack of external correctness, their limitation to few and generally crude materials, and their conventionalism, there clings to their works a charm such as belongs to the works neither of the most brilliant nor of the pronouncedly naturalistic periods. For, in the singleness of their effort to make their drawing as expressive as possible, without regard to any special kind of beauty or truth, these "primitives" discover a power of idealisation and a stylistic skill which, at a later period and with increased knowledge, are quite unthinkable. The conscious striving after beauty and symmetry detracts somewhat from the freshness of immediate observation, and deprives it of some part of its force; while, on the other hand, the attempt to imitate nature exactly draws the artist away from the true goal of art, for it leads him only too easily to forget that he is the creator, and not the copyist of nature. While, therefore, all subsequent endeavours lead only to this result, that after many and various attempts to bring beauty into harmony with truth, the flower of art blossoms for a brief season, to be followed immediately by decay, the "primitives," on the other hand, keep on their way unconcerned about the solution of such difficult problems, and unfold the powers that are in them in all their freshness, taking care only to infuse as much life as possible into their creations and to give them as much finish as is necessary to produce a harmonious artistic impression.

Thus the representations of Moronobu and his school combine a pronouncedly decorative effect, achieved by a symmetrical filling up of the surface and the strong contrast of black and white masses, with extreme animation of motion and expression. All the persons—and there is nearly always plenty of movement in these compositions—stand in relation to one another, react on one another, and thus produce an impression dramatic in the highest degree. Though essentially schematic in their construction, they are nevertheless full of a warm life not unfelt by the artist himself. Although the faces, especially the rounded faces of the women, with their diminutive features, are monotonous enough, and although the courtly etiquette which prevails in these representations demands all possible immobility and impassiveness, nevertheless the play of eyes and eyebrows betrays enough of the emotion that lies beneath. The figures, bounded by a firm, rounded, and in places slightly thickened contour, move in graceful attitudes and beautifully flowing lines. Scenes from history and legend, and also numerous representations from contemporary life, alternate with one another—a faithful mirror of the occupations of high society, its combats and love adventures, its games, pastimes, and pleasures, even its fashions in dress and coiffure. For a reduced specimen, see Anderson, *Japanese Wood-Engraving*, No. 6. Although the spirit of a new era of lax morality now first intrudes on these pictures, in the shape of easy beauties and celebrities of the stage, yet the artists never drop into vulgarity, but always preserve the forms of the highest propriety and good breeding. It is only in the crowded and lively street scenes, which Moronobu loved to draw on large oblong sheets, that he yields, always within the bounds of art, to a spirit of frolic which is absolutely enchanting. He never poses, but always remains simple and natural.

Hishikawa Moronobu 菱川師宣

Hishikawa Moronobu, known also by the name of Kichibei, was born about 1646–47[1] as the son of a celebrated embroiderer named Michishige, at Hoda, in the province of Awa. After he had learned his father's craft and had made a name for himself as a designer of patterned robes and embroideries, he left Yasuda, where he had lived until then, and went to Yedo, where he mastered painting, and then devoted himself chiefly to book-illustration. According to Fenollosa (*Outline*) he studied painting in the new Kano school of Tanyu, so that he was able to enter the field in competition with Tsunenobu, the Shogun's protégé. Although he distinguished himself as a painter by taking up again the popular style introduced by Matahei, with special attention to delicacy of detail and tasteful choice of colours, yet he achieved far greater influence through the new life which he imparted to wood-engraving by the untiring zeal with which he turned out series after series of illustrations, which he caused to be cut under his own supervision with more care than had hitherto been customary. This activity lasted from 1669 to 1695. Moronobu contented himself with ordinary types, but contrived to invest his figures with so much life that they appear to be all but actually speaking to the beholder. Further, he never neglected the decorative effect of his compositions, but made most felicitous use of the contrast between white and black spaces. Thus he became the real creator of the popular illustrative style. His most powerful work dates from the beginning of the eighties. Fenollosa says[2] that the contours became softer and more feminine in his later works. Soon a great number of pupils and fellow-workers of similar aims gathered around him, so that, toward the end of the

[1] Anderson Cat., p. 332; Fenollosa Cat., Nos. 3–6; Strange, p. 6.
[2] Tokio Cat., p. 13.

BING COLLECTION, PARIS

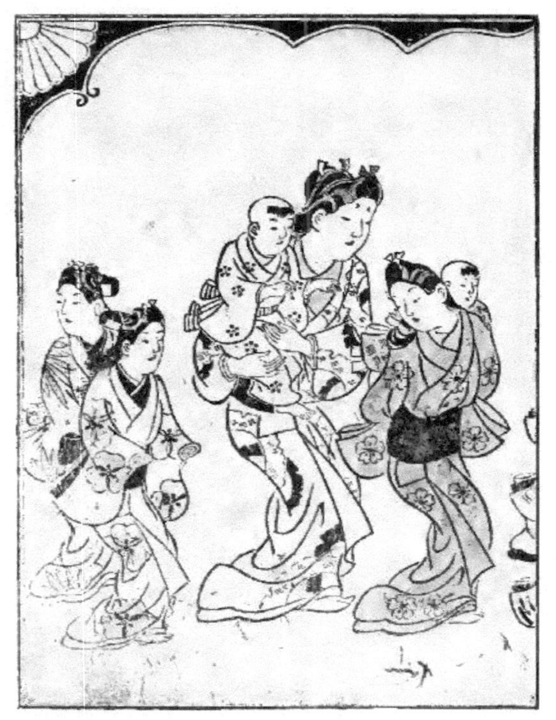

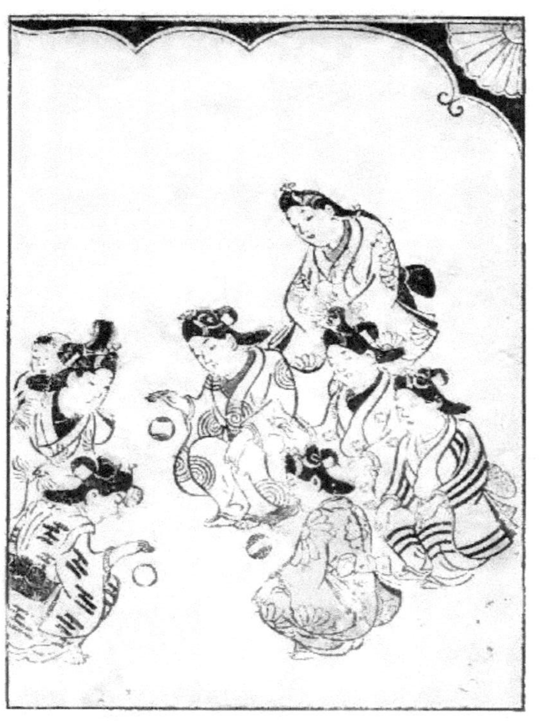

MORÓNOBU: A GAME OF BALL. From the third volume of "Yamato no ōyosei," of 1682. *Slightly heightened with colour.*

century, he stood as the absolute monarch in this domain. His sheets, which were always printed in bold and simple black and white, are seldom found coloured, and then only with a few broad effective blots of orange, brown-red, and green. One of his earliest productions is the *Ukiyo hiakunin joya*, or hundred female figures, thirty-one representations of women in their daily occupations, Yedo; further, the *Iwaki yezukushi*, scenes from aristocratic life, 1682; the *Yamato no oyosei*, 1682; in 1683 he published the pictures of fair women, *Bijin yezukushi;* in the *Hiakunun ishu sugata* (1685) he represents the hundred poets sitting facing each other in pairs, all different, full of movement and expression and individuality. Besides these, he illustrated the novel *Ise monogatari* (new edition, 1774, in two volumes), *Genji monogatari* (25 sheets), and edited a guide to the Yoshiwara in 1678, a topographical work (meisho) in 1687, a series of landscape gardens in 1691; and his life-work further includes an album of studies of animals, plants, and flowers, a set of designs for fans, 1682, flowers and birds, 1683, and *Yegata sennin yukushi* (ghost stories in the Chinese style), 1689. A very full list of his works may be found in Anderson's Catalogue, p. 334; and reproductions in the Hayashi Catalogue, No. 174; Duret, p. 53; Fenollosa, *Outline*, pl. ii. Single-sheet prints by him are very scarce. He is said in his old age to have renounced the world and shaved his head, and, taking the name of Yuchiku, to have spent the rest of his days as a monk, dying *circa* 1714–15 in the period of Shotoku (1711–16) at the age of sixty-seven. But a more credible version has lately been found on the first page of a book by his son Morofusa, according to which he died in 1695; and in fact no work by him later than that date can be proved to exist.

Moronobu left two sons, one of whom, Moronaga, is said to have distinguished himself as a colourist of wood-engravings. The other, Hishikawa Morofusa, followed absolutely the manner

E

of his father, manipulating it in flowing contours and with considerable spirit. As to his biography, see Fenollosa's *Outline;* he is mentioned as an artist as early as 1683, and was called Kichiza-yemon in ordinary life.[1] A book of dress patterns, with eighty-four plates, dated 1700, is his work. Reproduction in Hayashi Cat., No. 185.

Fenollosa (*Outline*) mentions Furuyama Moroshige as one of the best of Moronobu's pupils (like him he was also a painter), and suggests that he may have been the master of Kiyonaga.[2] Books illustrated by him date from the years 1692 and 1698. Frau Straus-Negbaur, in Frankfort-on-the-Main, possesses one of his prints.[3] A further pupil of Moronobu was Sugimura Masataka, who painted about 1700.[4] A book of 1684 contains magnificent illustrations by him, which are in no way inferior to the best work of the master himself. Another book of his was published at Kioto in 1716.

Two contemporaries of Moronobu were Hasegawa Toun, who edited the collection of legends called *Yehon hokan* in 1688, and Ishikawa Riusen, who illustrated country life in *Yamato kosaku gwasho.* Riusen is already found mentioned side by side with Moronobu as a celebrated artist. An illustrated book by him appeared in Yedo between 1692–96. A sheet dated 1714 is in the Hayashi Catalogue (No. 187). A sheet done by Ishikawa Riushu, a pupil of Riusen, is illustrated in the same catalogue (No. 188). Mention is further made about 1700 of the painter Wowo[5] who worked for wood-engravings as late as the period of Kioho (1716–35). Other illustrators are: Kawashima Shigenobu (1683), Kichi (1700), Yoshimura

[1] Tokio Cat., p. 14.

[2] *Ibid.*, p. 13.

[3] A follower of Moroshige was Furuyama Moromasa, who lived in the period of Horeki (1751–63)—at a very much later date, that is to say (Tokio Cat., p. 13). An illustration in the Hayashi Cat. (No. 186) represents a scene in a tea-house, in large broadside folio.

[4] Tokio Cat., p. 15.

[5] *Ibid.*, p. 14.

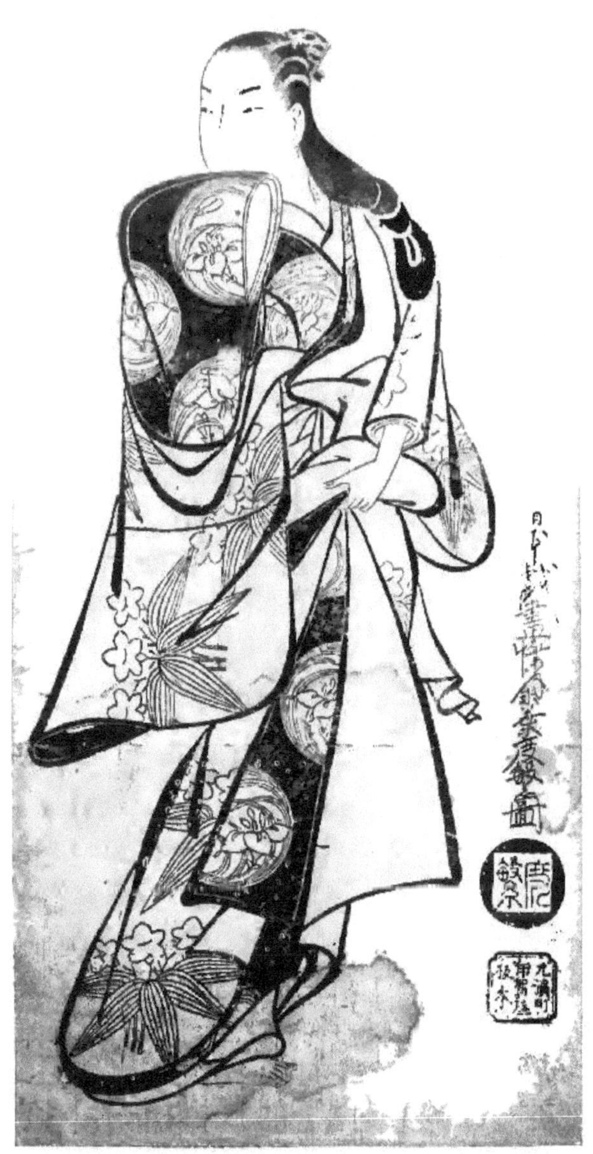

NORISHIGÉ: COURTESAN IN A ROBE FIGURED WITH IRISES AND PAULOWNIA FLOWERS. She holds up her dress with her left hand; her right hand is hidden. Kakemono. Signed: Nippon Kigwa Kwaigetsu Matsuyo Norishigé. *Black impression.*

Katsumasa (1718); the last mentioned is the author of *Taisei Shucho*, representations of animals and plants, 112 sheets, 3 volumes (Gillot Catalogue).

懷月堂 Kwai-getsu-do

The greatest of his fellow-workers, however, was Kwaigetsudo, whose chief activity synchronises with the first decade of the eighteenth century.[1] Although he does not equal Moronobu in creative power and fertility, and although, in contrast with the somewhat squat but well-proportioned figures of Moronobu, he yielded to a certain mannerism in drawing his heads, hands, and feet habitually too small, yet he understood how to impart to the female types that figure on his large, tall prints, clad in full, richly-patterned garments, a dignity of carriage, a flow of contour and of undulating drapery, which set them among the finest and most forceful specimens of their kind, while from the large black and white patterns of the dresses these pictures derive an incomparable decorative effect. Like Moronobu, Kwaigetsudo was also a painter. The Hayashi Catalogue gives Kwaigetsudo the cognomen Yasutomo, and adds that he was trained in the Tosa school and was the first Kwaigetsudo who produced wood-engravings (see illustration *ibid.*). In the Tokio Catalogue (p. 18 *seqq.*) the artist receives a detailed and judicious appreciation. He is brought into connection with Choshun (see *infra*) as the most brilliant member of his circle and the only one who worked at wood-engraving. He was principally active about 1707–14, and already shows the influence of Masanobu (see *infra*) and the first Torii. Although, says the Catalogue, his compositions were somewhat monotonous, he occupies an unapproached position among all these popular artists because of his excellent distribution of black patterns. Norishige, whose name accompanies that of Kwaigetsudo in the illustration here reproduced, seems to have been a pupil of his. About 1700 there worked also

[1] Fenollosa Cat., No. 15 ff.

Hane- 羽 gawa 川 Chin- 珍 cho 重

Hanegawa Chincho, of whom we have a few large pictures of women, coloured by hand, and in whose work brick-red strongly predominates. His designs are broad and distinguished[1] in style. A book illustrated by him and published at Yedo dates from about 1700.[2] This youthful period, however, which connects itself with Moronobu's activity, was followed in the subsequent decades by the artist's most important period, which marks him as a pupil of Kiyonobu. He lived from 1679–1754 and signed Hanegawa Okinobu.[3] An important sheet by him is in the possession of Frau Straus-Negbaur in Frankfort-on-the-Main.

As a painter of the popular school, Moronobu's pupil Choshun, called in Japanese Miyagawa Nagaharu, attained wide-reaching influence. A better colourist than his master, he favoured a similar range of subjects, but did not work for wood-engraving. He was chiefly active during the second decade of the eighteenth century. He kept more closely to the style of Tsunenobu than Moronobu to that of Tanyu. To the colours of the Kano school, red, yellow, blue, and green, he added the subdued shades, brown, olive-green, purple, and grey. He principally represented Yedo street scenes, and his activity and that of his school extended to about 1725.[4] One of his pictures is reproduced in Fenellosa's *Outline*, pl. iii. According to the same authority the school of Moronobu, which after 1710 fell more and more into decay, was followed, on the one hand, by Kiyonobu's freer school of wood-engraving, on the other, by the more conservative school of painting inaugurated by Choshun, to which the nobles, then beginning to separate more sharply from the people, were attached. His son, Miyagawa Choki, worked in the twenties. Another follower of Choshun, Tsuneyuki, who was perhaps trained in the Kano

[1] Epistolary communication from S. Bing.
[2] Hayashi Cat., No. 1450.
[3] *Ibid.*, No. 235 *seqq.*, with illustrations.
[4] Tokio Cat., p. 16.

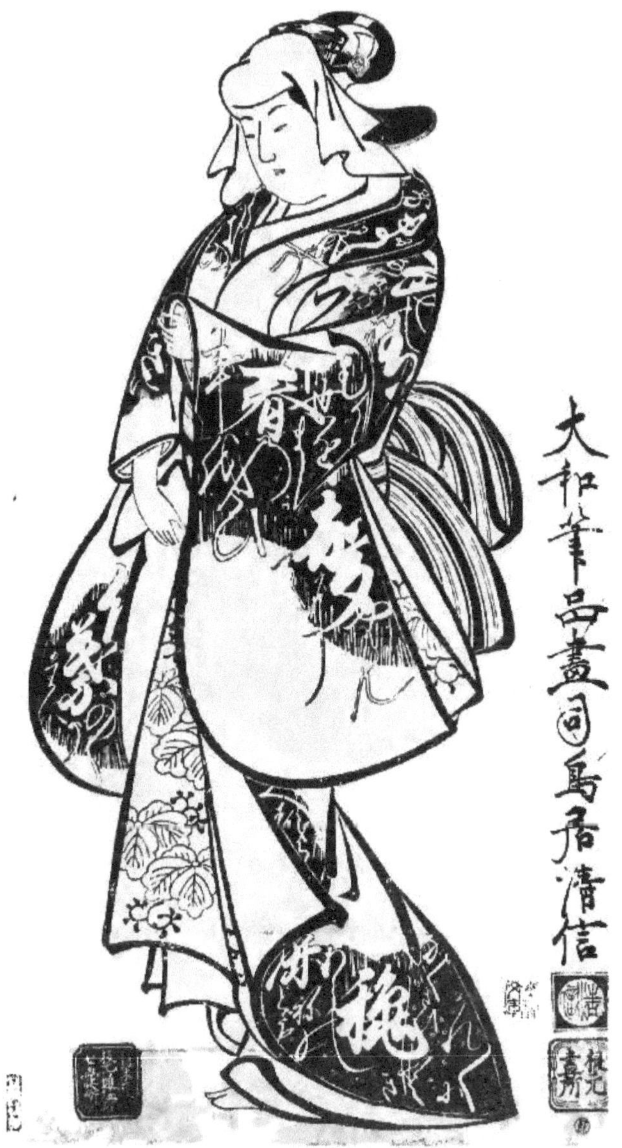

YAMATO TORIIKIYONOBU : BYÛN IN A ROBE FIGURED WITH WRITTEN CHARACTERS AND PAULOWNIA FLOWERS. Kakemono. Signed : Yamato Hippin Gwasgi Toriikiyonobu. *Black impression.*

school, belongs to the best painters of the popular style. He was probably a pupil of Tsunenobu, and painted about 1720.[1] But Choshun's pupil, Miyagawa Shunsui (Shinsui?) was a painter of especial importance, as influencing the further development of this style in the representation of graceful female figures, which reached its highest perfection in the second half of the century. Fenollosa, at least, thinks it very probable that he is one and the same with the Katsukawa Shunsui who was still at work in the second half of the century producing some not very important prints, and who made a name for himself chiefly as the teacher of the great Shunsho. In that case he must have changed his family name about the year 1750, and continued working until the year 1770, under Masanobu's influence. However this may be, he at any rate influenced Tsunemasa, who probably was originally the pupil of the above-mentioned Tsuneyuki, and whose significance lies in the fact that, as a painter, he prepared the way for the style of Harunobu and the others who depicted women during the second half of the century. Tsunemasa worked between 1730 and 1780; he seems to have perfected his peculiar style about 1750.[2] All the artists here named are remarkable only as painters.[3]

3. THE FIRST TORII: MASANOBU.—The art of the first half of the eighteenth century is mainly dominated by the influence of the Torii school, founded by Kiyonobu I., which devoted itself especially to representations of actors (the theatre having at that time reached its most brilliant development), and which continued to exercise its influence beyond the conclusion of the

[1] Tokio Cat., p. 21. [2] *Ibid.*, p. 22.

[3] Fenollosa Cat., No. 7–13. Fenollosa also discusses Shunsui in further detail in his *Outline* (p. 31) and in the Tokio Cat. (p. 24 *seqq.*), and suggests that he may have been a son of Choshun. He founded a large school of painting side by side with the Torii, which was distinguished for its realism, its intensity of colouring, and its delicacy of conception; the landscape background also began to develop in course of time. One of his paintings is reproduced in the *Outline*, pl. vii. It was only after 1765 that he worked for the wood-engravers once or twice.

eighteenth century. Formerly the opinion was that this time could be identified with that of the first appearance of the two-colour print, which had been fixed at about the year 1710; but since Fenollosa has established the fact that the production of these earliest coloured prints cannot well be assumed as prior to 1743, in which year the first dated and presumably the earliest print of this kind was published, we must take it that the whole previous period was entirely devoted to black and white. On the other hand, the painting of these sheets, which began to be done with artistic care quite early, at all events about the year 1710, deserves especial mention, as it developed the peculiar colour-scheme on which the true polychrome prints were afterwards modelled.[1]

Tori- 鳥 i 居 Kiyo- 清 nobu 信

Torii Kiyonobu I., according to his real name Shobei, was born in 1664 and lived until 1729.[2] From Kioto where he lived at first, he proceeded to Yedo where a more stimulating atmosphere was to be found, and gave himself up chiefly to the depicting of actors, and also to the preparation of theatrical programmes and posters. Whereas hitherto these subjects had only been occasionally treated, he elevated them to the rank of a permanent department of wood-engraving, which continued to be cultivated almost as a matter of privilege by the Torii school that he founded. His drawing was broad, bold, and decided, and calculated to produce its effect from a distance, as in broad-

[1] In my first edition I had assumed a parallel activity of, and a continuous rivalry between, Kiyonobu and Masanobu. Since then, however, it has been shown that we must assume the existence of two artists named Kiyonobu, the second appreciably younger than the first; and my former description has had accordingly to be completely recast, for although Masanobu began work at more or less the same period as Kiyonobu I., yet it was not until the latter half of his life that he became a determining influence in his art and entered into the competition as described with the second Kiyonobu.

[2] In the first edition his dates had been given as 1688–about 1756, on the authority of Anderson, *Japanese Wood-Engraving*, p. 23; Fenollosa Cat., Nos. 20–23, 29, 35, 61, 87; Strange, p. 21. The new dates are founded on the Hayashi Cat., No. 190 *seqq*.

brush painting. Simple rounded outlines sufficed him to express force. His faces are long and oval in shape. His large sheets[1] are remarkable for their admirable distribution of the black spaces, whose effect is made still more striking by being picked out with lustrous vermilion. A subdued yellow and a green approaching to olive are also used. About 1715 the large pictures of actors were at the height of their popularity, and through them, as the Hayashi Catalogue (Introduction, p. iii) rightly remarks, Kiyonobu became the true founder of the popular style, the courtly style of Moronobu having hitherto reigned supreme. Subsequently, however, and up to the invention of two-colour printing, these large sheets were more and more replaced by the smaller narrow prints called hoso-ye, which were employed for choice by Shunsho as late as the second half of the eighteenth century. In his first period Kiyonobu had also done book-illustrations — the Hayashi Catalogue (No. 1426 *seqq.*) instances several which appeared at Yedo about 1690, and again from 1700 to 1705.

In the beginning Kiyonobu coloured with the orange-red (*tan*, a lead pigment) then universally used for the purpose, his sheets coming thence to be commonly designated as tan-ye, orange paintings. From about the year 1715, however, he used instead of this a carmine-red (*beni*, a vegetable juice), with which he combined violet, blue, and a brilliant yellow.[2] In the second decade Indian ink was added, which was covered with a lacquer varnish, and this for two decades remained the characteristic of the colouring of that period. Gold dust and, for white surfaces, powdered mother of pearl (mica), were also used. These hand-coloured prints were called urushi-ye, lacquer pictures. It was just at this time, when the hand-

[1] Illustration in Hayashi Cat., No. 197.

[2] According to a statement in the *Kokka Magazine*, *tan* was displaced at the beginning of the period of Kioho (1716–35) by *beni* (Deshayes in *L'Art*, 1893, ii. 10).

coloured wood-engravings were at their highest perfection and circulated everywhere, that Masanobu, who had begun to work for wood-engraving about the same time as Kiyonobu, broke off this activity and devoted himself almost wholly to painting. At this time, too, the hair coiffure, after abandoning its elaborate style of the seventeenth century, and gradually becoming flatter and flatter, had changed yet again to continually squarer shapes distinguished only by a long flat queue.

According to Japanese custom, Kiyonobu's pupils adopted a part of his surname, which they completed by an additional syllable. Among these, Kiyotada was the most conspicuous. He began to work as early as 1720, but his activity ceased long before that of his master; for this reason his works are particularly rare.[1] An illustration in the Hayashi Catalogue (No. 219) rather reminds one of Masanobu. In the Tokio Catalogue (p. 33) thirty-three of his pictures are enumerated, varying in date from about 1714 to 1736. Perhaps he was a son of Kiyonobu.

Tori-i Kiyo-masu 鳥居清倍

Together with Kiyonobu I., Kiyomasu is generally spoken of as the second great master of this school.[2] As he was born about 1679,[3] he cannot have been a son of Kiyonobu, as was formerly supposed; rather he may have been his brother, as Fenollosa assumes. He is said to have died as late as 1763, and according to this account must have witnessed the activity of Kiyonobu II. (see below). A play-bill by him bears the early date 1693. Illustrated books by him appeared in 1703 (Kioto), and again in 1712 (Yedo), 1729, and 1747. The Tokio Catalogue (No. 37 *seqq.*) mentions sheets by him which are assigned to about 1711 and 1713; and one of these, in the judgment of Fenollosa, shows a distinction of draughtsmanship which may be sought for in vain among the works of Moronobu, and a sense of life which surpasses Kwaigetsudo.

[1] Fenollosa Cat., No. 31.
[2] *Ibid.*, No. 24.
[3] Hayashi Cat., No. 203 *seqq.*

VEVER COLLECTION, PARIS

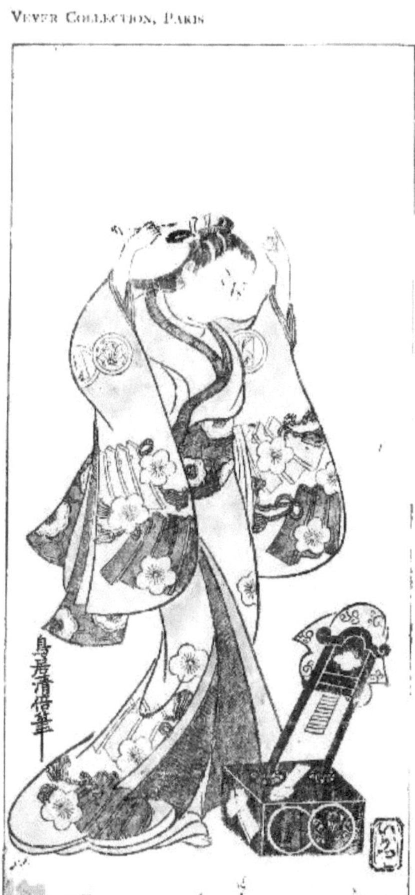

KIYOMASU: LADY AT HER TOILET. The dress figured with lotus. *Hand-tinted in yellow, green, and grey.*

BING COLLECTION, PARIS

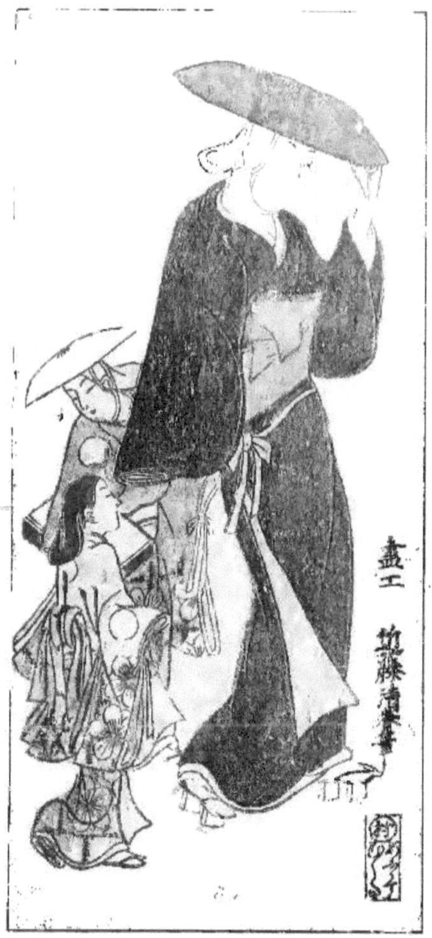

KIYOHARU: A YOUNG WOMAN TRAVELLING, WITH TWO SERVANTS. *Hand-tinted with black and yellow.* Medium size.

As a draughtsman Kiyomasu seems to have excelled Kiyonobu, and to have been altogether more productive than he. His compositions, consisting both of black and white and of two-colour prints, are replete with life and vigour. Bing (Catalogue, p. 2) gives a list of some of them. The Tokio Catalogue (No. 40) mentions an urushiya by him of about 1728, and two-colour prints of about 1744 and 1747 (Nos. 69, 70). A chess-board pattern first occurs in one of his prints towards 1748. The Gillot Catalogue even makes mention of a three-colour print, a falcon on its perch. Kiyoshige, also, of whom Bing cites an actor (Catalogue, p. 3), belongs to this period. He executed, as appears from a kind communication from S. Bing, almost exclusively actor prints, of larger or smaller size, together with some kakemonos. His period of activity extends from 1725 to about 1759. The Tokio Catalogue (No. 51) mentions a hand-coloured kakemono by him, dated about 1745, and also a two-colour print of about 1759 (No. 83). An illustrated book appeared at Yedo in 1754. There are two illustrations in the Hayashi Catalogue (Nos. 224 and 226), the first of which already reminds us very much of Harunobu.

Finally, we must name Kondo Sukegoro (also Hishikawa) Kiyoharu, who, during the first part of the eighteenth century, was specially active as an illustrator of books, particularly children's books. One of his picture-books appeared in Yedo in 1720. We have by him *Ginka-Zoshi*, poems on the girls' festival, Tanabata, of July 7th, according to the old calendar; a new edition, in colours, is supposed to have been produced in 1835, at Osaka, in 3 vols. 8vo. He also represented theatrical scenes.[1] The Hayashi Catalogue (No. 232) mentions a certain Kondo Katsunobu as his son or pupil, and illustrates a very graceful drawing by him, done in a broad style.

Further artists of this group are as follows: Torii Kiyosomo,

[1] Anderson Cat., p. 338; Cat. Burty, No. 152.

who was perhaps already influenced by Masanobu; his works are rare and distinguished. In the Hayashi Catalogue (No. 221), which also gives a reproduction, he is called a pupil of Kiyonobu I. In the Tokio Catalogue (No. 52) there is an urushi-ye by him of about 1739. Katsukawa Terushige, a pupil of Kiyonobu (illustration in Hayashi Catalogue, No. 531). Tamura Yoshinobu (illustration, *ibid.*, No. 233). Fujikawa Yoshinobu, middle of eighteenth century (illustration, *ibid.*, No. 294). Tamura Sadanobu (illustration, *ibid.*, No. 234). Shimizu Mitsunobu (illustration, *ibid.*, No. 292).

The second generation of the Torii is represented by Kiyonobu II., who worked from the thirties to the middle of the fifties, and so stood in the midst of the two-colour print period, which began in 1743. He is stated in the Gillot Catalogue to have been the third son of Kiyonobu I.[1] Bing (Catalogue, p. 1) mentions several of his sheets, but the question whether they belong to him or to Kiyonobu I. has still to be examined; the same applies to the lovers reproduced by Strange (p. 22). In the Jaekel Collection at Greifswald, there is an urushi-ye by him dating from the early thirties. On a colour-print of about 1752 there is already the suggestion of a landscape.[2] On the picture of an actor as Soga no Goro of about 1753 (illustrated in Fenollosa's *Outline*, pl. v.) the spots of red and green are as subtly distributed in their relations to the black and the white as the pattern on the shell of a tortoise; on a two-colour print of about 1754 (*ibid.*, p. 47) the black is already more prominent. Fenollosa (Catalogue, No. 61) singles out for special praise a triptych with figures under sunshades, printed in colours. He is perhaps identical with the Torii Shiro, one of whose sheets is illustrated in the Hayashi Catalogue, No. 227. Two

[1] In the first edition he had not yet been distinguished from Kiyonobu I., who was assumed to have lived to beyond the middle of the century.

[2] Tokio Cat., No. 46; *ibid.*, p. 27.

Royal Print Room, Dresden

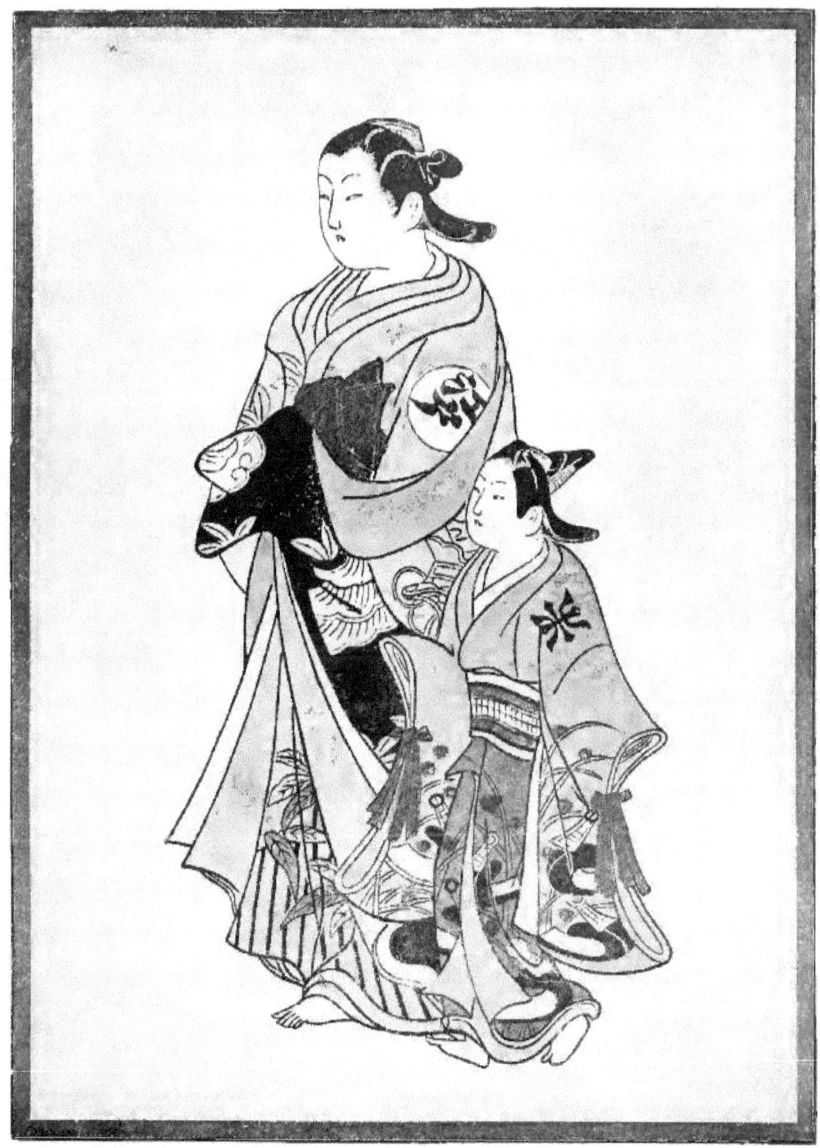

MASÁNOBU : Courtesan with a Servant. *Hand-tinted with red, yellow, brown, black, and gold-dust. On a mica ground.* Medium size.

celebrated artists, whose names were similarly formed, do not appear until long after—Kiyomitsu, about the middle of the century; and Kiyonaga, the most perfect representative of Japanese wood-engraving, towards the end of the century.

Beside this Torii school of the first period, and especially beside Kiyonobu II., stands Okumura Masanobu, whose life extended from 1685 to 1764, and who claims a special place by himself. He was also a publisher, and signed with the names Bunkaku, Kwammio, Tanchosai, also Genzoku, as well as with his real name.[1] He differs from the Torii in so far that, as a direct pupil of Moronobu and following his style more closely, he seldom produced actor prints, but devoted himself instead to the glorification of feminine charm and beauty; and in the end, his innate sense of grace and pleasing composition enabled him to bring the style of this early period to a perfection and finish not again equalled until the easier mastery of Kiyonaga.

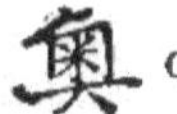 Oku-

村 mura

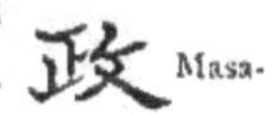 Masa-

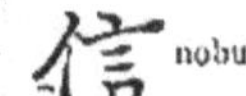 nobu

Masanobu's life falls into two clearly separated divisions, the boundary between them being formed by the second half of the thirties. At first he seems, as did his teacher, Moronobu, to have produced in the main book-illustrations (yehons), in black and white. Anderson (Catalogue, p. 338) cites several of them, among them a work which treats of beautiful women (bijin). The dates which he gives extend from 1690 to 1720, but the first of these (1690) is obviously much too early. In the Hayashi Catalogue (No. 1457 *seqq.*) Masanobu's illustrated books do not begin until 1703, and then follow some of 1706 and 1707. Single sheets coloured with *tan* are assigned by the Tokio Catalogue (No. 54 *seqq.*) to about 1710 and 1712. Fenollosa (*Outline*, pl. iv.) reproduces a hand-coloured actor of about

[1] In the first edition, 1751–52 had been given as the date of his death, on the authority of Fenollosa (Cat., Nos. 18–20, 36, 41, 48, 53–55, 66, 77). The biography of Masanobu has now assumed a very different aspect in the light of the above dates, which are taken from the Hayashi Cat., and in consequence of the separation of the two Kiyonobus from each other.

1725. But from 1715 to 1735 Masanobu devoted himself principally to painting, under the influence of Shoshun and then especially of Kwaigetsudo.

It is not until the second half of the thirties, in the period of Gembun (1736–40), that he again turns his attention to wood-engraving, in which branch of art he is influenced, like Shigenaga and Toyonobu (see *infra*), by the fertile and graceful book-illustrator Sukenobu. Illustrated books by him occur again from about 1740 to 1750, and in 1752 (Hayashi Catalogue), all published at Yedo. It was a new trend of national culture which led him to resume this kind of work, an outward sign of it being the gradual increase in the height of the central top-knot. He adapted himself even more closely than the Torii to the various changes of fashion.[1] After the invention of the two-colour print in the early forties he devoted himself to this work also with great assiduity. From this period began his rivalry with Kiyonobu II., each artist following the lead of his genius and training in a direction of his own. Masanobu principally represented graceful female figures and bright scenes of social intercourse, while Kiyonobu, for the most part, remained faithful to his representations of actors. A reproduction given by Anderson[2] shows his remarkable finish of composition and the grace of his figures. We miss the flashes of robust sensuousness that distinguish Moronobu, a more feminine and more elegiac temper discloses itself; but it is just this inclination toward delicacy that prepares the way for the subsequent development of Japanese wood-engraving. In a series of fifteen double sheets of mythological scenes, a varied picture of the life of the times is unfolded before us—boating parties, mandoline concerts, love scenes, the landscape scarcely indicated yet admirably suggestive. Single-sheet prints (ichimai-ye) are not wanting either; as, for example, a series of half-length female

[1] Tokio Cat., p. 38.   [2] *Japanese Wood-Engraving*, No. 7.

SHUNSHŌ

FAN

Monsieur G. Bullier, Paris

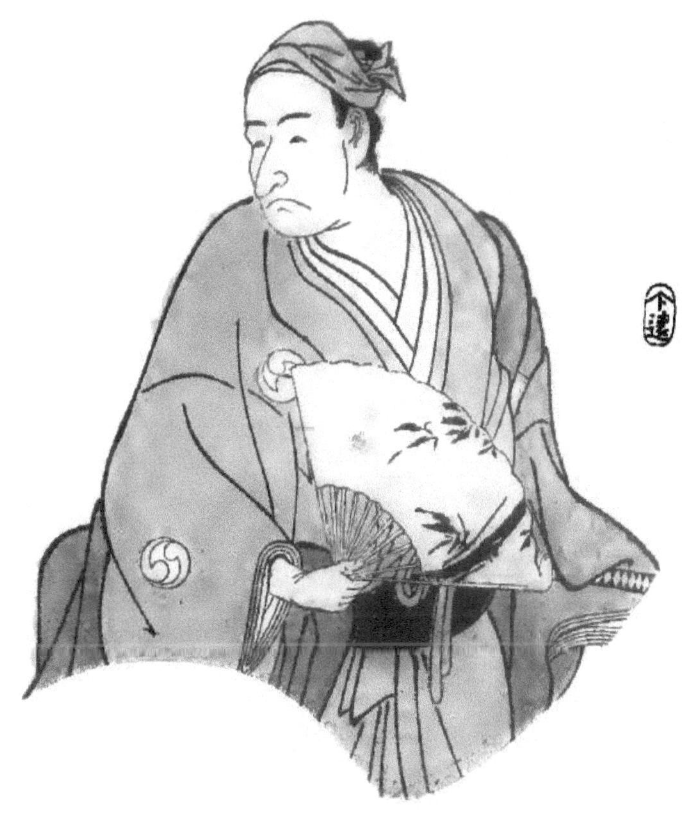

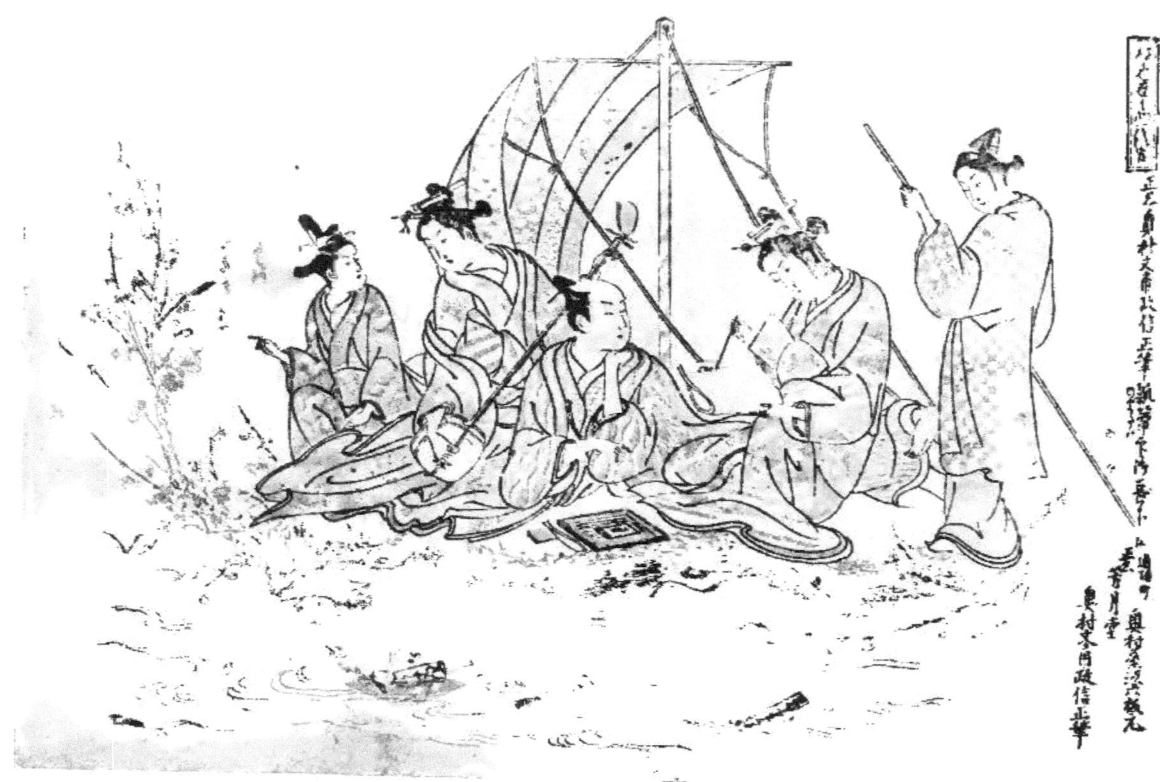

OKUMURA MASÁNOBU : A PICNIC UNDER CHERRY-TREES IN BLOSSOM.
Signed : Okumura Bunkaku Masánobu. *Green and pale pink.*

figures on fans. *Musachi no tsuki* (the moon in the province of Musachi) shows us a series of female figures, in black and white (Berlin, Kunstgewerbemuseum). Bing (Catalogue, No. 76) mentions some further sheets.

With Masanobu, too, begins naturalistic landscape, which attained its full development during the second half of the century. Besides small sheets, he now also produced large ones with single figures, or with populous interiors, such as had quite gone out of use since Moronobu's time. He reached his highest pinnacle, however, in the two-colour sheets, which he produced (partly with blind printing) between 1743–50; they are mostly compositions in three parts, with single figures or groups, and sometimes have an architecturally disposed background, in which the beauty of his grouping and the precision of his draughtsmanship are peculiarly evident. These two-colour prints were, like the hand-coloured black and white work, known as beni-ye, because the same red was used in both. But hand-coloured work continued to be produced along with them for some time longer, and even attained to its peculiar development about 1750, as is proved by several sheets of Masanobu which Fenollosa (*Outline*) assigns to this very period. In these his best days, when his figures were becoming rather longer and more elegant, he also produced his finest kakemonos. According to Bing he also turned out three-colour prints and might therefore be numbered among the inventors of that species.

The following is a list of other works by him, all hand-coloured black and white prints, unless otherwise stated :—

Long female figures, on large sheets, suggesting the work of Kwaigetsudo; young woman standing, playing with a cat; the three chief towns (Yedo, Kioto, Osaka) symbolised by three women, a large sheet; tiger crouching at the foot of a bamboo tree, worked out of a black ground; pheasant on branch of plum-tree; a book with double-page pictures of medium size, each scene containing two persons, very spirited, of strong vivacious contours, black and white (illustrations in Hayashi Catalogue, No. 275, where there are others besides); erotic scenes on oblong sheets.

Of Masanobu's pupils, Okumura Toshinobu is the best and

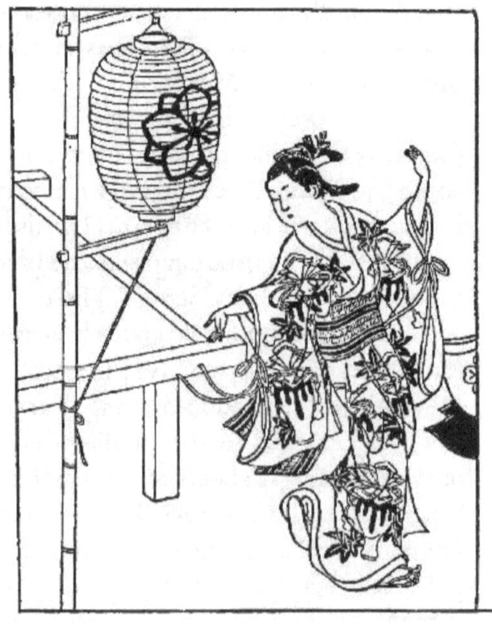

SUKENOBU. THREE DANCING-GIRLS.

best known; but the latter ceased working before the death of his master.[1] In the Hayashi Catalogue he is called the son of Masanobu. He must be reckoned among his early pupils, as his coloured sheets are still quite archaic in style. He also produced two-colour prints. According to Fenollosa[2] his work is generally very delicate; no large wood-engravings by him are known.

[1] Fenollosa Cat., No. 37. [2] Tokio Cat., p. 39.

Among the pupils and followers of Masanobu may be further mentioned: Kishigawa Katsumasa (illustrations in Hayashi Catalogue, No. 293). Ma(n)getsudo, by whom an excellent two-colour print of 1747 is known; illustration of a triptych of four women in the street in the Hayashi Catalogue,

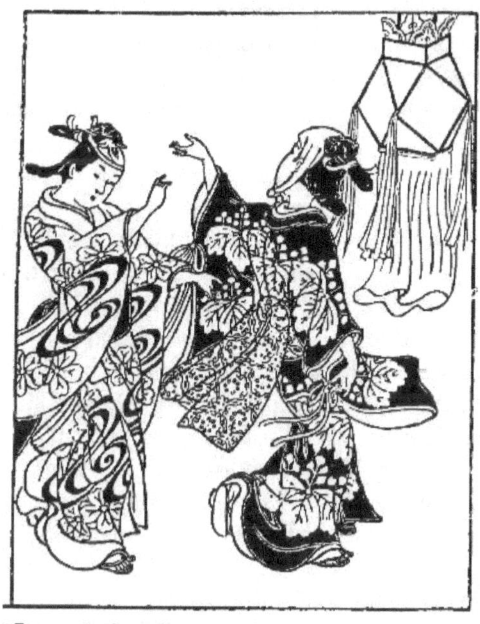

(*From a book published in* 1735).

No. 325; a two-colour print in large folio is in the library of the Berlin Kunstgewerbemuseum. Shuseido, coloured triptych with three women (Oeder Collection, Düsseldorf). An illustrated book by Okumura Bunshi Masafusa was published at Yedo in 1747.[1]

Finally, we must mention Nishimura Shigenobu as of this early period; he worked from 1728–40, and was probably

[1] Hayashi Cat., No. 1463.

the ancestor of the artist family of Nishimura.[1] At first he produced actor prints in the Torii style, then pictures of women after the manner of Kwaigetsudo, and thus gradually broke away from the Torii to found a school of his own. He possessed greater merit as a wood-engraver than as a painter, but his chief title to fame is the artistic training which he gave to his son, Shigenaga, the probable inventor of two-colour printing. A still greater artist was Nishimura Magosaburo. An uncertainty exists as to whether he was a brother of Shigenobu, or perhaps his son; in that case he would be identical with Shigenaga who is said to have styled himself thus, though only in cursive (Gillot Catalogue).

4. Book-Illustration in the First Half of the Eighteenth Century.—Besides the above-named masters, a number of competent but less original artists were active as book-illustrators. After Moronobu had, in the second half of the seventeenth century, brought book-illustration to a height not hitherto attained, and numerous pupils had followed him along this path, the demand for illustrated books (yehons) seems to have relaxed during the period from 1715 to 1735, when the interest of the people was more and more strongly diverted to the theatre, and representations of actors on single-sheet prints were eagerly sought after. But from about the year 1735 onwards, such books once more appear in increasing numbers, in manifest response to an enhanced desire for representations from life, as well as a heightened delight in romantic descriptions. The illustrations were almost uniformly printed in black and white, and very seldom coloured. We must here mention first Nishikawa Sukenobu, a pupil of Yeino Kano Sukenori. He lived from 1674 to 1754, and produced a multitude of illustrated books in the style created by Moronobu. He aimed at giving his readers continuous entertainment in

Nishi- 西
kawa 川
Suke- 祐
nobu 信

[1] Fenollosa Cat., No. 38; Tokio Cat., p. 32; Hayashi Cat., No. 318 *seqq.*

Bing Collection, Paris

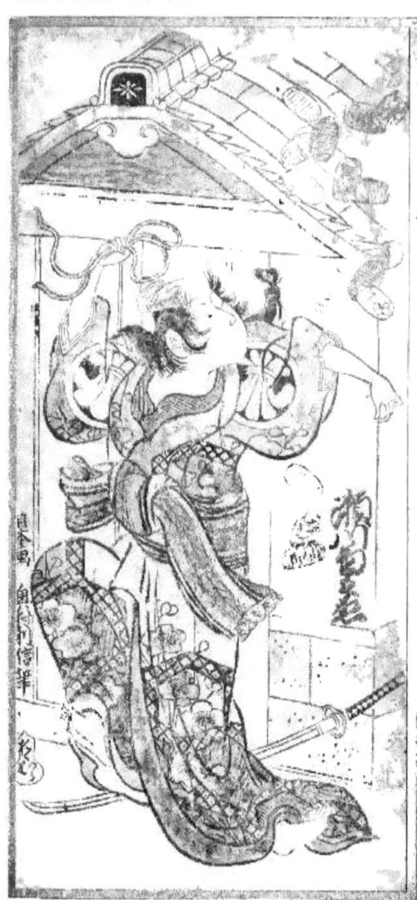

TOSHINÔBU : An Actor, in a Female Part, in a Shower of Gold (*Kobans*, little gold coins). *Hand-tinted with black, red, and yellow, and gold-dust.* Medium size.

Bing Collection, Paris

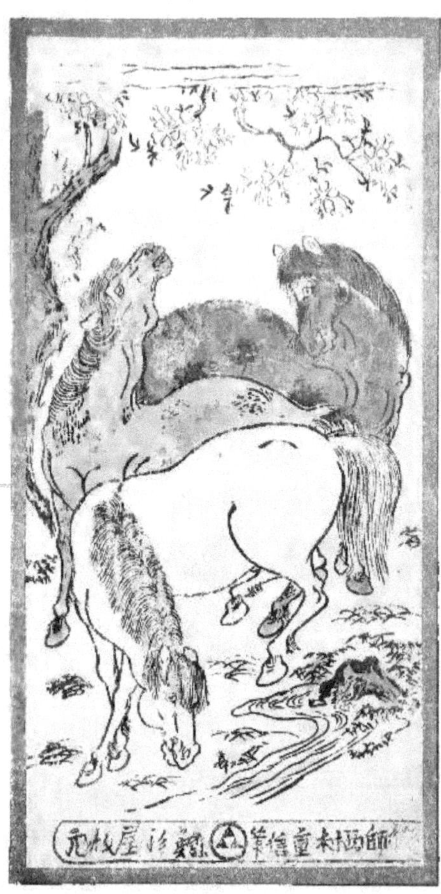

SHIGENÔBU : Horses drinking under a Cherry-tree. *Hand-tinted with black, grey, and yellow.* Medium size.

designs of facile invention, great vivacity, and excellent composition, lacking only in high seriousness and delicacy of detail. He was born in Kioto, and was known in private life as Nishikawa Ukio; his first work was done in the manner of the Kano school, from which he went over to the Tosa school. His importance for Kioto is the same as that of Masanobu for Yedo.[1] From about 1730 he seems to have settled in Osaka. The Hamburg Museum possesses a book by him called *Shotoku Hinagasa*, dated as early as 1713.[2] He was especially noted for his scenes from the life and occupations of women, of which a series appeared, as early as 1723, under the title *Hiakunin Joro shinasadame*:—

Yehon Hanamomiji. Undated.
Genji no yesho. 1730.
Wakoku hiakujo, hundred Japanese women, on 27 pictures.

In 1736 followed the widely known—

Yehon tamakadzura (Pl. no. 11 in Anderson's *Japanese Wood-Engraving*).
Yehon Asakayama. 1739.
1740, 1741, Yehon chiyomigusa, scenes from the life of women, 3 vols.

These books are followed by the scenes from social life, the *Yehon ike no kawazu*, an edition of which in 1768 is cited by Anderson. Illustrations of poems:—

1730, Yehon Tsukubayama; 1755, Yehon himekagami; and illustrations of the book of moral precepts:
Yehon chitoseyama. 1740.

He illustrated legends in his *Yehon Yamato-hiji* of 1742, and Japanese stories in his *Yehon Kame no Oyama* of 1747.

Besides these, the following books by him are mentioned:—

Yehon tokiwagusa, the life of court ladies, middle-class women, and courtesans, 3 vols. 1731.

---

[1] Tokio Cat., p. 41.

[2] Anderson Cat., p. 339. See Tasset. The new biographical dates (in lieu of "1671 to about 1760") are taken from the Hayashi Cat.

F

Yehon Fudetsubana. 1747.
Goriu yehonzoroye (various sketches). 1748.
Yehon Yoshinogusa, 3 vols. 1759.
An erotic work in 3 vols.

Reprints of his books continued to be published as late as the eighties of the eighteenth century.

Reproductions of his work may be found in Gonse[1] (weaving women) and Anderson[2] (genre-picture).

Tachibana Morikuni, Sukenobu's contemporary, was still more fertile, varied, and important; he gave his figures more life and expression, and paid more attention to the artistic execution of his wood prints.[3] He lived from 1670 to 1748. His numerous model sketches, as well as reproductions of his work, have already been detailed on p. 59. In his illustrations he follows the style of the Kano school; Tsuruzawa Tanzan is mentioned as his teacher.

He illustrated legends as follows:—

Yehon kojidan (ancient myths), 8 vols. Osaka, 1714. (Reproduction in Strange, p. 10.)
Yehon shahobukuro (legends, &c.), 9 vols. 1720. (A good specimen in Anderson, *Japanese Wood-Engraving*, No. 10, a dance of children).
Yehon Tsuhoshi, 9 vols. 1725. He here signs himself T. Yuzei. The first volume treats of agriculture, the chase, fishing; the second, of dancing and riding; the third, celebrated localities; the fourth, portraits; the fifth, tales and legends; the sixth, fantastic representations; the rest, landscapes. A later edition in 1772.
Gwaten tsuko (legends), 10 vols. Osaka, 1727.
Yehon Oshikubai, 7 vols. Osaka, 1740. (Rep. Strange, p. 11.)

Illustrations of poems are to be found in the following works:—

Wacho meisho gwazu, 4 vols. 1732
Fuso gwafu, 5 vols. 1735. Treats of the celebrated localities of Japan. A later edition, Kioto, 1784.

[1] Vol. i. p. 123. [2] *Pictorial Arts*, i. p. 171.
[3] Anderson Cat., p. 339; Hayashi Cat., No. 1599 *seqq.*; Duret:

Yokioku gwashi (the No dance), 10 vols. Osaka, 1732.
Honcho gwayen, 6 vols. 1782.

Ooka Shunboku, who died about 1760, at the age of eighty-four, also illustrated legends:—

Wakan koji Bokuo shingwa, 5 vols. 1753.
Hisei Musha Suguri. 1736. Reproductions after his works by an anonymous pupil.

As a copyist of ancient paintings he has already been mentioned (p. 56).[1]

Other illustrators are:

Kokan, who published in the year 1722 a collection of popular sketches called *Jimbutsu sogwa*. Duret mentions a work of 1724 in three volumes.

Hokio Tachibana Yasukuni, a son and pupil of Morikuni:

Yehon Noyomagusa, studies of flowers. 1755, 5 vols.
Yehon Yabutsusen, illustrations of historical poetry. Osaka, 1778, 5 vols.

Tsukioka Masanobu, died 1786:

Yehon Komei futubagusa, stories of the childhood of famous men. Osaka, 1759, 3 vols.
Onna buya Kebai Kurabe, heroines. Osaka, 1766, 3 vols.

Hayami Shunshosai, about 1775:

Korobanu sakino zuye, very spirited scenes with landscapes. Kioto, 3 vols.

Roren:

Roren gwafu, facsimiles of expressive brushwork drawings. Yedo, 1763.

Tsukioka Tange (1717–86), of whom the following works are mentioned:[2]

Yehon musha tazuna, also named the Yehon Komio futubagusa 1759, representations of heroic deeds.

---

[1] Anderson Cat., p. 341 *seqq*. [2] Duret, p. 97.

Yehon hime bunko 1760, ladies' book.
Togoku meishoshi 1762, landscapes of Eastern Japan.

In the Tokio Catalogue (p. 41 *seqq.*) the two following pupils of Sukenobu are mentioned: Nishikawa Suketada, probably a son of Sukenobu, more original and imaginative in his colouring than the latter; illustrated books by him occur from 1748 onwards (Hayashi Catalogue No. 1477 *seqq.*); and Tsukioke Settei, who represents the transition to the following generation which is already influenced by Yedo.

Further names to be mentioned are: Nakaji Sadatoshi, of the Kano school; he published drawing exercises in Kioto about 1730 (Hayashi Catalogue, No. 355).—Kitao Sekkosai, from Osaka, a pupil of Buncho? Illustrated books by him are dated 1754 and 1767; in the latter of these a separate plate for the general tint is first employed. A large broadside folio sheet of 1764 represents, in forty-eight divisions, women of various classes and professions (illustrated in Hayashi Catalogue, No. 479).—Kanyosai in Kioto, called also Tatobe Riosai and Mokio (1712–74), one of the best draughtsmen of the period. One of his works is *Kanyosai gwafu*, Yedo 1762, 5 vols. of plants, birds, and landscapes, in the style of the old Chinese masters (Hayashi Catalogue, No. 1612); *Mokio wakan zatsuga*, after old pictures (1772), 5 vols., new edition 1802; drawings of fishes, 1775 (Duret, No. 462 *seqq.*).—Ippo, collections of drawings, Osaka 1752 and Yedo 1758—Rinsho, drawings, Yedo 1770.—By Ito Jakunobu are: *Gempo Yokua*, plants and animals, black and white (1768), 55 sheets, a work of unusual power and largeness (Hamburg Museum). The artist lived from 1716 to 1800. He studied the Kano school to begin with, and then the Chinese school and Korin.

CHAPTER IV

THE DEVELOPMENT OF COLOUR-PRINTING (1743–1765)

1. The Two-colour Print—2. The Three-colour Print—3. The Polychrome Print

1. The Two-colour Print. — Our mental picture of the development of Japanese wood-engraving has taken on quite another aspect now that we do not, as until recently, date back the beginning of colour-printing, first with two, then with three, and then with several colour blocks, to 1710, but place it, on Fenollosa's authority, in the beginning of the forties of the eighteenth century. It follows from this modification that during the whole interval between these two dates black and white still predominated exclusively, though with growing importance and perfection of hand colouring.[1] When then, about the year 1743, colour-printing with two blocks, rose and green, was introduced—an invention that we perhaps owe to Shigenaga—it was at once generally adopted among the leading artists, so that it may be regarded as a distinguishing mark of the fifth and sixth decades. The colouring of black and white prints did not cease at once, but gradually retired to the background. Towards the end of the fifties a third block was added, perhaps yellow in the beginning, changing later to blue; then followed in quick succession several attempts to heighten the colour effect by modifying and combining the colours, and it was not long

[1] Prints coloured by hand are called urushi-ye; colour prints nishike-ye.

until, about the year 1765, the number of blocks was increased, and thereby the foundation laid for wood-engravings unrestricted as to colour effect. The period of transition from the primitive two-colour to the completely developed polychrome prints, which for us represent Japanese wood-engraving *par excellence*, was very short. It embraced not much more than the first half of the sixties.

The colour print, like Japanese art in general, was probably brought over originally from China.[1] True, a statement is reported by Satow, in the *Transactions* of 1881, on the authority of an author named Sakakibara, that coloured prints of a likeness of the celebrated actor Ichikawa Danjuro, the founder of an actor-clan that still flourishes, were sold in the streets of Yedo in the year 1695. But this should doubtless be interpreted as referring to woodcuts coloured by hand.[2] Prints in another colour than black seem to have been produced very early, although only quite exceptionally; at least, Strange cites (page 3) a book that appeared in the year 1667, containing patterns for kimonos (outer robes) which are engraved in pairs on one block, and printed alternately in black, olive-green, red, and a fourth colour (reprod. *ibid.*). Even granting, however, that we are not here dealing with a new edition of a much later date, there would still be no connection with the printing from several blocks successively adjusted, in which process lies the essence of the colour-print. It may be considered, indeed, that the deepening and softening of the tint on different parts of the

[1] Binyon (*Painting*, p. 232) mentions that there are Chinese colour-prints in the British Museum, representing bouquets, flowers, birds, &c., which were brought home from Japan by Kaempfer as early as 1692. They are printed from several blocks and their technique is already fully developed.

[2] In the *Kokka Magazine* we are informed that, according to the statement of the celebrated romance writer Kioku Ichio, a wood-carver, Kinroku, invented the colour print, but employed it only in the production of calendars (Deshayes in *L'Art*, 1893, ii. 10).—Compare Anderson, *Japanese Wood-Engraving*, pp. 22, 64; Strange, pp. 3, 4.

KOEPPING COLLECTION, BERLIN

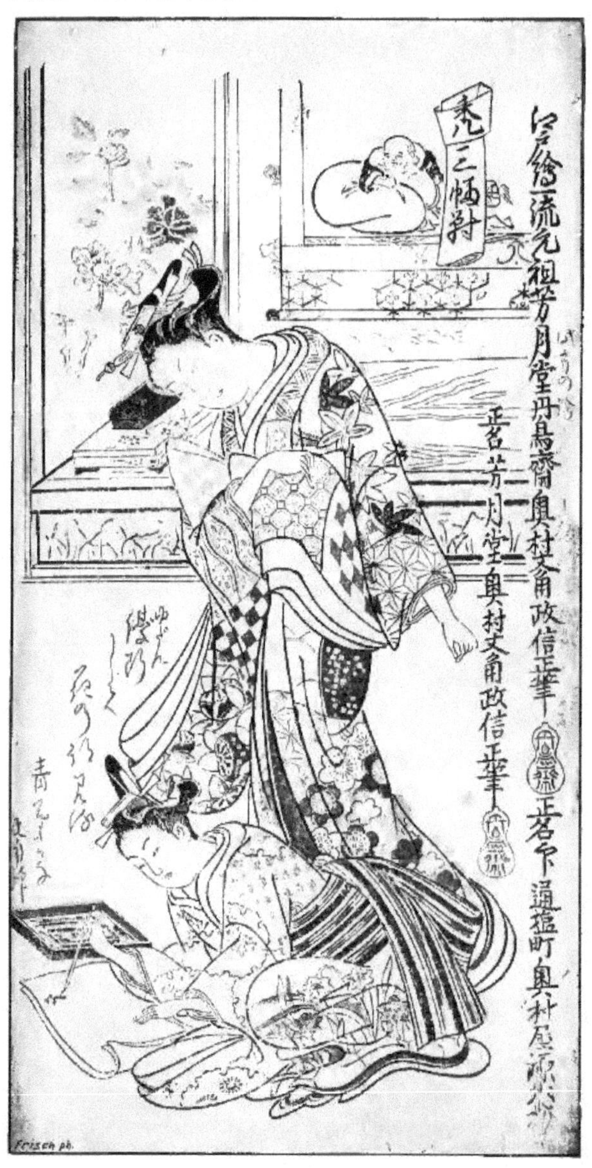

MASÁNOBU : *Kamuro* (SERVANT) WRITING A LOVE-LETTER, HER MISTRESS WATCHING HER. Behind, in the *tokonoma*, a picture of the god Hotei. *Two-colour print in red and green.* Part of a triptych representing "The Audacities of *Kamuros*."

same block (as was done, for example, in landscapes in *Gwako senran* (1740), where the distance is lighter and the foreground darker in tone[1]), was a first step toward colour-printing. But it does not seem to be proved that the application of different colours to the same block, which was often done in the nineteenth century, was known in the early period. As we have not been able to prove the existence of an earlier colour-print than that dated 1743, of which we shall speak immediately, and as the internal evidence of other two-colour prints does not point to an appreciably earlier origin, it follows that Anderson's statements,[2] according to which a certain Izumiya Gonshiro, towards the end of the seventeenth century, was the first to use a coloured block, besides the black, in order to colour certain parts of his drawing with carmine red (*beni*), must be referred to hand colour; at any rate, prints of this kind have not come to light. The first book illustrated with coloured wood prints is said to have appeared as late as 1748.

The sheet dated 1743, representing a young man in the rain, is by Shigenaga. Whether it is the first colour-print ever produced in Japan, we do not know; nor has the name of the inventor of this new process been handed down to us. But from the circumstance that it is dated at all, forming thus one of the few exceptions among Japanese single-sheet prints, we may doubtless conclude that it was the first sheet produced in this technique, and that the youthful artist gave expression by this signature to his pride in his new invention, precisely as did his pupil Harunobu twenty-two years later, when he succeeded in inventing the full polychrome print. At all events, prints in two colours are not hitherto known to have been produced appreciably earlier. Why the artist chose precisely these two tints, rose and green, for his colour blocks (to be sure a very happy choice), has not yet appeared. The colours which were

[1] *Japanese Wood-Engraving*, p. 64. [2] *Ibid.*, p. 22.

employed up to that time for hand colouring afford us no explanation, as they were quite different in kind and far more various. It is also a surprising circumstance that through nearly two subsequent decades these two colours were employed virtually unchanged, even in tone and strength, by all the other artists of the period, and that it was not until a third colour-block was introduced (about 1760) that these sheets presented a greater variety of aspect.

Fenollosa (Tokio Catalogue, 1898, p. 43) says that two-colour printing was, up to the beginning of the fifties, only employed for small prints. He estimates the total number of two-colour prints at about 10,000. On page 5 of the same work he gives an admirable characterisation of the two-colour print. Professor Jaekel in Greifswald writes to me: "The first red and green prints seem to me to be those in which these two colours are only printed in the form of delicate patterns on the spaces of the dresses and the salient parts of the background. These pattern-blocks were probably technically most nearly akin to the stencil plates which had been in use from ancient times for pattern printing on cloth and continued to be used long after. The tinting of the dresses to their whole extent only came in later."

Nishi- 西 mura 村 Shige- 重 naga 長

Nishimura Shigenaga, the son of Shigenobu, lived from 1697 to 1756, and distinguished himself especially in the middle of the thirties.[1] The rudiments of his art he learned from his father, and then assimilated himself very closely to the style of Masanobu. Although the affinity of mind and temper that attracted him to this artist entitles him to be regarded as his follower, and from the fifties as his legitimate heir and successor, he yet deserves quite as much, at a certain period of his life, probably in his youth, to be called a disciple of that excellent

[1] Anderson Cat., p. 388; Fenollosa Cat., Nos. 40, 57, 80, 92. The dates are taken from the Hayashi Cat.

KOECHLIN COLLECTION, PARIS

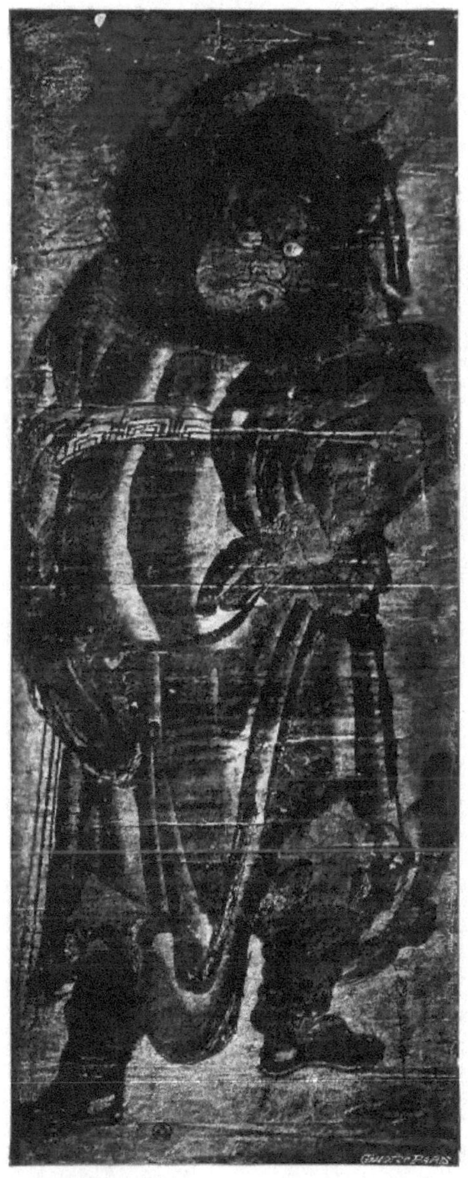

SHIGÉNAGA: SHŌKI, THE DEVIL-QUELLER.
Hand-coloured black and grey, the flesh dark red. Large.

actor-painter, Kiyonobu. For there exist prints by Shigenaga with representations of wild deities which belong entirely to the forceful style of the Torii school. Although, like Masanobu, he took especial delight in the delineation of graceful women, nevertheless he did not disdain to try his hand on actor-pictures as well. The versatility of his talent is further shown by a hand-coloured sheet representing a mandarin duck among iris, on the water's edge (Bing Catalogue, No. 89). It is incorrect to attribute to him, as Anderson does, colour-prints produced with four blocks, and to date this activity as far back as 1716. He began, as all artists hitherto mentioned, with black and white prints. As early as the middle of the fourth decade his style showed a great affinity with that of Masanobu, approaching, however, more closely to the personal peculiarities of the latter than to the broad style handed down from the school of Moronobu. What distinguished him was the striving for individuality, and that in a new, fresh, youthfully sensitive spirit, which he passed on to his pupils also and which gave its stamp to the woodcuts of the great flowering which now began. In this rôle of mediator between the old and the new art, as well as in his more personal qualities, lies Shigenaga's essential significance. It is sufficient to mention here that Harunobu was his pupil.

The year 1743, as we have seen, forms the one decisive turning-point in his life, as it brought with it the invention of the two-colour print. The beautiful specimen of this process which Anderson gives at the beginning of his *Japanese Wood-Engraving*, a young girl walking under a sunshade on the bank of a river (signed Senkwado Nish. Shig.), is therefore dated by him much too early (1725). But it proves clearly enough to us how Shigenaga's strength lies in the artistic rendering of a general impression, though Masanobu excels him in precision, beauty, and individuality of drawing. In any case, the invention of the two-colour print was of such revolutionising importance that all, even the older generation of masters still alive, immediately took up the production of such prints. Shigenaga himself never tired of developing this technique further, endeavouring after ever new effects by varying the grading or contrasts of the colours, by change in the patterning, by blind printing. In the beginning of the fifties his art reached its high-water mark, while Kiyomitsu at the same time continued the style of Kiyonobu. The subjects that he treated were similar to those of Masanobu, single figures of women and scenes of social life, mostly in triptych form, which, however, were no longer rigidly divided into three separate parts, but represent a continuous composition. As he also produced three-colour prints and died as early as 1756, it is clear that they must have been invented before this time and not towards the end of the fifties, as was assumed in the first edition. Fenollosa mentions one of his large sheets printed in this style, representing the interior of a hall, in which, besides the two colours, rose and green, yellow is employed by way of transition to white, in addition to the black contour-block. He thinks it very probable that Shigenaga, having invented the two-colour print, may have discovered the three-colour print as well. It is true that a print of this kind cannot be assigned to about 1759, as Fenollosa assumed, but must have been produced several years earlier. Illustrations of his works in the Hayashi Catalogue (Nos. 304, 305, 313), which also mentions books illustrated by him (Nos. 1464 *seqq.*), beginning with about 1735. As to his possible identity with Mangosaburo, see the end of Chapter III., § 3.

As his pupils, Toyonobu and, later on especially, Harunobu and Shigemasa are to be mentioned. It is not certain that Akiyama Sadaharu was a pupil of Shigenaga, but Fenollosa thinks it possible; he cites a black and white print by him dating from the middle of the fifth decade, and gives him the testimonial that, had he worked longer, he would very

ROYAL PRINT ROOM, DRESDEN

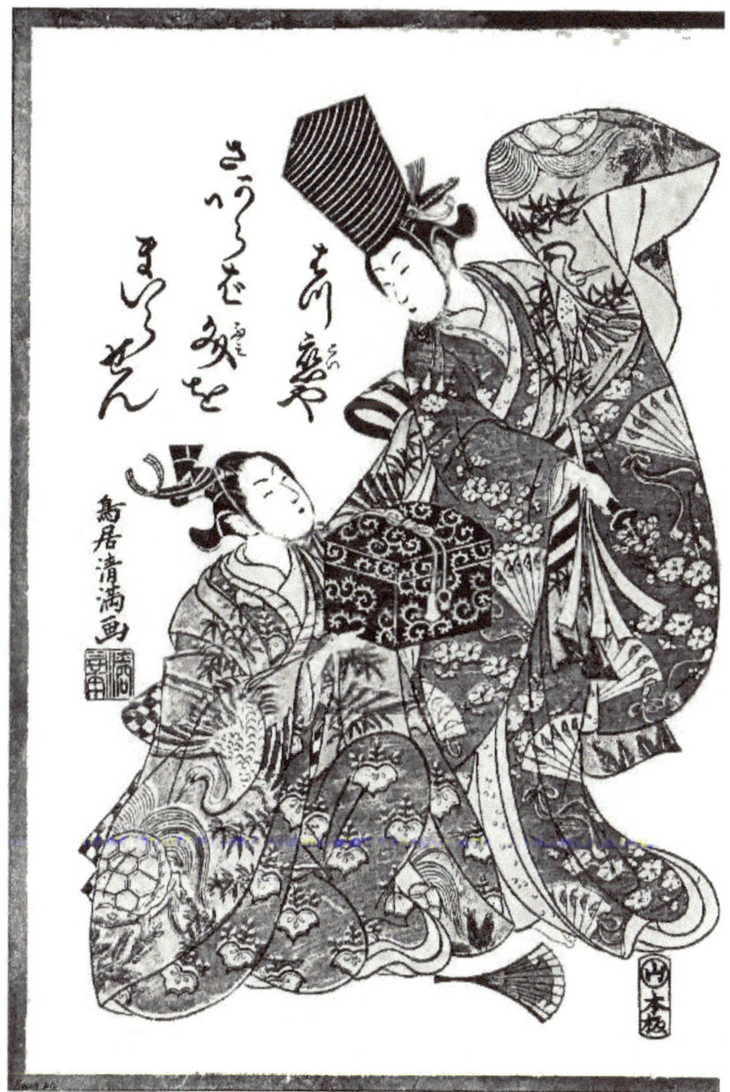

KUJÓMITSU: NEW YEAR'S DANCE, EXECUTED BY TWO *Shirabiōshis* (SINGERS). The standing figure, whose robe is figured with pine, bamboo, and almond-blossom (happiness), cranes and tortoises (long life), wears the *sambasa* on her head and holds a rattle in her hand. The other, whose gown is figured with paulownias, wears the *mintai* on her head, and holds up the *membako* (mask-coffer). *Three-colour print in green, red, and grey.*

likely have become a dangerous rival of Harunobu's.[1] Ishikawa Toyonobu was born in 1711 and was therefore only about ten years younger than his teacher Shigenaga; he lived, however, much longer than the latter, namely, until 1785, and remained vigorously active even in old age.[2] He also called himself Ishikawa Shuha. He began his career with black and white work, and then, like Shigenaga, continued Masanobu's manner in two-colour prints, producing numerous continuous triptychs, which are noted for the grace of their female figures. The earliest attempt to produce new tones by printing red over green originated with him. He was also one of the first to practise full polychrome printing; thus, for example, his large horizontal sheet in four colours, the parody on the seven sages in the bamboo grove, who are here represented by singing-women, is dated 1765. He also produced book-illustrations; the Hayashi Catalogue (No. 1488 *seqq*) mentions some published at Yedo in 1763 and 1779. Contemporaneously with Kiyomitsu and Shigenaga he practised three-colour printing by using first yellow, then blue, as a third colour. The Tokio Catalogue (p. 40) calls him the chief rival of Kiyomitsu (see below), but seems wrong in assigning him to Sukenobu's group. His pupils are mentioned below in connection with Shunsho. Harunobu and Shigemasa also, who already belong to a younger generation, and Yoshinobu and Toyoharu, the pupils of Shigenaga, will be dealt with later.

石 Ishi-
川 kawa
豊 Toyo-
信 nobu

The Hayashi Catalogue further mentions, as pupils of Shigenaga, Hirose Shigenobu (No. 324); Yamamoto Shigeharu (No. 348); Yamamoto Fujinobu (No. 349), whom Fenollosa calls a pupil of Harunobu; Tomikawa Fusanobu, who worked from 1741 to 1763 and then called himself Ginsetsu (No. 353).

[1] Fenollosa Cat., No. 62.

[2] Fenollosa Cat., Nos. 64, 75, 88–91, 101, 169; Anderson Cat., p. 342; Bing Cat., No. 92 ff. The dates are taken from the Hayashi Cat.

We have already seen, in the preceding chapter, how Masanobu, Kiyonobu II., and Kiyomasu, immediately after the invention of the two-colour print, devoted all their powers to its development.

Tori- 鳥 i 居 Kiyo- 清 mitsu 滿

2. THE THREE-COLOUR PRINT.—While the method of Masanobu found a propagator in Shigenaga, a follower of the Kiyonobus and Kiyomasu arose in Torii Kiyomitsu, who generally passes as a son of Kiyomasu, but owing to his later appearance in the history of art, is looked upon by Fenollosa rather as the successor, adopted late in life, either of Kiyonobu or Kiyomasu.[1] He lived from 1735 to 1785, and began to work in the early fifties. There are no known hand-coloured sheets by him. As Shigenaga and Toyonobu entered upon the inheritance of Masanobu, so did Kiyomitsu carry on the traditions of the Torii, followed meantime, from 1750 to 1765, like a shadow by Kiyohiro. Kiyomitsu's draughtsmanship is broad, but not always as delicately worked out as that of the ancients. He is noted for the exceptional grace, fulness, and finish of his compositions; his figures are generally long, with small heads and small features; the ample draperies cling close to the bodies.

Like Shigenaga, he cultivated the three-colour print as early as the fifties; in fact, this technique is especially indebted to him for its further development and completion, since the first half of the sixties, at which time he took the lead of all other artists, was his most fertile period. He was the first to give blue a permanent place in the synthesis of colours, so that the treatment of this colour formed a distinctive characteristic of his work. He did not, however, use it pure in the beginning, but shading strongly into grey, and thereby achieved a beautiful gradation of tone, as is shown in an early kakemono-ye[2] repre-

[1] Anderson Cat., p. 341; Fenollosa Cat., Nos. 83, 92, 99, 100, 102, 104–107, 110–112. The dates are taken from the Hayashi Cat.

[2] In Japanese these narrow sheets, which are fastened on the door-posts, are called hashira-kakushi.

VEVER COLLECTION, PARIS

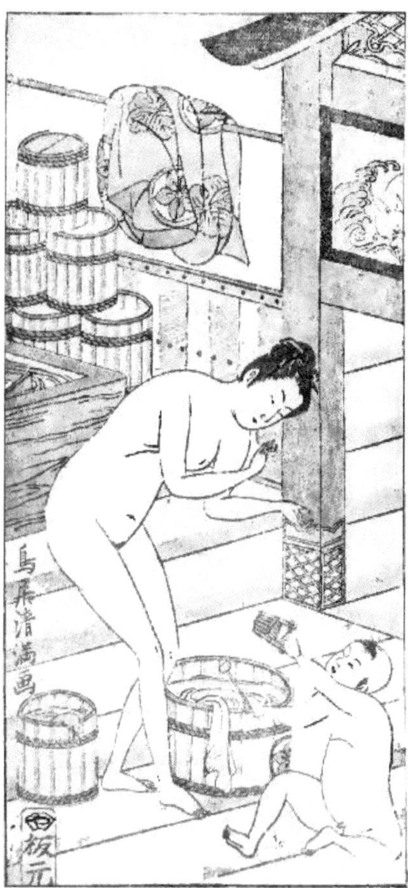

KIYÓMITSU: A BATHING SCENE IN A HOUSE. The bath in the background. The child holds a pail and ladle. *Three-colour print in pink, yellow, and grey-brown.*

VEVER COLLECTION, PARIS

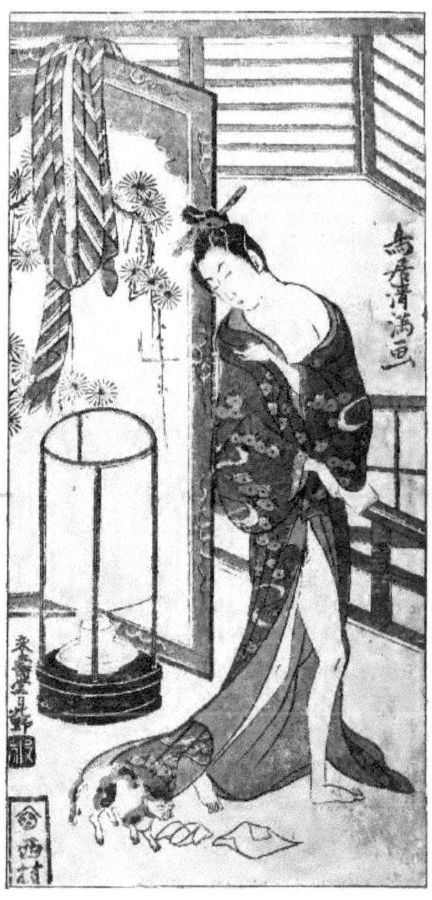

KIYÓMITSU: WOMAN IN A DRESSING-GOWN WITH A CAT. She holds a paper in her hand. On the floor a paper lantern with an oil-can. On the screen a sash. *Two-colour print in red and green.*

senting a mother and child. By the addition of brown he even occasionally changed his blue into an olive green, as in the large and beautifully composed sheet of the two dancing girls, in which the green and red is also modified. In part he achieved the mild and subdued, yet powerful elegance of his tones by special mixtures of colour, partly also by printing them one over the other, whereby he enriched his scale of tints. It is remarkable that in his rather heavy treatment of colour, neither black nor white plays a considerable part. He too was active in book-illustration; illustrated works by him appeared at Yedo in 1760 and 1776. In his productions actors predominate; see the sheet of about 1760 illustrated in Fenollosa (*Outline*, pl. vi.). In addition, however, he drew scenes of daily life, bath scenes, and in Bing's Catalogue (No. 19) there is also mentioned a print with birds. Strange reproduces, on page 24, a woman preparing tea. In the Jaekel Collection at Greifswald there is a large oblong three-colour print by him, which is composed as a triptych, but printed undivided from a single block; it represents a gentleman promenading with two ladies, with Fuji in the background. The same collection possesses a four-colour print, large oblong, in which red and green predominate; it was probably done about 1760, and represents three geishas sitting in a room and playing with cushions. About the year 1763, following the example of Harunobu, who in the meantime had been making his experiments, his blue appears perfectly pure; but the cheerfulness of this young pioneer's colour-scheme was never quite attained by the older artist. He remains the chief master of the short ascendancy of the three-colour print, the general effect of which was apt to be somewhat sombre. As no black and white prints, so also no genuine polychrome prints by him seem to be known.

According to Fenollosa (*Outline*), the fundamental colours of the three-colour print, which seems to have developed in the middle of the fifties, were red (*beni*), blue, and the newly added yellow, that is, colours resulting from the decomposition of the green hitherto used. Professor Jaekel, on the other hand, in a personal communication, is of opinion that the third colour was the result of blue being printed over red in the case of the caps of the actors, which appear to have been of a vivid violet; he is acquainted with such prints by Kiyonobu II., Kiyomitsu, and Kiyohiro. This third colour, a late introduction, was then, he thinks, at once generally made use of to enrich the colour-scheme in every direction.

The introduction of three-colour printing also brought the kakemono-ye to full perfection. The number of figures represented on them rose occasionally to eight or ten. The fact that one colour could now be printed over another made it possible to vary the colour-scheme almost infinitely.

Tori-i Kiyo-hiro 鳥居清廣

Torii Kiyohiro, who, like Kiyomitsu, was active from about 1750 to 1765, was perhaps more gifted than the latter, but his achievement was less.[1] The Hayashi Catalogue calls him a pupil of Shiro Kiyonobu (see under Kiyonobu II.). Fenollosa suspects that he was a younger brother of Kiyomitsu, but the fact that he published an illustrated book, *Serifu*, with five black and white prints, in Yedo, as early as 1738, is against this assumption. Another book, called *Tomimoto*, appeared in 1754, with eleven illustrations (Gillot Catalogue). For the rest, only two- and three-colour prints are known by him also, partly in the form of triptychs, with beautiful drawing of the patterns on the robes and tasteful application of a delicate olive-grey. Like Kiyomitsu, he affected especially the delineation of actors (illustrations in Hayashi Catalogue, Nos. 259, 263, 254). Tanaka Masunobu is mentioned by Fenollosa (Catalogue, No. 94) as a late pupil of Kiyonobu II. in his old age, who produced about the middle of the fifties actor prints in two colours. But there exists

[1] Fenollosa Cat., Nos. 85, 93, 103; Tokio Cat., p. 50.

VEVER COLLECTION, PARIS

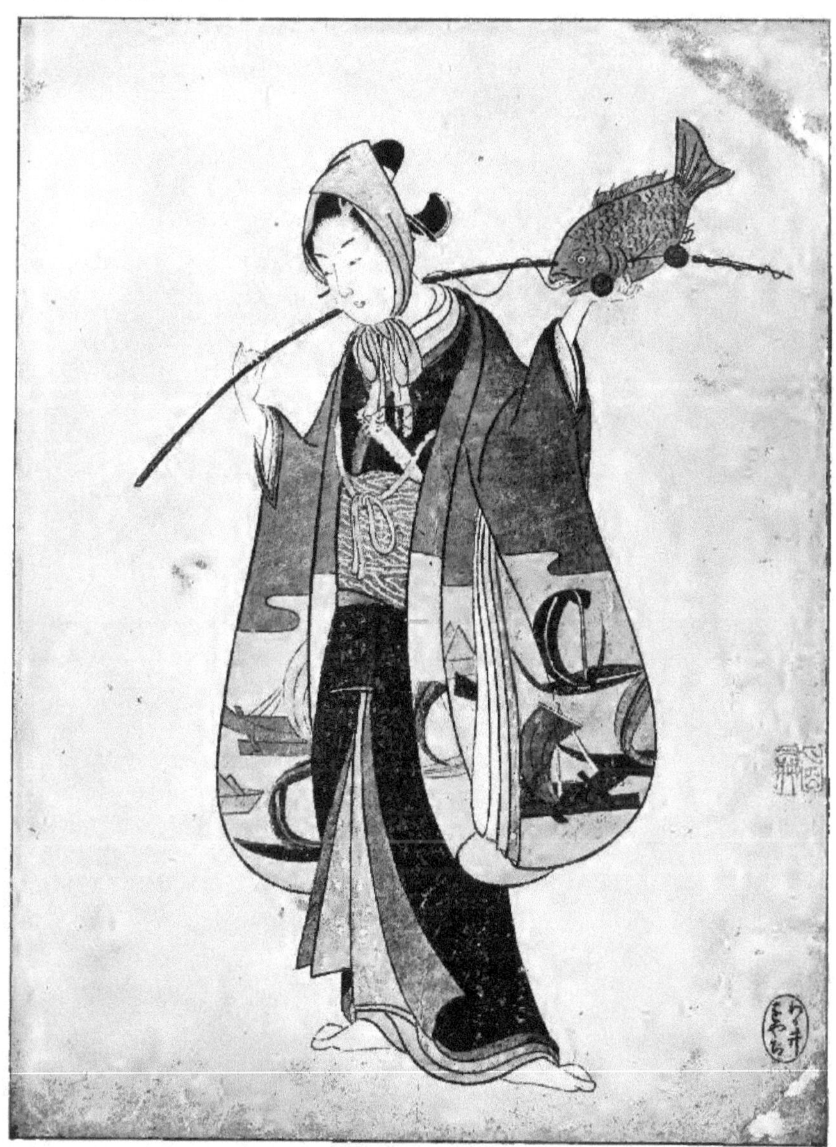

HARUNÔBU : A DANCER WITH A KERCHIEF ROUND HER HEAD, HOLDING A LARGE FISH ON WHEELS. Yellow robe, figured with ships; a fan in the grey sash. *Grey background.*

a two-colour print by him dated as early as 1746: two children in a saké-bowl with a sail (Hayashi Catalogue, No. 290). According to the Hayashi Catalogue, on the other hand, he is said to have probably been a pupil of Shigenobu, and later to have followed Shigenaga and Harunobu. He also called himself Sanseido. The Hayashi Catalogue gives specimens of his work (Nos. 291, 289). In Bing's Catalogue (No. 33), under the date 1760, is mentioned a theatre scene by Torii Kiyotsume. According to the Hayashi Catalogue he was a pupil of Kiyonobu II.; for reproductions see the Catalogue (Nos. 249, 252). He reminds one of Harunobu. Works illustrated by him appeared in Yedo in 1777.

Other artists of the period are: Torii Kiyoharu (illustration in the Hayashi Catalogue, No. 223); Torii Kiyosato, probably a pupil of Kiyomitsu (Tokio Catalogue, No. 86; illustration in Hayashi Catalogue, No. 263 *bis*). The Hayashi Catalogue further mentions: illustrated books by Torii Kiyohide, 1772 and 1775, and by Torii Kiyomoto, about 1786–94.

3. The Polychrome Print.—Without doubt, we owe to the amiable and cheerful genius of Harunobu the invention of prints entirely unlimited in the number of blocks and choice of colours. As, twenty-two years earlier, Shigenaga had dated the first two-colour print, so also Harunobu placed the date 1765 on several of his delicate and richly coloured prints, square and of medium size approximating to that of the later surimonos, evidently intending thereby, in just exultation over the final success of his invention, to fix its date for all succeeding ages. Before, however, he succeeded in this great step, he had spent half a decade endeavouring to produce new effects by means of the three-colour blocks then in use, which gradually led up to his invention. Indeed, his activity extends back into the time of the two-colour print, although only into its closing years.

Suzuki Harunobu, the founder of the Japanese wood print in the style familiar to us, and thus the first of the moderns, was a pupil of that Shigenaga who invented the two-colour print and probably also the three-colour print, and who, after Masanobu's death, upheld his heritage through a decade. In this case, the inheritance of the artistic tradition, and its gradual transformation in the direction of an entirely new ideal, is clearly in evidence. For as the grace and peculiar charm of Masanobu here continue to live on in their specifically Japanese fashion, to be transmitted as an inalienable heritage from the time of the "primitives" to the whole following half-century of the great moderns, so, on the other hand, the special peculiarities of drawing and colour which constitute the characteristic style of the "primitives" come to an end with Harunobu, and give place to an entirely different conception of the outer world, which, in contrast with the decorative method hitherto current, must be described as essentially naturalistic; although the faithful reproduction of the real world is by no means the positive goal of this art movement. The causes of this new phenomenon are not to be sought for in any particular progress made by art, for the older art was able, as Moronobu's creations prove, to reach with its simple means a degree of expressiveness and vivacity which later times in some ways never recovered; nor could the invention of the perfect polychrome print have influenced it decisively, for this was not immediately followed by an increase in power of artistic representation. Rather must it have been due to the spirit of the age, to the changed direction of the outer as well as the inner life of Japan, that minuter detail and greater variety of representation was now required of her art. This, indeed, and this alone, can account for the falling off in strength, fulness, and robustness, which is noticeable henceforward.

But Harunobu forms not only the beginning of a new, but

7

Vever Collection, Paris

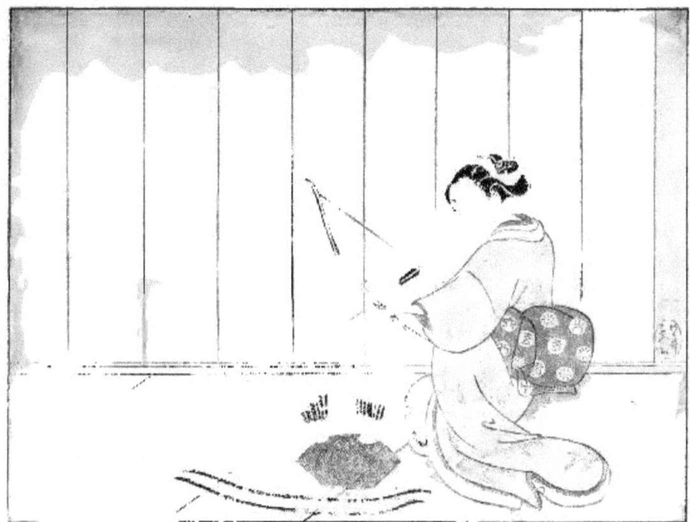

HARUNÓBU: A Young Girl with Bow and Arrows (*Yokiu*). Date, 1765.
Yellowish-grey dress with greyish-green sash; yellow floor.

Koechlin Collection, Paris

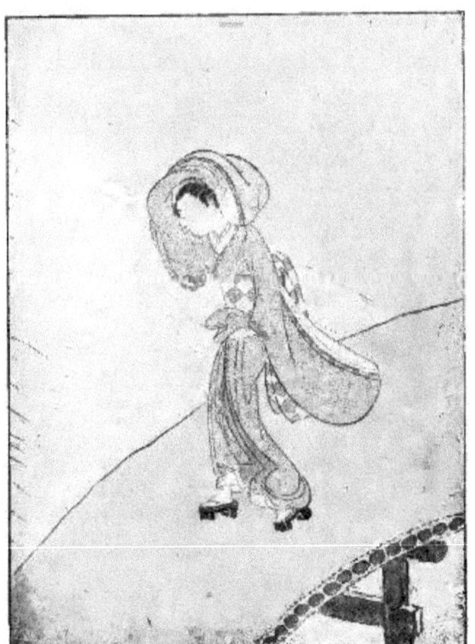

HARUNÓBU: Lady on a Bridge in the Snow, wrapping herself with her Sleeves. Reminiscent of the tale of the Sano Ferry. Date, 1765. Water light yellowish tone, sky and bridge blue, the piles of the bridge brown; dress yellow.

also the close of an old period in this respect as well, that he himself, in the first years of his activity (towards the end of the fifties) produced a few things still entirely in the style of the old school. Those worth mention are principally two-colour prints (only a few of these exist), for example, a picture of wrestling actors of such power and fierceness that we can hardly recognise in it the refined and delicate master of later years; further, a triptych with single figures. In the employment of broad black masses he shows a sense of grandeur in style which goes beyond his teacher and points directly back to Masanobu himself.

His three-colour prints also are few in number, but of especial importance as a preparatory step toward the complete polychrome print. He produced in this style chiefly kakemono-ye, long, very narrow sheets, which, like the paintings, could be fastened on the pillars of the houses. Masanobu had already attempted this species, and with success, but it was left for Harunobu to establish finally this form, which remained a special favourite until the end of the century. Peculiar skill was demanded in order to dispose a single figure on an extremely limited space so as to keep it both life-like and natural, while yet at the same time producing a decorative effect. Gradually two, three, and at length even more figures were introduced. It was especially the most celebrated artists, Kiyonaga, Utamaro, &c., who cultivated this style by preference. Now Harunobu attempted even in these cases to attain new colour-combinations. On one sheet, representing the delivery of a letter, he employed as his third colour (besides red and blue) not green but yellow, in small spots to heighten the effect of the red; but along with this he obtained a green and a violet by over-printing. In this way he had already five colours at his disposal. But on another sheet, which Fenollosa dates about 1763, a young girl with a monkey, the same three colours are used, the red very deep and

G

the yellow very soft, to achieve a still richer effect. If we include both black and white, which he could dispose in small scattered parts very effectively, to accentuate the effect of the main colours, it is already possible to distinguish nine clearly separate tones, and—this is characteristic of Harunobu—every colour already appears in perfect purity, as do also the tones produced by over-printing. Moreover, they all stand in perfect balance with one another. From this it was only a short step and a mere question of technique to arrive at a colour-print with any desired number of blocks and colours.

This end Harunobu achieved in a series of particularly beautiful compositions, rich in colour and finely cut, of square surimono size, some of which, as, for example, the woman on a white elephant, and another walking over a snow-covered bridge, he dates 1765, to show, by stating the year in which they were made, his justifiable pride in the final success of his invention. He here used five or six wood blocks, and by employing principally light but vivid colours in combination with very delicately blended grey and brown tones, as well as by excellent blind impression, *e.g.* for snow, he produced a chromatic effect the purity and delicacy of which has hardly been excelled by any subsequent work. Thus we have here one more instance of what has so often been observed, as, for example, at the invention of printing, of the European chiaro-scuro-print, and of oil-painting (Van Eyck), that the first products of the new art were also the most perfect, and that subsequent generations have seldom been able to follow them up with adequate success. The further development of colour-prints now no longer depended upon technique, but must be sought exclusively in the idiosyncrasy of each artist, in the way in which he was able to give expression to his peculiar point of view and to his peculiar sense of colour. Here also the chief aim was to secure the distinctest possible effect with the simplest

VEVER COLLECTION, PARIS

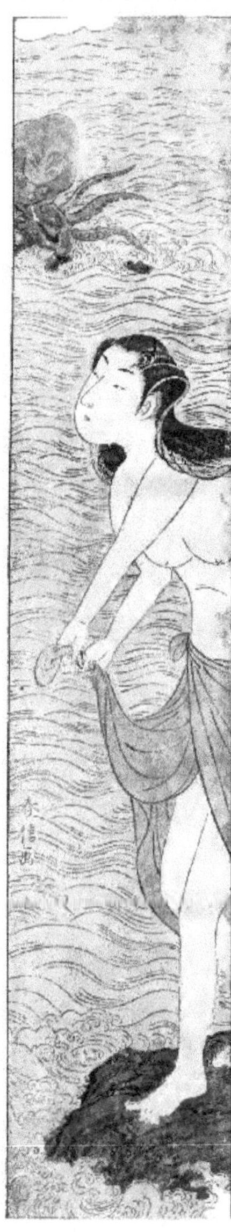

HARUNOBU: *Ama* (FISHER-WOMAN) WITH *Tagò* (POLYPUS) Water and drapery grey brown, the drapery darker in tone Kakemono.

OEDER COLLECTION, DÜSSELDORF

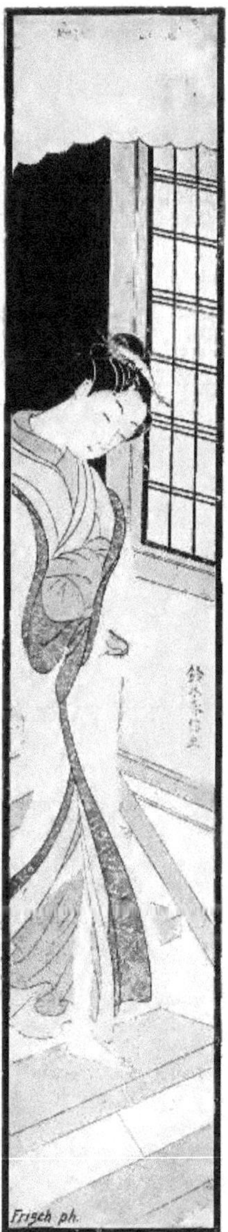

HARUNOBU: GIRL COMING DOWN STEPS. Kakemono.

possible means. Harunobu himself sometimes augmented the number of his blocks to seven or even to ten, but what makes him most famous, besides the subtle harmony of his colours, is their purity and unimpaired brilliancy. This radiance, which is peculiar to him and which contrasts most strongly both with the dull colouring of the primitives and with the subdued tones of all the later great masters of the colour-print, Shunsho, Kiyonaga, Utamaro, reminds us forcibly of the gay and sensuous colour-scheme of the Chinese, and leads to the conclusion that Harunobu received the impulse of his revolutionary innovation from the common birthplace of all Eastern-Asiatic culture. The fact that he borrowed the material for his pictures of woman's life from masters like Shunsui and Tsunemasa also points to such a connection. Colour-printing underwent a further development in the beginning of the nineteenth century, in the surimono, a square congratulatory picture, printed sometimes with as many as thirty blocks, and with the aid of all imaginable metallic tints. However admirable this may be in technical respects, it cannot be regarded as especially productive from an artistic point of view, inasmuch as such multiplication of means is after all no more than a *tour de force.*

CHAPTER V

THE FIRST FLOWERING OF THE POLYCHROME PRINT

1. Harunobu—2. Shigemasa—3. Shunsho

Suzu- 鈴 ki 木 Haru- 春 nobu 信

1. HARUNOBU.—Suzuki Harunobu, the inventor of the polychrome print, was a pupil of that Shigenaga who, in the beginning of the forties, had founded two-colour printing, and towards the end of the fifties, very likely three-colour printing also; but it has already been pointed out that he took his subjects of female life, which made him so famous, from the older masters, Shunsui and Tsunemasa (Tokio Catalogue). In Professor Jaekel's opinion (conveyed to me in a letter) he connects in his older books immediately with Toyonobu, who had already fully developed that graceful female type which attracts us so greatly in the youthful work of Harunobu. In his later prints, on the other hand, the influence of Kiyomitsu makes itself felt.

His life extended from 1718 to 1770, and, according to the Tokio Catalogue (Introd., p. iv.), he stood at the head of a group of artists which apparently styled itself Kiosen. The master himself seems also to have employed this name.[1] Harunobu, who lived in Yedo, began his activity as early as the fifties, first with two-, then with three-colour prints; but it was not until he had brought the latter to perfection, and had thus found the connecting link with the true polychrome print, that, from the

[1] Fenollosa Cat., Nos. 96, 98, 109, 117-133, 142; Anderson Cat., p. 342; Strange, p. 29; Cat. Burty, No. 178 f. The biographical dates are taken from the Hayashi Cat.

KIYÓNAGA

GIRLS ON SEA-SHORE

British Museum

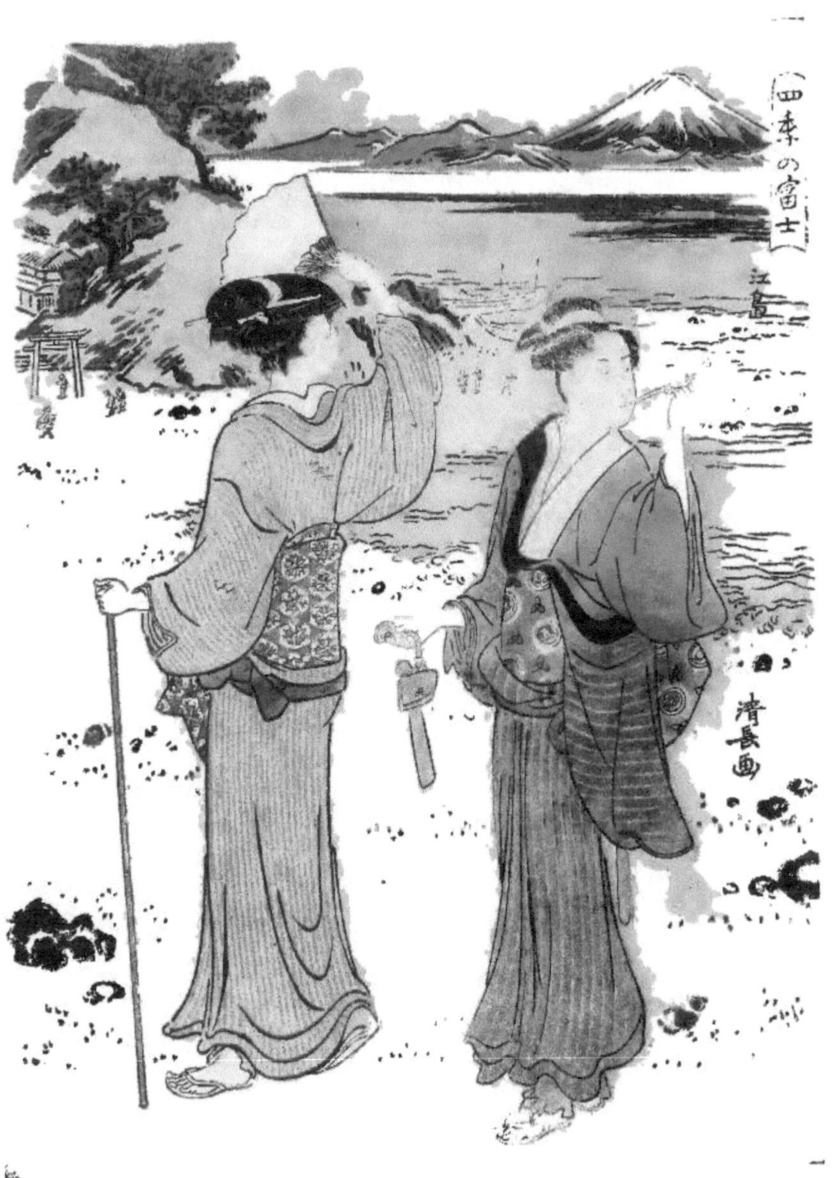
四季の富士
江島
清長画

year 1765 on, he put forth his full powers and created in the following lustrum an almost countless number of the richest, the most graceful, and the most varied polychrome prints. In the last years of his life he took up painting in addition to his woodcut work. A youthful, amiable disposition distinguishes this renewer of Japanese wood-engraving, and leads him to choose the life of youth, fair women, and lovers as his favourite subjects; actor-prints he produced but seldom, and, as it would seem, only in his earliest years.

If the works of the primitives, with whom background, as such, had no existence, can justly be compared with mosaic (Fenollosa), Harunobu may be said to have created space for his compositions by imparting depth to them through the addition of a background. Instead of leaving the background blank as heretofore he gave it a delicate grey or soft green tint. After he had succeeded in bringing his colours to perfect purity, notably a brilliant blue and a red of oxide of lead which did not turn black as readily as that of his successor Koriusai, he developed, partly by over-printing, partly by the employment of additional blocks, the rest of the tone-series in equal purity, to the number of some fifteen. As the colours which he employed were generally opaque, he endeavoured to obtain his effects less by the manner of their application than by the harmonising of shades and the use of neutral mediating tones. His works of the period round 1767 may be recognised by the fact that the side-wings of the hair are again beginning to project and to form an almost horizontal line below, just over the ear. The year 1768 forms the high-water mark of his activity; thenceforward he signs his prints regularly. Towards 1769 his figures, which until then had been very symmetrical, became longer, the faces, too, changed from a round to an oval shape, and the nose increased in length. Herein he follows a fashion that had become pretty well universal at that time. At the same time he began to use white as the basis of his draperies. Finally, he elaborated his landscapes with loving care, further emphasising details, such as water and snow, by blind printing.

Besides the single sheets, which we shall presently refer to, he illustrated in his early days some books in black and white, such as :—

The occupations of women, 16 sheets.
The seven gods of fortune, 8 double sheets.
An anthology of Chinese poetry, 2 or 3 vols. 1763.

A book of 1762 is mentioned by the Hayashi Catalogue (No. 1491).

Of his colour books, the following are especially worth mention :—

Pretty women of the Yoshiwara. Yedo, 1770. (Illustrated in Duret, p. 92.)

Yehon haru no nishiki, spring scenes, 2 vols. (Yedo, 1771), 17 double sheets, light in tone, principally in grey and brown, the landscapes carefully elaborated, but the faces expressionless; probably his last work.

Wedding scenes, 7 oblong sheets, very delicate in colour and contour.

Various series of fanciful designs, of oblong shape.

Occupations of women, 30 sheets.

Of his single sheets, those in the style of the primitives are very scarce, as also the medium-sized colour-print. Of especial beauty are his kakemono-ye, mostly representing a single figure, but not, as Fenollosa states, without background, as the contrary is proved by the very charming work here reproduced, which shows a young girl descending a staircase. Of unusual shape and monumental beauty is a bridal procession, on a black background, in ten broadside folio sheets. Most of his sheets are of a medium quarto form which he was the first to introduce, and usually represent two figures. A representation of cranes in the reeds is exceptional. His prints of the year 1765

Bing Collection, Paris

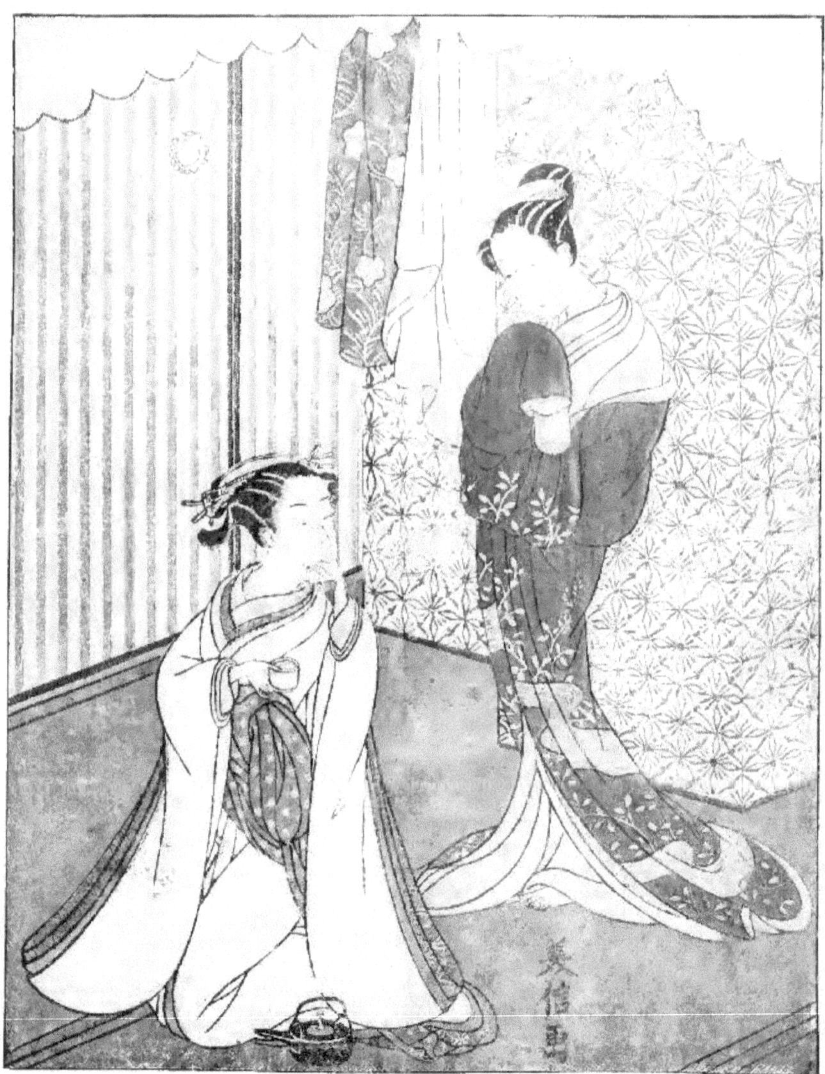

YOSHINOBU : Two Women in a Room.
Pink and yellow predominate.

have already been mentioned in the preceding chapter; to them belongs, among others, that of a young girl reading a letter. Strange reproduces (plate 2, page 30) two women; Anderson (*Japanese Wood-Engraving*, plate ii.), a woman with a vessel of water on her head, who turns, in the act of walking, toward a child that she is leading by the hand. Fenollosa (*Outline*, pl. viii.) reproduces a print of about 1768–69, for which ten wood blocks, exclusive of the black and white block, were employed. Among other compositions may be mentioned:—

A youth discovering bamboo shoots in snow.
Sennin Kinko in the shape of a woman, seated on a carp.
Washerwoman tripping gracefully through a brook.
Dancing girl with a large Tai fish.
A young woman at her door with two youthful companions and a dog.
Two little girls at a temple gate—one of his most delicate creations.
Two women standing in the water, one of whom is catching small fish by the aid of a cormorant, while the other keeps them in a bowl.
Two female water-carriers, one of whom is standing in the water and filling a bucket.
Two women under a large umbrella, protecting themselves from a heavy shower.
Two girls on the seashore, picking rush-leaves.
A youth leading a girl on horseback—one of his most perfect creations.
Sedan-bearers at night by lantern light.
A parrot on its perch, large and simple (Berlin Kunstgewerbe-museum).

Other sheets are mentioned by Bing (Catalogue, No. 133), and the Leroux Catalogue.

A word of warning may be added concerning the reprints of Harunobu's works, as they appear to have been made from re-cut blocks; they can be recognised by the thickness of the contours, the deep impression of the lines, the dirty dull colours and especially the sooty black. Blind printing is also employed with particular frequency.

Harunobu is said to have left a son or pupil, Harunobu II., who learned to draw in the Dutch (European) style (Anderson Catalogue, p. 342). Fenollosa names another pupil of Harunobu, Fujinobu (Catalogue, No. 163; see under Shigenaga), also Kuninobu (No. 164). Suzuki Haruji, of whom we have kakemono-ye, was very similar to the master, and therefore probably his pupil. The following are further mentioned as his pupils: Harushige, his son, who worked principally in the seventies (Hayashi Catalogue, No. 415); Harutsugu (*ibid.*, No. 419 *seqq.*); Haruhiro, *i.e.* Koriusai (see below); Muranobu (*ibid.*, No. 422); Uchimasa (*ibid.*, No. 423).

Among contemporaries of Harunobu may be mentioned: Miyagawa Tominobu (Hayashi Catalogue, No. 354); Minko, of Osaka, who came to Yedo in 1760 (*ibid.*, Nos. 406, 407) and illustrated books about 1765 and 1770; Uyeno Shoha (*ibid.*, No. 408); Soan (*ibid.*, No. 409); Morino Sogiku (*ibid.*, No. 410); Kogan (*ibid.*, No. 411); Shoshoken (*ibid.*, No. 412); Soshosai Seiko (*ibid.*, No. 413).

Yamato Yoshinobu, often confused with Harunobu, was very likely also a pupil of Shigenaga (Hayashi Catalogue, No. 350), and worked at two-colour prints of very delicate and naïve character towards the end of the fifties (Fenollosa, No. 95); he was perhaps the same person as the later Komai Yoshinobu (Fenollosa, No. 167). Another pupil of Shigenaga was Shigemasa, who began with three-colour prints about the middle of the sixties, and soon after, at the same time with Harunobu, turned to polychrome prints, continuing thenceforward, beside Harunobu, as one of the principal masters of this school. Before, however, we give our attention to him and the remaining contemporaries of Harunobu, it will be necessary to speak of an artist who, as the immediate continuer of Harunobu, so completely assimilated

湖 Ko-
龍 riu-
齋 sai

his style of drawing, though not his colour, that some have thought they could recognise in him a new phase of Harunobu under another name. This man is Koriusai, whose real name was Isoda Shobei, a samurai of the Tsuchiya family, who also called himself Masakatsu Haruhiro, or the hermit of Yagenbori; he lived in Yedo and was very probably a pupil of Harunobu.[1] Their similarity lies chiefly in their drawing, but as the colouring of the two men is absolutely different, the idea, alleged to be that of the Japanese themselves, that there were two Koriusais, the one being simply identical with a certain phase of Harunobu's development, is probably a mistaken one. Koriusai was at work through the whole of the seventies, but about 1780 turned to painting, which he probably abandoned in 1782. He is especially remarkable for his deep and most original colouring, in which predominate a dark orange red, a deep, somewhat mottled blue, and also a black admirably applied in broad masses. This colouring lends a dignified and serious aspect to his presentations, which, like Harunobu's, are especially occupied with delineations of women. His *genre* pictures, agreeable but rather lifeless, are very numerous; but his activity lay chiefly in kakemono-ye, on which he introduced first two, then three, and at length several figures; indeed, his output in this line is more considerable than that of all other artists combined, and in point of finish and fulness of composition may be regarded as the highest achievement in this species of print. In this style he produced eight views of Lake Omi, typified by figures; a youth of rank with a falcon on his wrist, and Fuji in the background, and many others. According to the Tokio Catalogue (p. 65) almost two-thirds of all kakemono-ye are from his hand. During the time of his activity a further change in coiffure begins to take place; from about 1772 the middle coil projects in its full breadth,

[1] Strange, p. 32; Fenollosa Cat., Nos. 143, 147, 151, 154–160; Bing Cat., No. 146 ff. The Hayashi Cat. speaks of him as a pupil of Shigenaga.

from about 1775 the side-wings, which so far had stood off stiffly, begin to bend over, and from 1776 the little queue at the back disappears entirely. About the middle of the seventies begins Harunobu's rivalry with Kiyonaga, against whose influence, however, he was unable to hold his ground. In 1777 he stood at the height of his powers, but by the end of the same decade his types began to get common and monotonous. About 1787 he even began to imitate his rival Kiyonaga. His books with black and white illustrations were published from 1777 to 1780.

Koriusai, like Harunobu, was a master in the use of blind printing, especially for indicating dress patterns. He employed it in a specially masterly manner on a series of original representations of the zodiac, drawings of animals of wonderful variety and with a splendour of colour that makes them perhaps the most triumphant success of Japanese colour-printing and certainly stamps them as the high-water mark of this artist's work, to which none of his other productions can be compared. In this style we have by him fighting cocks, red and white, parrots which are left in white on a ground of a beautiful brick red. He was noted for his representations of animals in general: among others may be mentioned a crane's nest, an eagle which has seized a pheasant, a white crane in the snow, the Howo bird above clouds, cranes at sunrise, ducks in the reeds, pheasants, and lastly, a fat white cat about to pounce on some butterflies, partly in blind printing.

Especially celebrated is his series of fifteen medium-sized sheets, in which the black of the background plays an important part, each depicting a courtesan in a magnificently patterned robe, with two young attendants; this series he began about 1777 and brought to a close about 1780. Of his early period there is a series of eight charming sheets representing the different periods of the day by female figures. A series of erotic prints, small oblong, are very delicate in colour.

VEVER COLLECTION, PARIS

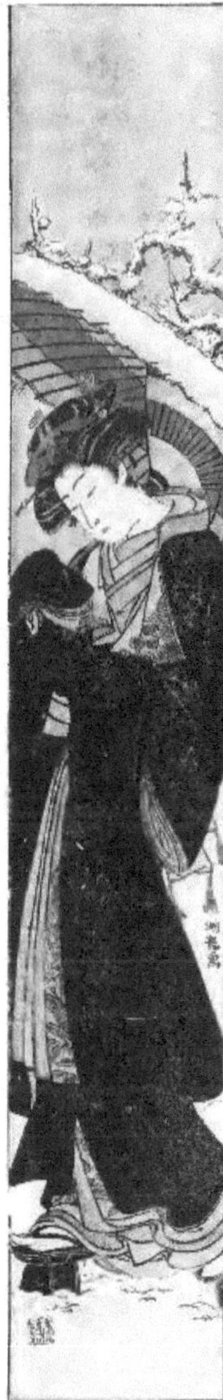

KORIUŠAI: LADY IN THE SNOW. Kakemono.

VEVER COLLECTION, PARIS

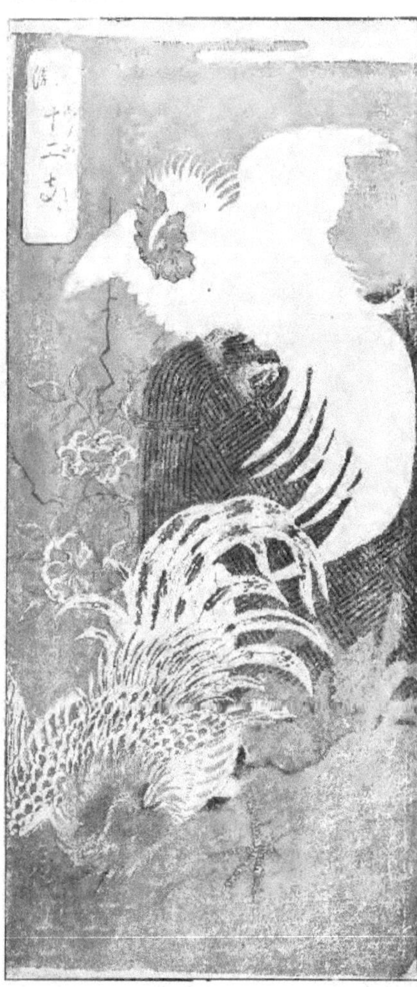

KORIUŠAI: FIGHTING COCKS. The tenth of twelve plates forming an animal series.

R. WAGNER, BERLIN

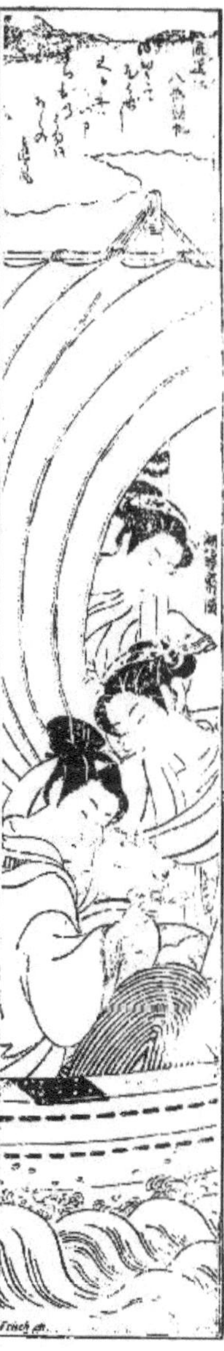

KORIUŠAI: THE RETURNING SAIL. A gentleman with a *saki*-bowl and two girls in a brick-red boat. From the series of eight subjects of Lake Omi. Kakemono.

The following list shows how original are many of his other productions:—

A child playing with a tortoise, which it is trying to submerge in a bowl of water.
Five children playing with a rat.
A child struggling with a polyp.
Kintoki blowing the flute (Berlin Kunstgewerbemuseum).
Young women standing on a balcony at sunset.
Two young women on a balcony lighted by red lanterns, looking down upon a throng of people who are trying to shelter themselves from the rain under a large umbrella.

Strange reproduces, on page 32, a young man holding on his shoulder a young girl, who is trying to set a striking clock.

The cause of the discoloration of the orange-red containing lead, which occurs more frequently with Koriusai than any one else, has been attributed to artificial oxidising, and also to the application of black by means of the ball of the thumb; but it is probably the usual entirely unintentional oxidising of a not very permanent colour, as the manner in which this black appears and the way it passes over into the red has every appearance of being due to accidental variations, according to the degree of thickness with which it was laid on. Just herein lies the inimitable charm of colour that attaches to these prints. In the surimono-like animal designs, which were executed with great care, this peculiarity is not found, obviously because better colours have been employed. Similar changes may be noticed in other much-faded prints of this period, which, after they have been long exposed to the light, have sometimes scarcely a trace of colour left, but for this very reason have charmed our painters in the highest degree. Though such a predilection may attest an almost morbid over-refinement of the human mind, still it has a certain justification, and may even, considering how shy our time is of colour, be a normal phenomenon. For that reason, painters will not easily be convinced that in neither case are the changes intentional.

2. Shigemasa.—In the year 1764, one year before the invention of the polychrome print, there first appear those artists whose vocation it was, as followers of Harunobu, to control and direct Japanese art in its further development: Shigemasa, Shunsho, and Kiyonaga. The first two of these will be treated of in this chapter, as their principal activity, like that of Koriusai, the immediate follower of Harunobu, falls in the seventies. Kiyonaga, however, whose full influence was not felt until the beginning of the eighties, simultaneously with that of Shunsho's pupils, will be discussed in a separate chapter, more especially as he represents, on his own merits, the high-water mark of Japanese wood-engraving.

Shunsho, like Hokusai, is apt to be overrated, as he is better known and especially pleasing to the eye. The merit, however, of having, after Harunobu, effected the transition from the style of the old period to that of the new, belongs undoubtedly to Shigemasa, who, besides, deserves especial attention as one of the best draughtsmen among Japanese artists. Like Harunobu, Kitao Shigemasa, also called Kosuisai, was a pupil of the aged pioneer Shigenaga. He also signed himself Sekkosai, Kwaran, Tairei, and, as calligrapher, Ichiyosai. Born in 1739, he began about 1764 with actor prints in three colours, and went over in 1765, together with Harunobu, to the polychrome print, which he cultivated until the beginning of the eighties without having to fear the rivalry of Kiyonaga, who had now come to his full powers, and before whom all other contemporaries retreated.[1] He was still painting as late as the middle of the eighties, but then seemingly retired, though he

Kita- 北
o 尾
Shige- 重
masa 政

[1] Fenollosa Cat., Nos. 114, 204–216; Anderson Cat., p. 344; Cat. Burty, No. 197 ff.; Strange, p. 86.

VEVER COLLECTION, PARIS

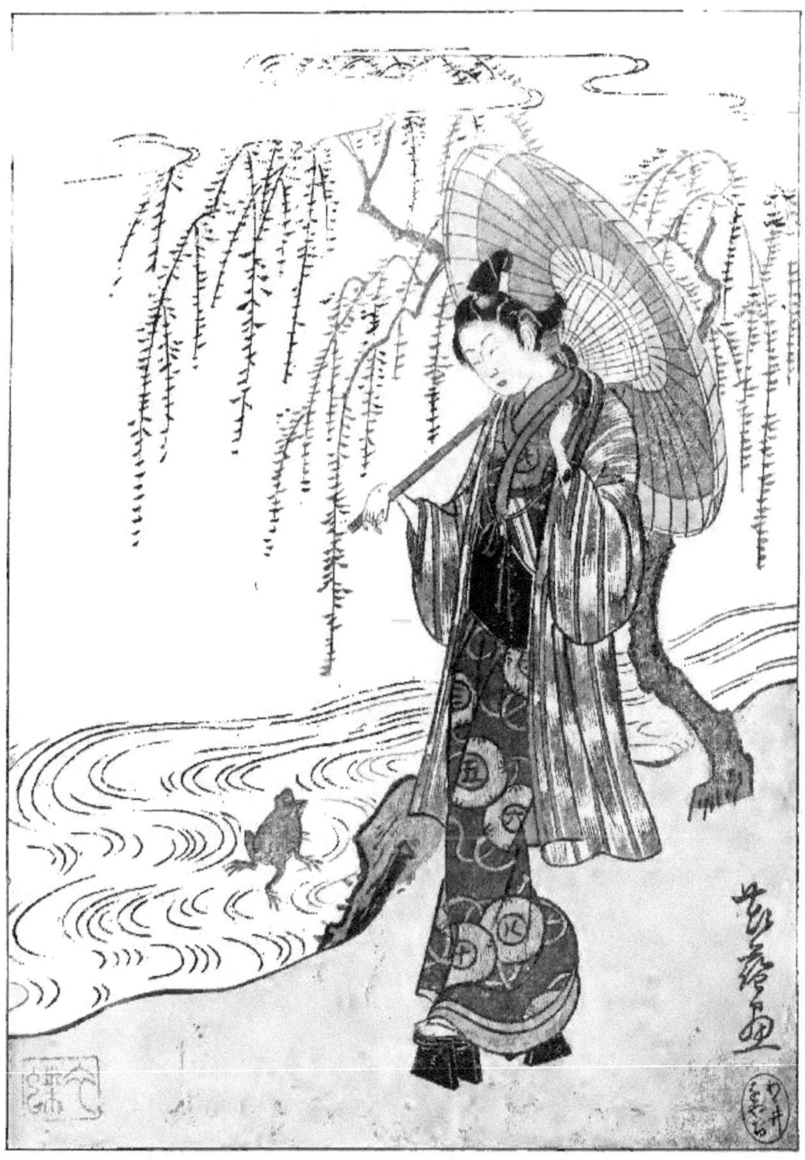

SHIGÉMASA : ONO NO DOFU, THE FAMOUS CALLIGRAPHER, AS A YOUNG MAN. He watches a frog snapping at a branch of willow. *Yellow and brown predominate.*

is said to have only died in 1819; if so no works from his hand during these last decades of his life are extant. He progressed slowly and did not develop his full activity until the seventh decade, producing little, but dedicating himself with comparative zeal to book-illustration. Then, at last, toward the end of the seventies, he reaches his full height. His works are rare, and only the early ones are signed with his name, but still his unsigned productions show his characteristics unmistakably. His kakemono-ye are also rare, but among them are some very beautiful things; Fenollosa considers the sheet with two lovers and a man holding an ape (Catalogue, No. 215), which he places about 1781, as perhaps the most beautiful of this class. As he is simpler in his drawing than Koriusai and Shunsho, so he is also softer in colouring. The best draughtsman of the generation active in the seventh decade, he is particularly happy in rendering with perfected art the sinuous movement of garments, as, in general, he is unexcelled in lively movement, *e.g.* in his print of the No-dancer with the fox mask of about 1777. He collaborated with several of his contemporaries in the illustration of books.

Of his single sheets Fenollosa cites among others (Catalogue, No. 208) a series of geishas, which he dates *circa* 1775, and which form a kind of pendant to Koriusai's series of courtesans. From his very early period there dates a three-colour print of a young man acting as umpire at a cock-fight.

Besides the ordinary *genre* pictures, he also did animal representations; Bing (Catalogue, No. 299 ff.) cites a cock with a hen, horses (with blind printing), an eagle on the alert; further, irises on the edge of a brook down which drinking-cups are floating, a view of the river Sumida in Yedo. Beautiful renderings of plants on large oblong sheets are to be found in Gonse's collection. Strange gives a reproduction of one of his prints at page 24.

He distinguished himself to a marked degree as an illustrator. Besides the excellent polychrome illustrations which he executed in collaboration with Shunsho, and of which we shall speak when we treat of the latter, the *Seiro Bijin awase sugata kagami* (Beauties of the Yoshiwara), 1776, and the twelve representations of sericulture, he also produced independently the following :—

Yehon fuku jiro, illustrations of legends. Yedo, 1791.
Tales for children. 1791.
Kwacho shashin zuye (flowers and birds), 1805, 3 vols.
Album with fish, Yehon tatsu no miyako.

In black and white he produced :—

Yehon biwako, representations of women. 1775.
Yehon yotsu no toki. 1775.
Yehon yasu Ujikawa, celebrated Chinese and Japanese heroes. 1786.
Yehon Kamagadake, celebrated horses and their owners. 1802.

His pupil was Kitao Masanobu, called, as poet, Santo Kioden, his family name being Iwasi, his personal name Denzo; he lived from 1761 to 1816 (the dates: 1775–1830 given in the first edition are corrected according to the Hayashi Catalogue). He signed himself Kitao Shinsai, Risai, Kankoku, Seisai, Hosan, &c. He did not produce much, as he followed also the vocation of poet. His activity began in 1778 (Fenollosa Catalogue, No. 217). Fenollosa reproduces, on pl. xi. of the *Outline*, a print from the Illustrations of Pretty Women (*Shin Bijin Awase Jishitsu Kagami*, 1784).

By him we have:

A series of the Fifty Poets, printed in deep but very harmonious colours.

A pamphlet, New Illustrations of Pretty Women, seven double sheets in large folio; on each are two or three women, sometimes with children, with a slightly indicated landscape background; the colour is gay, the drawing careless, the expression defective.

Eight landscapes of Kanazawa, represented by women.

KIYÓNAGA

GIRLS TYING POEMS ON BLOSSOMING TREES IN SPRING

British Museum

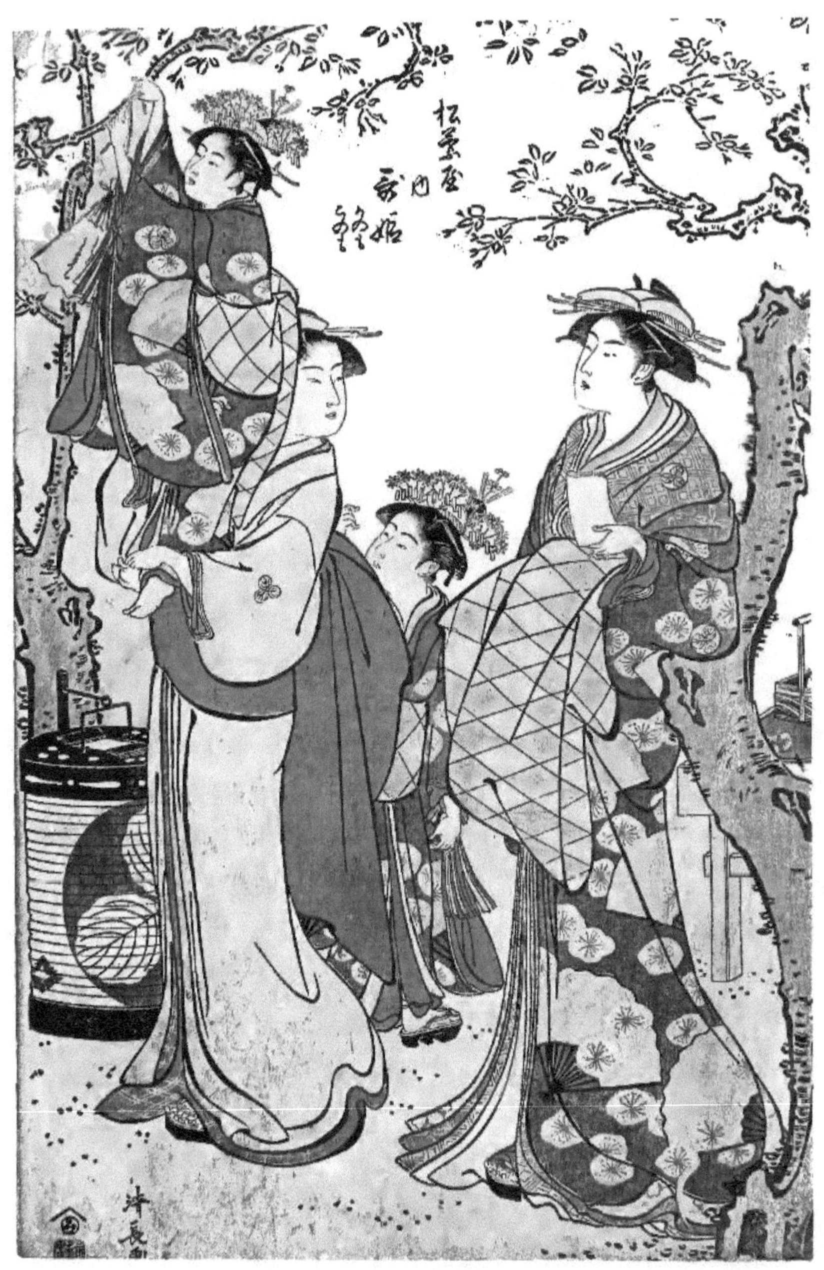

Kioka gojunin isshu (fifty humorous poems), 1786 (Yedo).
A small work in black and white, of the year 1802, humorous tales of wise men and fools in the baths.

Other illustrated books are mentioned by Duret.

Yenkoan seems to have been a pupil of Shigemasa (illustration in Hayashi Catalogue, No. 1006), and Nagabide a contemporary, who produced about 1770 a number of very graceful prints of single female figures. Kurth (*Utamaro*, p. 87) makes him a pupil of Nagayoshi, and accordingly puts his active period later, saying that he worked in Kioto and Osaka and that his pictures of actors were influenced by Sharaku. The *Yekon Chuko teijo kagami* (the Mirror of the Faith of Virtuous Women) (Jackel Collection) is by him. Further research is needed on Nagabide.

Later on we shall mention two other pupils of Shigemasa, Shumman and Masayoshi.

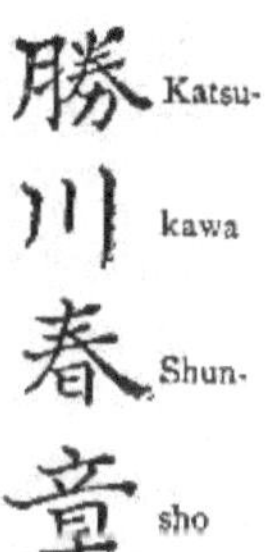

3. SHUNSHO.—Katsukawa Shunsho, who dominated wood-engraving during the seventies and trained a numerous school of pupils, was born in 1726 and died in 1792.[1] His artistic name was Jusuki. It was not he who founded this new artistic clan, but his teacher, Shunsui, the son or pupil of Choshun, who about the middle of this century had assumed the name of Katsukawa, but had been active only a short time as wood-engraver.[2] On the other hand, it is Shunsho's merit that he took up again the representations of actors, which had already gone somewhat out of fashion, and now continued the activity of the Torii with the additional aid of polychrome printing.[3] His activity began in 1764, when he followed Harunobu principally. From about 1770 his figures, like those in all the art of the time, became longer. Towards the end of the seventies the colouring

[1] Fenollosa Cat., Nos. 178–201; Anderson Cat., p. 343; Bing Cat., No. 235 ff.; Cat. Burty, No. 189 ff., 196; Strange, p. 33 f. The biographical dates are taken from the Hayashi Cat.

[2] Fenollosa Cat., No. 117. See also *supra* under Choshun.

[3] Fenollosa, *Outline*, p. 35.

of his dress-patterns became almost too rich. Almost all his pupils followed him in the representation of actors; among them Shunko and Buncho rank high, also Shunyei, Shunzan, Shuncho, and Shumman; but he achieved his highest renown by numbering among his pupils Shunro, who afterwards, under the name of Hokusai, rose to such great importance. When Kiyonaga became supreme in the eighties, Shunsho, like his contemporary Toyoharu, devoted himself entirely to painting.

His first print, about 1764, represented the five actors known by the name of Gonin Otoko. Towards the end of the sixties this artist develops his fullest activity. He produced innumerable actor prints all of them noted for their vivacity of movement and strength of colouring, although the expression of emotion was of less consequence than in Harunobu or Kiyonaga. With an extremely simple yet effective arrangement of draperies, Shunsho succeeded, by his clever distribution of black masses, in producing an admirably decorative effect, for which the rendering of actors in women's parts—which in Japan are always taken by men—offered him special opportunities. Strange reproduces a picture of this class (plate iii.), and also one with two actors at page 94; also Anderson (*Japanese Wood-Engraving*) on plate iii. Fenollosa (*Outline*, pl. x.) reproduces a print from the *Seiro Bijin Awase* of 1775.

Other works by him are:

Five representations from the play Sembonzakura.

Likenesses of actors in quarter length, in frames, oblong octavo, very delicately coloured.

Sheets of wrestlers, such as Shunko, Shunyei, and others produced.

Beautiful surimonos.

A kakemono-ye, two young women playing with a monkey.

A Buddhist winged angel, playing the lute, reminding us of Italian Renaissance compositions.

A horse under a cherry tree in blossom.

No-dancer, of larger size (Berlin Kunstgewerbemuseum).

R. Wagner, Berlin

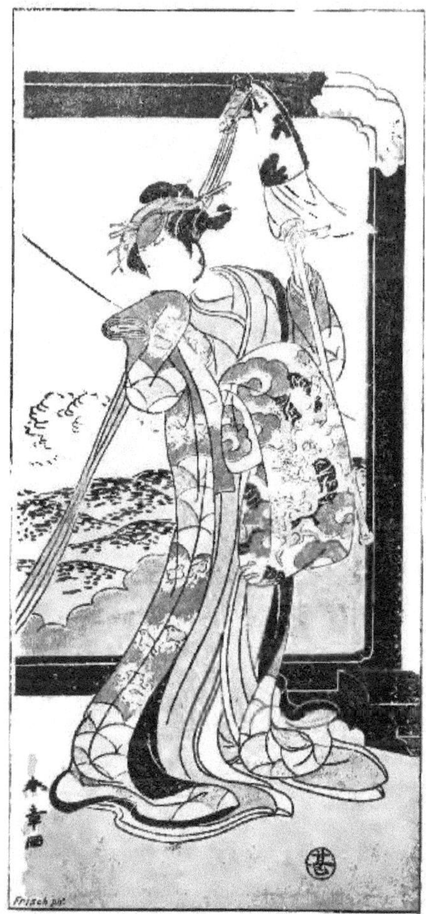

SHUNSHŌ: Actor in Female Costume executing a Dance with a Hobby-horse. On the screen the mountain Fujiyama. *In red, grey, green, &c.*

Vever Collection, Paris

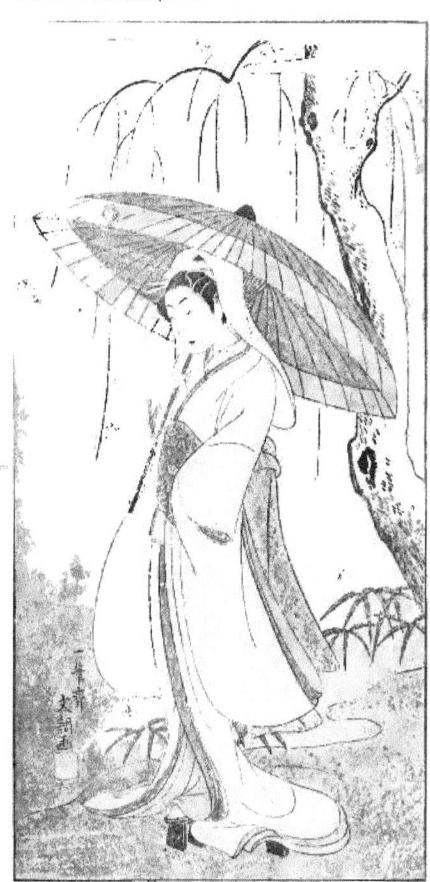

BUNCHŌ: A Lady in the Snow. *Grey and yellow.*

Of his illustrated works in polychrome, the following may be mentioned :—

Theatre fans. Yedo, 1769.

Kobi no Tsubo, a collection of actor likenesses, 1770, still somewhat conventional, but very effective in colour.

Nishiki hiakunin isshiu azumi ori, the hundred celebrated poets (Yedo, 1774), one of his principal works.

Sairo bijin awase sugata kagami, mirror of the beauties of the Green Houses, in collaboration with Shigemasa, 3 vols. Yedo, 1776.

Sanjirokkasen, the six-and-thirty poets. Yedo, 1775.

Other works in Duret.

The *Green Houses* is probably the most beautiful illustrated work that Japanese art ever produced. The beauties who dwell in the green-painted houses of pleasure are here generally represented in fours on a double sheet, engaged in the various occupations of their daily life, playing, smoking, at music, painting, poetry, in the garden. Also some sheets with very beautiful conventionalised plants. A characteristic of this work is a special light rose colour which predominates with violet, grey-brown, and yellow, and gives a very delicate effect.

Another celebrated work, in which he likewise collaborated with Shigemasa, is the illustrations of Sericulture, in twelve sheets, each usually representing three people at work, with explanatory verses above.

With Buncho he edited, in 1770, a series of actor likenesses in quarter length, each represented on a fan : Yehon butai ogi ; the earliest book of polychrome prints, after those of Harunobu.

Lastly, with his contemporary Toyoharu, he edited a folio representing the twelve months, the sheets divided diagonally, with landscapes on the upper part and groups mostly of three figures on the lower ; the slender figures are very graceful in movement, the shading very soft ; evidently a work of his early days.

A very numerous flock of pupils was educated by him, and it is difficult to differentiate them, as they followed his style with

H

fidelity, and most of them, like their master, cultivated actor prints. But it will be necessary, before speaking of the individual pupils, to advert to two contemporaries and rivals of Shunsho, who can hardly be separated from him, as, though working entirely in his spirit, they form, through the peculiarity of their nature, a necessary complement to the manner of that artist. They are Buncho and Toyoharu.

Itsu- 一 hitsu- 筆 sai 齋 Bun- 文 cho 調

Ippitsusai Buncho, like his rival Shunsho, reached his culmination in the beginning of the seventies. He died in 1796. His surname was Kishi, his name in art Uyemon. He was a pupil of Ishikawa Kogen. But whereas Shunsho aimed at violent motion and robust colour in his actor representations, and therefore often became angular and hard, though always impressive, Buncho strove to achieve a soft flow of line and delicate colouring, to which his favourite subject, actors in women's parts, was more especially adapted. His sheets are perhaps the most delicate and gracious of all Japanese art and are distinguished both by exceptional sharpness and fineness of drawing, and by a harmony and elegance of colour grouping which can scarcely be surpassed. With a lustrous, yet restful green and red he was fond of combining the most delicate gradations of grey, so as to produce an extraordinarily harmonious whole. The strong effects of black and brick red, which appear particularly in the early part of Shunsho's work, are seldom to be found in Buncho. As, like Harunobu, he chose the colours for his prints with great care, they have generally preserved their full freshness of tint, and yet their effect is as mild as that elsewhere attained only by works whose colours have been gradually harmonised by exposure to light. As examples of his *genre* pictures, the following may be given :—

A girl smoking on a balcony.
A girl looking at a hototogisu (night cuckoo).

---

[1] Fenollosa Cat., Nos. 181, 182, 184 ; Bing Cat., No. 170 ff.; Hayashi Cat.

BING COLLECTION, PARIS

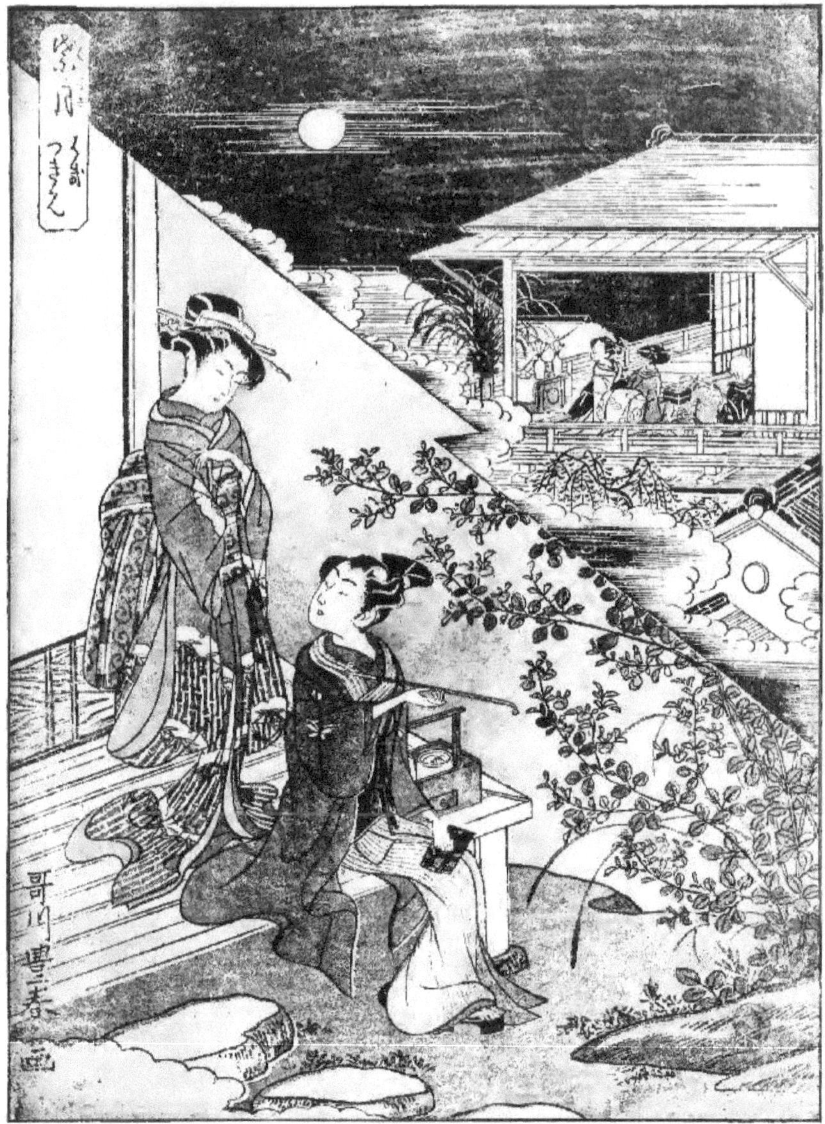

TOYŌHARU: THE EIGHTH MONTH (SEPTEMBER). From the series of the Months. *Pink and green predominate.*

Fenollosa (*Outline*, pl. ix.) reproduces the picture of an actor of about 1772.

Reproductions of drawings by Buncho were given in the *Buncho Sensei Gwafu* (Yedo, 1816), black with some colour.

His pupil was Kincho Sekiga (illustration in Hayashi Catalogue, No. 477).

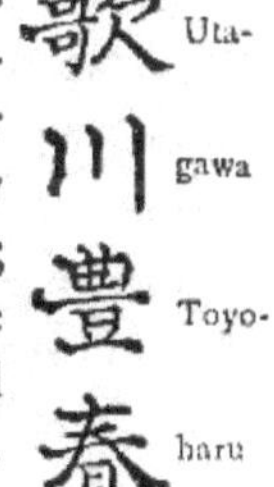

Utagawa Toyoharu lived from 1733 to 1814, and began work towards the end of the sixties.[1] He was a pupil of Shigenaga, and, according to Fenollosa (Catalogue, No. 171), a brother of the gifted Utagawa Toyonobu, who worked in the early seventies, but died young, so that his work has become very rare; on the other hand, the Hayashi Catalogue, which reproduces one of Toyonobu's prints (No. 1017), is of opinion that he is identical with Toyoharu, whose youthful period he in that case represents. Toyoharu's ordinary name was Tajimaya Shozabro, and he also signed himself Ichiriusai. His prints, especially of the early period, are very rare. His second style began about 1773, but after 1776 he produced but little. A delicately strung nature, he shrank from competition with the newly arisen style of Kiyonaga, and, like Shunsho, devoted himself principally to painting from the eighties onward. At the same time, he possessed, in contrast to Buncho's pronouncedly decorative talent, a most sensitive and individual gift, in virtue of which he became the founder of a special clan of artists, that of the Utagawas, which was destined to take the lead in place of the Katsukawa clan. Fenollosa (*Review*, p. 42) is right in inclining to put him even above Shunsho in genius. The designs for the Months, done in collaboration with Shunsho, have already been mentioned. Besides this, one of his most beautiful series is that consisting of four sheets representing the Perfections. One

[1] Fenollosa Cat., Nos. 173-177; Anderson Cat., p. 347. The biographical dates are taken from the Hayashi Cat. (my first edition made him reach the age of sixty-nine years).

of the works of his early period, when he was competing with Harunobu, is a large and beautiful print, representing two lovers playing *go* on the terrace of a garden, while a woman stands and looks on. He borrowed his orange-red from Koriusai. He was one of the first to learn the rules of perspective from the Europeans, and employed them, *e.g.*, on the large oblong print of the performance of a No-dance at the court of a nobleman. He was, moreover, one of the founders of landscape renderings, and could also represent crowds with great ability (Tokio Catalogue). His pupils were Toyohiro and particularly Toyokuni, of whom we shall treat later. Another probable pupil of Ishikawa Toyonobu is Ishikawa Toyomasu, who worked at the same time as Harunobu, Shunsho, Toyoharu, and Shigemasa, and is dated by Fenollosa [1] about the year 1770. He executed a series of the twelve months. The Hayashi Catalogue (No. 347) contains a reproduction of one of his works. Toyohisa is also mentioned as a pupil of Toyoharu (illustration in Hayashi Catalogue, No. 1015).

Here we must also mention a contemporary of Toyoharu, Shiba Gokan (or Kokan) who was born 1747 and died 1818.[2] He signed himself Shun, Shumpa, Fugen Dojin, and Kungaku; in daily life he was known as Katsusaburo. He was a pupil of Harunobu, whose manner he continued after the death and under the name of the master. He is mentioned as the first Japanese artist who learned the rules of perspective from the Dutch and applied them in his book of travels, *Gwato saiyudan*, 1781. He is also said to have been the first to execute copperplate in Japan, but Burty (Catalogue, No. 455) mentions as the first attempt in this technique a *meisho* (book of travels) consisting of thirty-one oblong sheets, of the year 1849, which would thus

[1] Cat., No. 170.

[2] Anderson Cat., p. 344: *id., Japanese Wood-Engraving;* Strange, p. 32; Bing in the *Revue blanche*, vii. (1896), pp. 314, 315 note.

Bing Collection, Paris

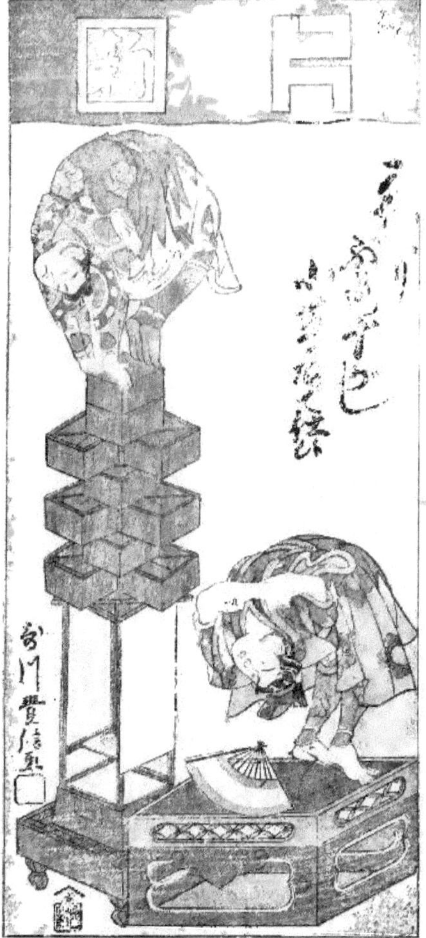

UTÁGAWA TOYÔNOBU: Acrobats. "Artists of Osaka." *Brick red predominates.*

Vever Collection, Paris

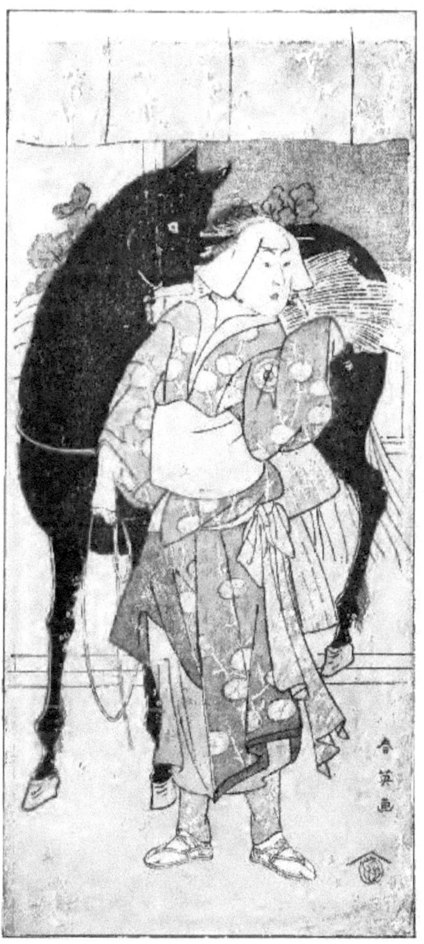

SHUNYEI: Peasant Girl in Trousers and Sandals leading a Horse loaded with Rice-straw.

be half a century later. The knowledge of perspective, which is distinctly traceable in Toyoharu, and is seen again in Hokusai, may, however, have been passed over to these artists by Gokan. The Hayashi Catalogue (No. 462) gives a (coloured) landscape which he is said to have drawn on stone; but this is most improbable, as lithography was only invented in Europe about 1800.

One of the most faithful pupils of Shunsho's early period was Katsukawa Shunko, who worked chiefly from the latter half of the sixties to the middle of the eighties; towards the end the proportions of his figures became exaggerated.[1] The Hayashi Catalogue (No. 585) gives 1827 as the year of his death. An illustrated book by him appeared at Yedo in 1795. Besides representations of actors and wrestlers, a blind man dancing is cited as by him (illustrated in Hayashi Catalogue, No. 588). One Kichosai Shunko (illustration in Hayashi Catalogue, No. 788) belongs to the nineteenth century. Perhaps he is identical with Shunko II. (*ibid.*, No. 787), who already shows European influences.

There were also engaged in actor representation Katsukawa Shuntoku, Shunyen, and Shunki; of the latter we have a dancing actor, reproduced by Strange, page 34.

Among the pupils of Shunsho's later period Katsukawa Shunyei takes a prominent place.[2] He was born in 1762 and died in 1819. His family name was Isoda, his name in art Kinjiro; he also called himself Kutokusai. It is not without reason that many rate him even higher than his master. Besides his effective and grandly conceived actor likenesses, which remind one of Sharaku, he produced large pictures of wrestlers, which are noted for their excellent drawing; for fans he drew very gay popular compositions, which are effective with very

勝 Katsu-
川 kawa
春 Shun-
英 yei

[1] Fenollosa Cat., Nos. 189, 193, 195, 203; Strange, p. 36; Bing Cat., No. 278 ff.; Tokio Cat., p. 74.

[2] Fenollosa Cat., No. 202; Strange, p. 36; Bing Cat., No. 259 *seqq.*

few colours; he also produced small popular sheets toned in pink and grey only, as well as kakemonos. Illustrated books by him appeared about 1789 and 1801 (Duret).

One of his pupils was Shunto (illustration in Hayashi Catalogue, No. 786), a successor (?) about 1830 of Shunwa (*ibid.*, No. 789). As his pupils, we shall also have occasion to mention Shunsen and Shuntei, the contemporaries of Hokusai.

Three other pupils of the latter part of Shunsho's life, Shunman, Shuncho, and Shunzan, came entirely under the influence of Kiyonaga, the victorious successor of their master, thus following the tendency of the times. They can thus be postponed to the end of the chapter on Kiyonaga. With respect to Gakutei, see under Hokusai.

As further pupils of Shunsho may be mentioned: Katsukawa Shundo, who also signed himself Rantokusai. An illustrated book by him appeared at Yedo in 1790 (illustration in Hayashi Catalogue, No. 622 *seqq.*). Katsukawa Shemkaku (*ibid.*, No. 625), Katsukawa Shunsui II. (*ibid.*, No. 628), Shunri (*ibid.*, No. 771), Shunjo, who published an illustrated book at Yedo in 1782 (*ibid.*, No. 618).

Probable pupils of Shunsho are: Angiusai Yenshi, who, according to the Tokio Catalogue (No. 163), worked in the eighties in the style of Kiyonaga (Hayashi Catalogue, No. 766), and Shoyu (*ibid.*, No. 770).

Other contemporary artists are: Katsukawa Kinjiro (Hayashi Catalogue, No. 629). Ikku, whose family name was Shigeda and whose artistic name was Yochichi, was specially famous as a novelist (*ibid.*, No. 769); illustrated books by him appeared at Yedo from 1799 to 1813. Rinkusai, who published a book of actors (Yedo, 1790), 3 vols. (Duret).

YEISHI

A LADY HOLDING SAKÉ-CUP, WITH ATTRIBUTES OF GOOD-LUCK

BRITISH MUSEUM

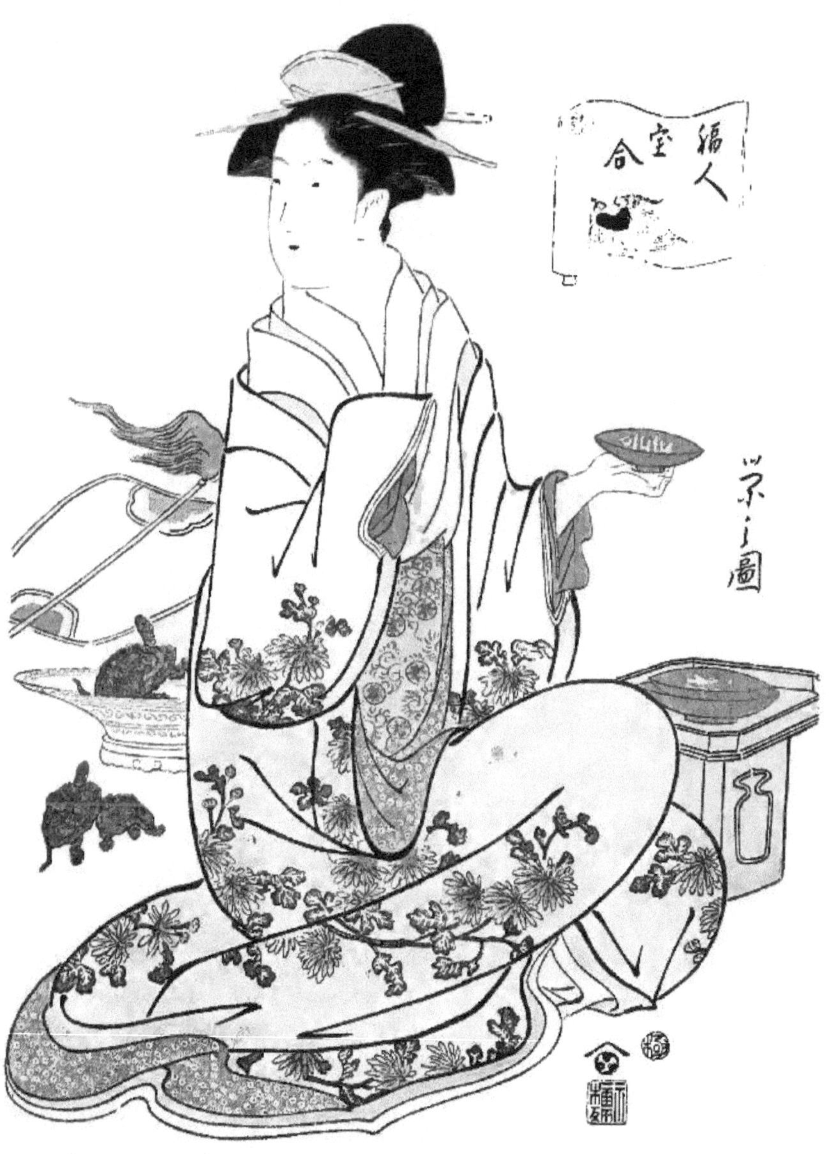
婦人宝合

CHAPTER VI

THE CULMINATION: KIYONAGA

THE great and aristocratic school of the Torii, which had stamped its impress upon wood-engraving in its primitive stages, and had played a determining part in all its subsequent changes and developments, from the hand-coloured black and white print through the two- and three-colour prints, had for a decade past been rather relegated to the background, when, about the middle of the seventies of the eighteenth century, Torii Kiyonaga took the lead, thenceforth to dominate the art of Japanese wood-engraving through two decades, and to bring it to such a culmination as only Moronobu had achieved equally undisputedly, just one hundred years before. The far-reaching innovation brought about by the invention of the perfect polychrome print (1765) had meanwhile diverted the aim of this art, which till then had consisted in realising as fully as possible an entirely personal intuition, in the direction of a pleasing play of form and colour. Such must have appeared to the old school incompatible with its hitherto so simple and yet so vigorous activity. More suddenly even than in ancient Florence the school of Giotto yielded to the victorious onset of the new generation, the Torii school disappeared before the revolutionising activity of the three young masters, Harunobu, Shigemasa, and Shunsho. The creative energy of this school, cultivated and perfected through generations, was, however, destined to receive, after a decade of repose devoted to careful preparation, a final and supreme incarnation in Kiyonaga, who brought to

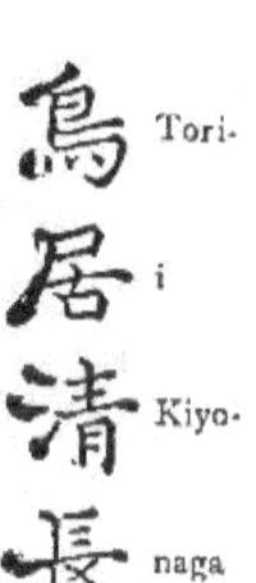

the service of an art aiming only at the simply great and beautiful, all the means of expression that had meanwhile been perfected. It is significant that his teacher, Kiyomitsu, the last of the pure Torii masters, did not influence the full unfolding of his nature so much as did the most versatile of the newly arisen school of artists, Shigemasa. It is true that Kiyonaga, who was the son of a publisher, had produced, shortly before the beginning of this new period, three-colour actor prints in the old style, but no one could have divined from these productions the future greatness of the man. During the time that Shunsho turned to the neglected field of actor representation and cultivated it in a new style notable for its charm of colour effect, Kiyonaga was collecting his strength while following this new movement with intelligent sympathy. Then he suddenly appears as the fully matured artist, who, thanks to his inherited loftiness of aim and nobility of taste, found it easy to surpass these meritorious yet more or less superficial innovators, to put them aside without an effort, and himself, as it were unintentionally, in their place. In the second half of the seventies he had already brought his own peculiar style to full maturity; from the beginning of the eighties he was the autocrat of wood-engraving, and saw the pupils of his predecessors pass under his banner.[1]

Kiyonaga was born in 1742 and died in 1815 (Hayashi Catalogue). His family name was Seki, his artistic name Ichibei. According to the Tokio Catalogue his activity began about 1760. He became, along with Koriusai and Harunobu, the most important designer of kakemono-ye. Fenollosa[2] has written a good estimate of his art, and reproduces[3] a fine print of about 1786. With the beginning of the seventies he came under the influence

[1] Fenollosa Cat., Nos. 113, 124–61; Anderson Cat., p. 342; Strange, p. 26; Bing Cat., No. 34 ff.; Goncourt Cat., No. 1238 ff.

[2] *Outline*, p. 39 *seqq*.

[3] *Ibid.*, pl. xii.

VEVER COLLECTION, PARIS

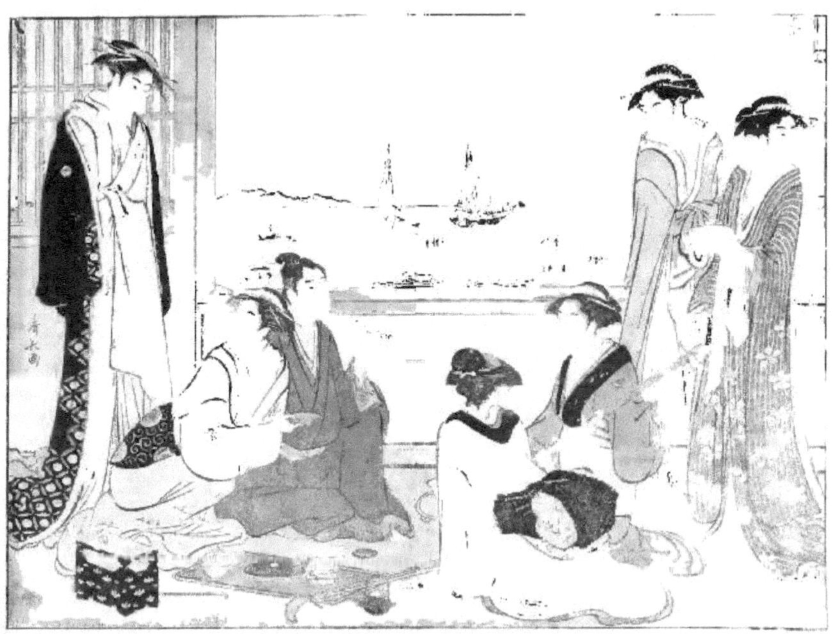

KIYÓNAGA: A TERRACE BY THE SEA. A young man and a geisha in blue; two servants near them; behind him his betrothed; to the right two friends. *Pink, grey, and black predominate.* A diptych in a series of twelve.

of both Harunobu and Shigemasa, but the latter finally gained the upper hand towards the end of the decade. An early actor print, in three colours, is quoted by H. E. Field in *The Art of Kiyonaga*.[1]

What then are the innovations which he introduced and to which Japanese art owed its advance beyond all previous efforts to the summit of its achievement? First of all, complete liberation from all conventionalism. Of the arbitrary treatment which the primitives had allowed in dealing with the human body, there had remained a trace even up to his time; for the sake of a stronger decorative effect, or greater gracefulness, hands and feet had been drawn too small, or the body too slender and too flexible, or the features too delicate. To all this Kiyonaga now, guided by a highly developed sense of beauty, opposed normal proportions of the body. His figures, during the period of his highest power—for he too, later, following the tendency of the time, leaned toward exaggerated proportions—are absolutely symmetrical, of a healthy roundness and well set up. They move with a natural quiet grace and dignity which has caused them to be compared not unjustly with the noble figures of the most highly developed Greek art. They have been purged of all the mannerisms that played so great a part in the creations of the primitives, without, it is true, prejudicing their artistic effect, as the goal of these artists was not at all the exact rendering of nature, but only the presentation of single characteristic motives of movement. But even that affectation which prevailed in the works of the first artists in free polychrome, and which resulted from insufficient study of nature, was in his case almost non-existent. Knowledge of reality and reverence for it led to a complete renovation of style.

This healthy realism in the creations of Kiyonaga points to a revolution in Japanese art, as from now on—until new

[1] *Burlington Magazine*, xiii., p. 241, July 1908.

mannerisms arose—the one-sidedly decorative element in drawing receded, effects of this kind being attempted by colour rendering only. We must not, indeed, suppose that any naturalistic imitation was aimed at; this latter remained, as appears from the lack of perspective and shadows, absolutely foreign to Japanese art during its highest period. But something essentially new had been acquired by the mere fact that, as the figures were conceived in relation to natural realities, it was necessary to give them a fixed position in a real space. By this means the representation was rounded off into a pictorial whole. In place of the background, hitherto only adumbrated by a single tint, there now appeared a definitely indicated interior or a finished landscape, which formerly had been done only incidentally and without full recognition of its necessity. In contrast with previous attempts, Kiyonaga may be regarded as the first real landscapist of Japan. By the choice of his colouring, and especially by the well-considered admixture of yellow tones, he imparted to his representations of outdoor life the charm of a cheerful sunshiny aspect.

The pictorial rounding-off of the design also finally led to an entirely new manner of composition. So far, thought had been given only to the balance of the individual parts, both in black and white and also in the colour-scheme generally; but now the aim was to fill out the given area completely in a manner pleasing to the eye. This Kiyonaga did with perfect mastery. As he had found perfect symmetry for the figures themselves, so also he introduced it, with effortless ease, into the composition as a whole, so that in his representations everything is rendered as with the inevitableness of nature. Each of his compositions, mostly representing women in conversation, following their daily occupations, walking out of doors with their children, forms a completely rounded whole, and yet how many of them form only parts of those great triptych represen-

VEVER COLLECTION, PARIS

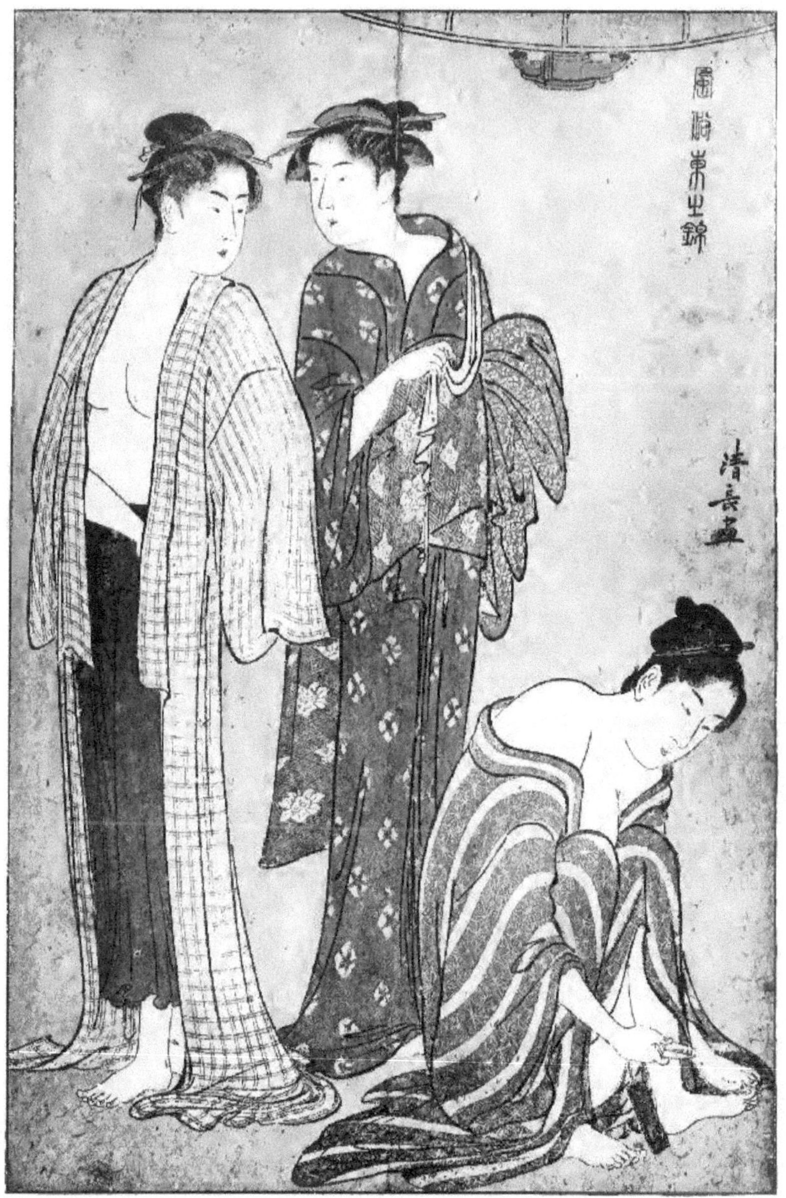

KIYÓNAGA : THREE SINGERS AT THE BATH. *Grey ground.*

tations, closely interconnected in their parts, which henceforward achieved an ever greater vogue. Of Kiyonaga it is really true to say what many collectors seek to persuade themselves of in respect to such fragments in general, that his sheets have been so composed in the beginning that, according to choice or necessity, they may be used singly, or in pairs, or as triptychs; although, as a rule, the full effect intended by the artist is only attained in the complete composition. The colour strives as little as the drawing for independent effect in Kiyonaga's work, for it too aims only at giving clear and graceful expression to the object; but in its plainness and simplicity it contributes as much toward the general effect of monumental greatness as does the design. Unfortunately, it is especially in the works of Kiyonaga that the colours have seldom retained their full strength, whether on account of their chemical composition, or because the sheets were much in request as wall decorations and have therefore been much exposed to the decomposing action of the sunlight; on their greatly faded appearance is probably based the idea that in the reduction of colour to the merest trace we may recognise a refinement purposely introduced by the artist.

All these qualities that result from a beautiful equilibrium of forces would doubtless have given the master an eminent historical position even without the addition of any pronounced originality, though they would not alone have lifted him to the first rank of the artists of his country. But a still more important quality of Kiyonaga's work consists in the singular charm which emanates from his creations, and which, in contrast with the effeminacy prevailing in most of the works of his predecessors, may be designated as the breath of an eminently virile spirit, sure of itself, and aspiring to high achievements. Without aiming at any special charm or refinement of soul-portrayal, that is, without informing his figures with any strong emotion, gentle or forceful, nor indeed individualising them in any remarkable way, he was yet able to impress the stamp of life and movement upon all his compositions; it is precisely in the outward repose, equable and graceful, with which he endowed them that he shows himself the truest embodier of that ideal of propriety, so highly valued among the Japanese as among all Asiatic nations of culture, which celebrates its highest triumphs in the greatest possible restraint of the emotions, without ever petrifying into a senseless formalism; on the contrary, through this manner of expression, the consciousness of the natural dignity of man appears all the more clearly and inspires the spectator to rise superior to the vulgar agitations of passion and desire. It was only as uniting in himself all previous aspirations, and now as master in addition of all the treasures of grace, charm, magic, and beauty meanwhile discovered, that Kiyonaga was enabled to achieve once more a style as powerful as that of Moronobu, the founder of Japanese wood-engraving one hundred years earlier, when the latter, without special preparation and without the facilities of later times, stood facing a whole world of phenomena unexplored.

When Kiyomitsu died Kiyonaga assumed the name of the fourth Torii, to show that he was the head of the fourth generation of Torii. Later, however, when he had perfected a style of his own, he abandoned the designation Torii. With the end of the ninth decade there came for Kiyonaga also, in one direction, a decline. The proportions of his figures became long and inclined toward an exaggerated elegance, and particularly his faces took that oval form which thenceforth became almost universally prevalent, and is especially frequent in the works of Utamaro, but which is sharply distinguished from the rectangular formation which Kiyonaga preferred in the days of his strength. The arbitrary virtuosity of his contours increased more and more, but, on the other hand, he still preserved his other excellences;

Koepping Collection, Berlin

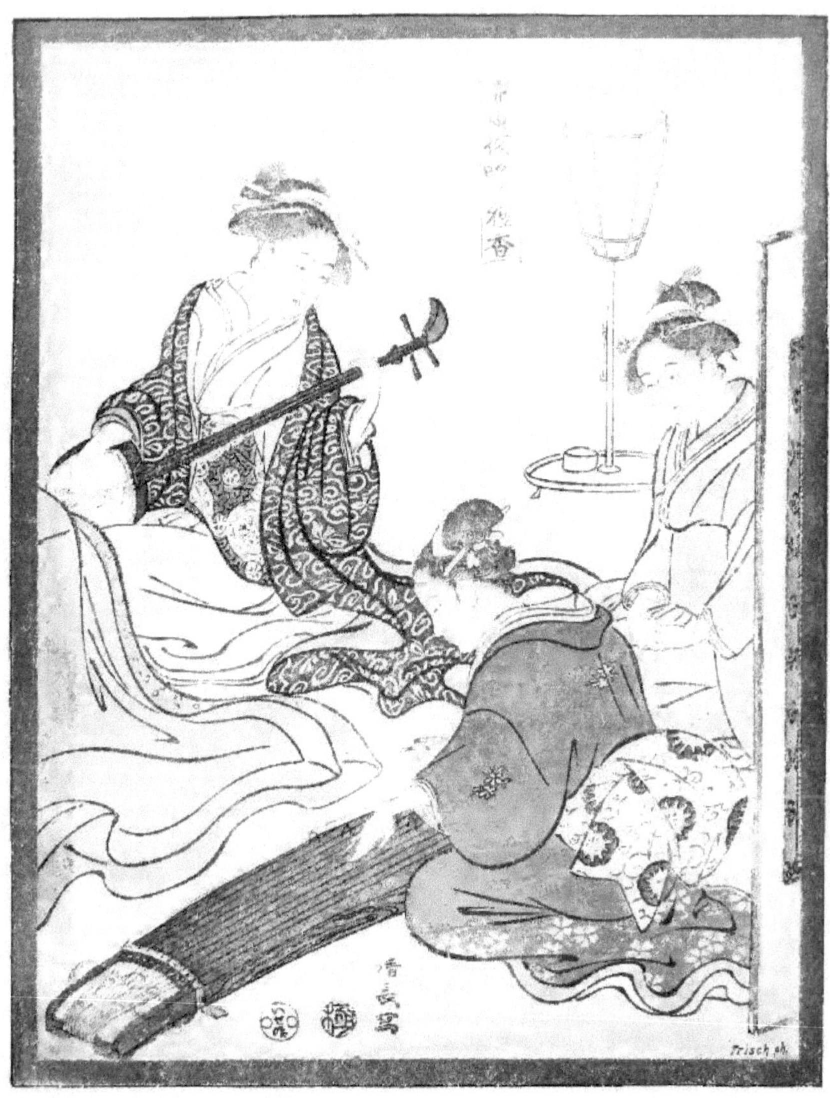

KIYÓNAGA: Musical Entertainment with the *Kōto* (below) and the *Šhamižen*.

the strong distribution of black and white, the rich and yet restrained patterning of the dresses, and the pure outline of the nude. Towards the end of his career he turned again to the representation of actors, resuming the tradition of his school and entering into direct and victorious rivalry with Shunsho. Theatre-programmes in black and white by him date from 1785 to 1799. Although he began to retire from the field in the nineties, probably feeling that a new day was dawning which could conduct him no higher but only into regions where his co-operation was not absolutely needed, he yet continued at work as late as 1801 at least, from which year dates a still extant print of children at play (Hayashi Catalogue, No. 701). He transferred the successorship to Toyokuni, and retained for himself, as the last great representative of the brilliant Torii school, only the part of chief leader and master of the school. Fenollosa is accordingly mistaken in assuming that he gave up working for the wood-engravers as early as the beginning of the nineties.

Among his numerous works, some especially beautiful kakemono-ye deserve mention :—

The woman under the umbrella (according to Fenollosa, No. 233, about 1782).
The woman in the storm (about 1787).
A woman standing, and one crouching on the ground, engaged in writing.

Of other single sheets the following may be mentioned :—

Actors, early three-colour print.
Temple festival, eight geishas carrying a lion. 1783.
Woman in bath-robe, with a little dog.
Kintoki playing with young tengus.
Kintoki with two bear cubs.
Boy seated, playing with mice.
Children at play. 1801.
The actor Danjuro making up ; oblong surimono.

Toilet scene, six figures, oblong (Berlin Kunstgewerbemuseum).

The Suruga Street in Yedo on New Year's Day, 1780, black and white, intended to be coloured by hand; probable the largest print ever produced by a Japanese wood-engraver.

Of series:

The twelve months of the year, represented by women.
Another set of the same.
Eight landscapes of Yedo, in lateral form.

Reproductions of his work are given by Strange, plate i. and at page 28, and more especially by H. E. Field on four plates in the *Burlington Magazine* (see *supra*), where works typical of every stage of Kiyonaga's development are brought together. Especially notable are his compositions in triptych form :—

Three actors, about 1779 (Fenollosa, No. 229), dating from the earliest time of his independent activity, reminding us of Shunsho; a rarity in this kind of representation.

The celebrated boating party on the Sumida, the river running through Yedo (reproduced in Bing's Catalogue from his *Japon Artistique*).

Women stepping out of a boat; one of his most beautiful works.

Women on verandah, looking down upon river.

Women in garden, dyeing cloth.

Pouring rain.

Women's bathing house (interior).

A flute player before a company of women.

A young prince with falcon, surrounded by women, Fuji in background.

A party in a boat enjoying the tricks of a monkey.

His few illustrated books are called incomparable by Fenollosa. The Hayashi Catalogue (No. 1577, *seqq.*) tabulates such books of the years 1777 to 1791. Duret cites a further book of 1798, 3 vols., Yedo.

Kugai junen irojigoku, Ten Years of Torment in Love's Inferno, 1791.

UTÁMARO

GIRLS GATHERING MULBERRY LEAVES

(Part of the twelve-sheet print of Silkworm Culture)

BRITISH MUSEUM

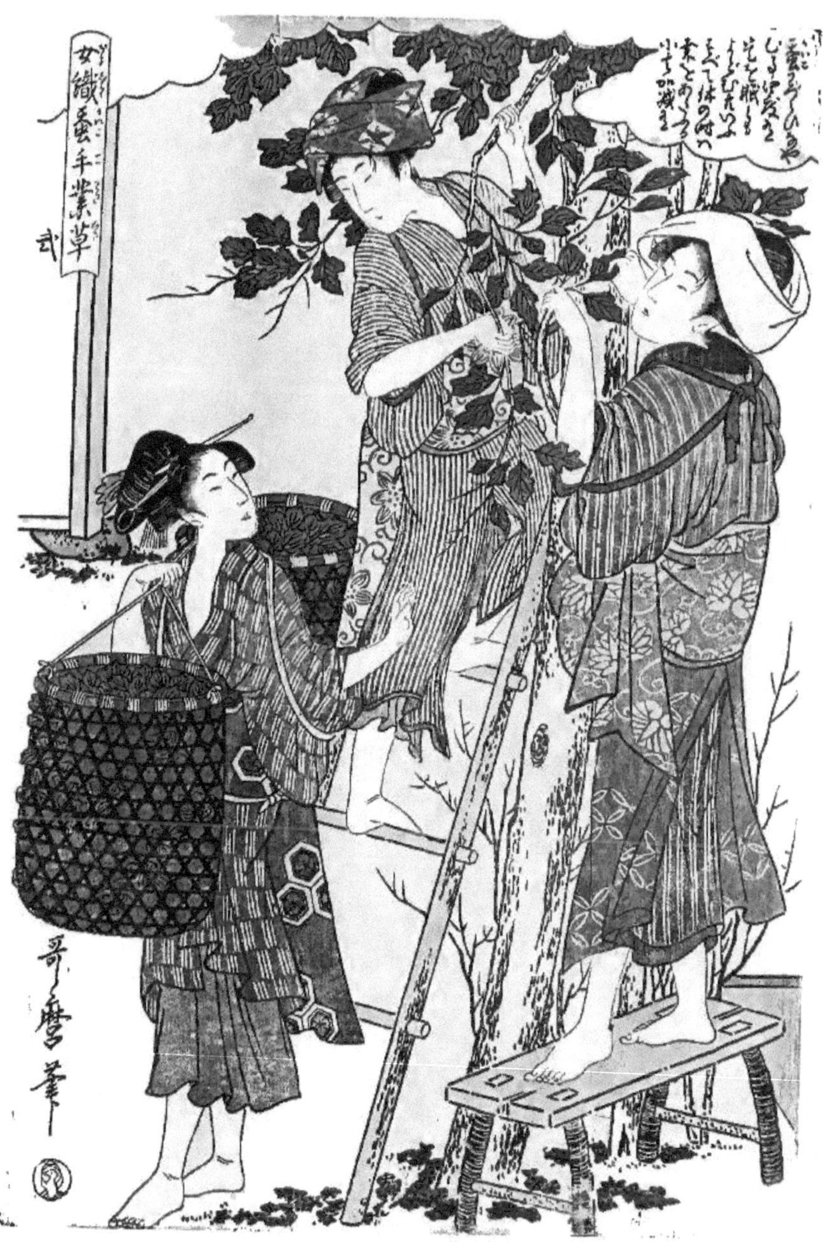

Burty (Catalogue, No. 181) attributes to him, doubtless quite correctly, a charming book, the *Yehon monomigaoka*, excursions according to the season (Yedo, 1785) 2 vols., small, with illustrations in black and white, signed Seki Kiyonaga.

The three pupils of Shunsho named in the preceding chapter who wholly adopted Kiyonaga's style, are the following:—

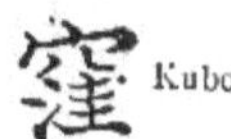
Kubo

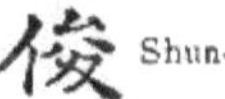
Shun-

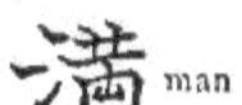
man

Kubo Summan (Shunman) was originally a pupil of Shigemasa and then went over to Shunsho, but when Kiyonaga came into full supremacy he took from him his method of composition and form, without however subjecting himself blindly to his influence.[1] The time of his activity began with the close of the eighties and lasted until about 1820. According to the Hayashi Catalogue (No. 510) his name in art was Yasubei. A peculiar personal magic which attaches to his nature preserved him from slavish imitation. Though his sheets closely approach those of Kiyonaga in general appearance he yet stamps each detail with his own individuality. His work was very unequal; even during his best period, in the beginning of the tenth decade, it was alternately refined in expression and delicate in drawing and then again full of arbitrary mannerisms. To him must be referred the attempts to ground the large tripartite sheets on a principal tone of grey, with a sparing but intelligent addition of other colours. Books illustrated by him appeared in Yedo, 1795–1815. A very fine polychrome book, called *Goju nirishu*, the Fifty-one Poets, 1801, is also his work (Gillot). He is also supposed to have occupied himself with the illustration of humorous verse. A New Year's visit in the snow, in the environs of Yedo, is reproduced by Gonse, *Art Japonais*, i. p. 218.

Of his triptychs, one with a woman in landscape is highly praised (Fenollosa No. 281), as also the sea-water carriers; of his

[1] Fenollosa Cat., Nos. 279–283; Anderson Cat., p. 344; Strange, p. 36; Bing Cat., No. 319 ff.

surimonos, a series of flowers; further, representations from the animal kingdom: starlings flying across the red sun, 1815 (reproduced by Gonse, i. p. 266), butterflies, &c.

Katsu- 勝 kawa 川 Shun- 春 cho 潮

Katsukawa Shuncho was probably in the beginning a pupil of Shunsho, but attached himself most closely to Kiyonaga from the beginning of the eighties on.[1] He was gentler by nature than his first teacher, and became a most faithful imitator of the latter's mighty conqueror. He was active until the end of the century; later on he is said to have retired from the field of art, but to have lived on until 1821 at least. The change which he made in the direction of his style must have been the result of conviction, for he is by no means lacking in individuality, and could turn his gift to good account. In the matter of drawing, clear and clean though he always is, he was not able entirely to overcome the influence of his first teacher, which tended to give his contours a certain calligraphic-decorative character; on the other hand, he created for himself, in the treatment of landscapes enlivened with figures, a wholly original means of expression. At times, indeed, the manner in which he renders his landscapes is purely impressionistic. When in the further course of his activity he began to draw near to the new-risen star of Utamaro, he could still steer clear of direct imitation. Strange reproduces at page 36 the bust of a beauty treated in this style. A representation in Kiyonaga's style is reproduced by Anderson.[2]

He also signed himself Kichizayemon and Churinsha or Kisado Shuncho (Hayashi Catalogue, No. 630). Illustrated books by him date from 1786 and 1790, Yedo (*ibid.*, No. 1536 *seqq.*). A diptych is dated 1786 (*ibid.*, No. 630). The book called *Growing Herbs* (Yedo, 1790), 2 vols., gives a good

[1] Fenollosa Cat., Nos. 262–274; Anderson Cat., p. 363; Strange, p. 37; Bing Cat., No. 282 ff.

[2] *Japanese Wood-Engraving*, pl. iv.

series of pictures from woman's life from childhood to motherhood (Berlin Kunstgewerbemuseum).

Of Shuncho's single sheets, the following may be mentioned:—

Pictures of wrestlers.
Triptych (about 1790, according to Fenollosa, No. 272), women stepping out of a boat; one of his most beautiful things.
A little girl journeying on horseback.
Promenades and feasts.
Young prince taking riding exercise.
Two princes shooting with the bow.
A print in five sections: travellers, with Fuji in the background.

Katsukawa Shunzan also began as a pupil of Shunsho, and later followed closely Kiyonaga; nor was he either lacking in force and originality.[1] He worked from the middle of the eighth decade till the end of the century. Of his triptychs, one which represents a scene at the gate of a temple is celebrated. Reproduction in Strange, page 80; a triptych in the Hayashi Catalogue (No. 772). Fenollosa (*Outline*, pl. xiii.) reproduces a print of about 1777.

Fellow-pupils of Kiyonaga were the following artists: Torii Kiyotsune, who is wrongly cited by Burty (Catalogue, No. 148) as a pupil of Kiyonaga.[2] On the contrary, he betrays everywhere his descent from Kiyomitsu by the graceful formation of his figures and by their very small feet and hands; he also exhibits the influence of Harunobu. Besides actor prints he produced book-illustrations; one of his books, in two volumes, appeared in Yedo in 1774 (Duret). There are mentioned as being by him:—

Twenty-four examples of filial love; from the Chinese.

---

[1] Fenollosa Cat., Nos. 275–278; Bing Cat., No. 297; Strange, p. 81. In the Hayashi Cat. (No. 772) he is called a pupil of Shunsho and Shunyei.

[2] Anderson Cat., p. 342; Fenollosa Cat., No. 168; Burty Cat., No. 150; Bing Cat., No. 33; Strange, p. 24.

Dozi gamatsu (?), the story of a child named Maruko, small size, in black and white.

A reproduction in Strange at page 26. *Cp. supra*, p. 95.

Of Torii Kiyohiro[1] Bing cites some sheets (Catalogue, No. 29).

As contemporaries of Kiyonaga we may further mention: Torii Kiyomasa (a sheet in Bing's Catalogue, No. 72), who is called the son of Kiyonaga in the Hayashi Catalogue (No. 736 and illustration), and Utagawa Kunimasa, a member of the painter-family founded by Shunsho, and a pupil of Toyokuni, *q.v.*, of whom Bing (Catalogue, No. 231) cites:—

Half figures of three actors.
Saint praying before a waterfall.

With Kiyonaga's pupil, Kiyomine, who styled himself fifth of the Torii, and with Kiyomitsu, the Torii line, that great school of actor representation, comes to an end after an existence of a hundred years. Kiyomine (Shonosuke), who married the granddaughter of the old Kiyomitsu, began his activity in the beginning of the nineteenth century. He was still living in 1830, and apparently died at the beginning of the forties.[2] He worked in a style that reminds us of Toyokuni and Utamaro, and is at times very elegant, but often lacking in animation of expression. He also produced copies, *e.g.*, after Kiyonobu and Kiyomasu. A print in five divisions, *Imayo Gonin Bayashi*, represents five female musicians (Hamburg). Strange reproduces, at page 28, a woman in half length. Another print is reproduced in the Hayashi Catalogue (No. 739). Kiyoyasu was one of his pupils (illustration, *ibid.*, No. 740).

The following appear to be connected with Kiyonaga: Santoun (illustration, *ibid.*, No. 765); Riuunsai (*ibid.*, No. 767); Gentei Munataka, late (*ibid.*, No. 768).

[1] Anderson Cat., p. 342.
[2] Strange, p. 27; Fenollosa Cat., No. 304; Bing Cat., No. 73.

BING COLLECTION, PARIS

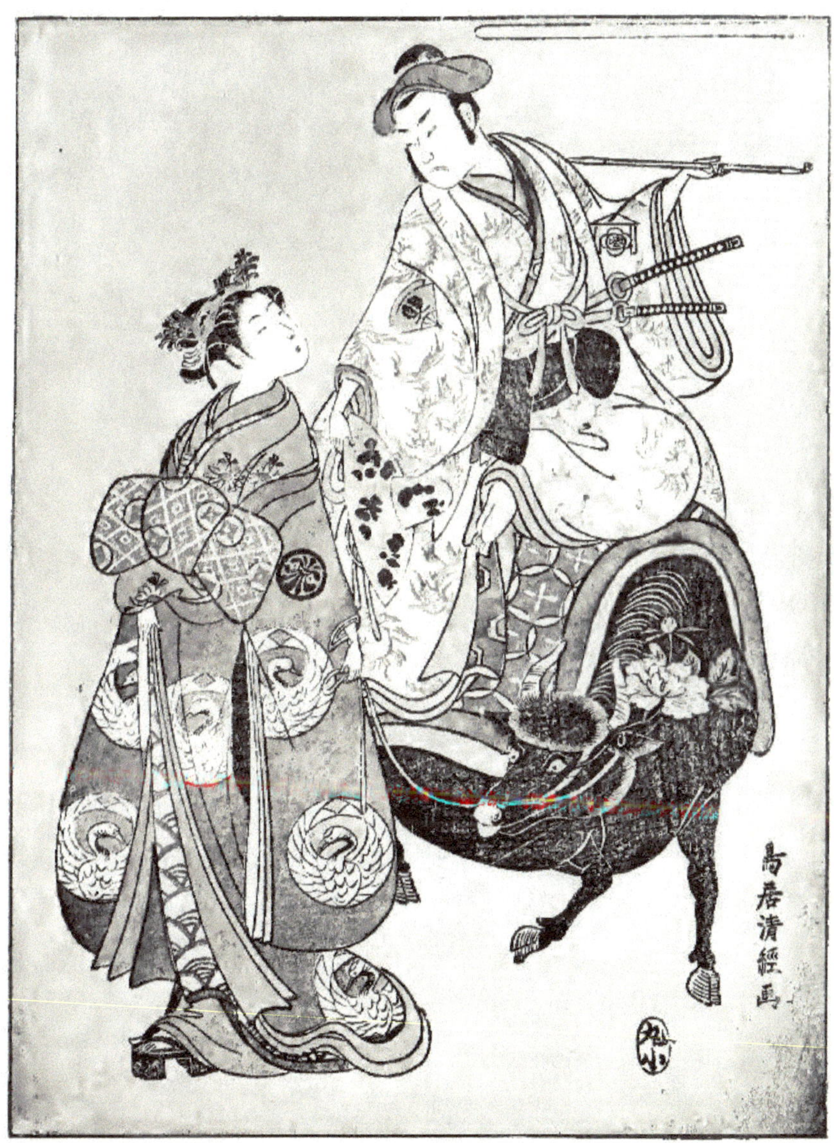

KIYŌTSUNE: AN ACTOR AS THE POET BOTANKWA ON AN OX LED BY A COURTESAN. *In dull green and pink.*

Illustrated books were produced by the following: Yamaguchi Sojun, album of drawings, Kioto, 1804; caricatures, Yedo, 1799, 3 vols. Keisan Takusho, drawings of bamboo plants, Yedo, 1804.

This is the place to revert to an artist who, like Korin a hundred years previously, occupied a position entirely unique in the development of Japanese engraving, namely, Kitao Keisai Masayoshi (not Keisai Kitao Masayoshi). A son and pupil of Shigemasa (Kosiusai), he was born in 1761 and began work about 1780, at the time when Kiyonaga was at his zenith.[1] Between 1787 and 1823 he produced a number of books with reproductions of his sketches overflowing with life and esprit (see page 59), through which he influenced, not inconsiderably, the young Hokusai who, from the end of the century, was coming rapidly to the fore. He died in 1824. With him awoke anew the love of and reverence for nature, and the conscientiousness in the rendering of details which had slumbered since the days of Korin. Simultaneously with Utamaro he began to give an independent significance to landscape, and to observe carefully the shapes of animals and the formation of plants; but he does not render them with the almost meticulous accuracy of Utamaro (who always remained before all things a draughtsman), but with the strength and boldness of a painter who keeps in view the total colour impression and understands how to render it with a few broad strokes, without, however, neglecting accuracy of detail where it is essential. He often signed his books Joshin. Especially famous is an album of sketches of flowers in bloom, without contour, Yedo, 1813 (Berlin Kunstgewerbemuseum); and also the *Choju riakugwashiki*, representations of animals, 1797. His

北 Kita-
尾 o
政 Masa-
美 yoshi

[1] Anderson Cat., p. 347; Cat. Burty, No. 204 ff.; Bing. Cat., No. 305 ff.; Fenollosa Cat., No. 222 ff. The date of Masayoshi's birth is taken from the Hayashi Cat. (No. 499).

earliest work is the *Yehon Miyako no nishiki*, views of Kioto, twelve coloured pictures, Kioto, 1787 (Gillot). In 1800 he published some very impressionist sketches of landscape; the eight views of Lake Biwa he represented in pairs, of oblong shape.

Vever Collection, Paris

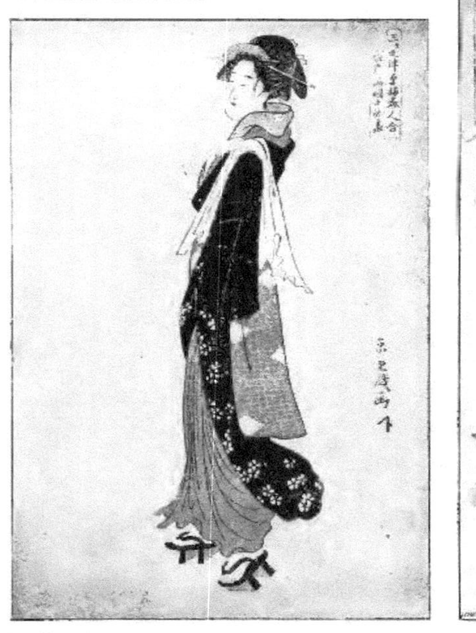

YEIRI: A Singer. From a series of pretty girls. Black gown, figured with cherry-blossom; pink petticoat, brick-red sash. *Grey ground.* Medium size.

Royal Print Room, Dresden

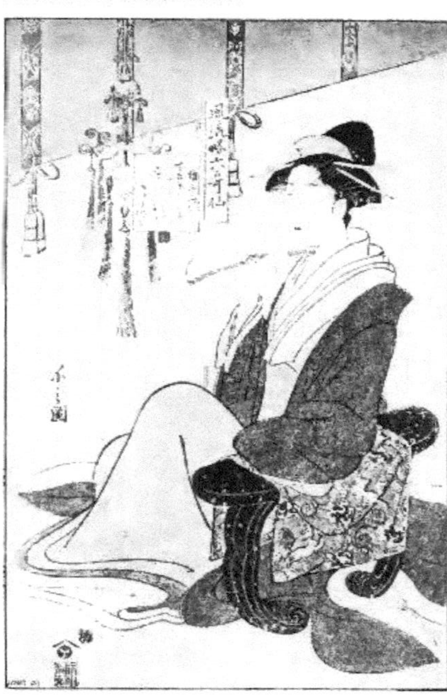

YEISHI: A Lady of Rank seated and leaning on the *hijikake.* From a series of six plates *Yellow ground.* Medium size.

Royal Print Room, Dresden

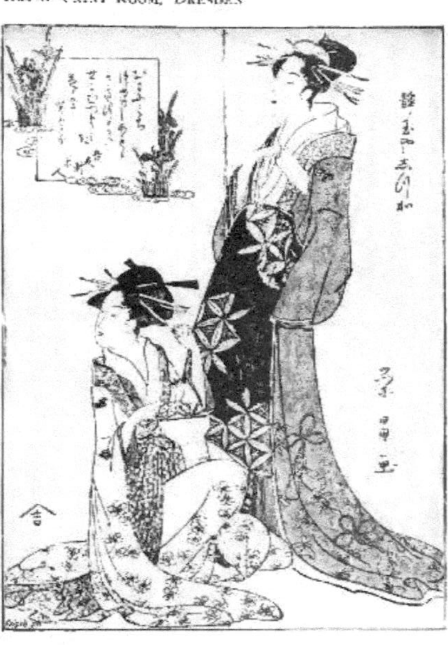

YEISHŌ: Two Courtesans. *Yellow ground.* Medium size.

CHAPTER VII

THE PERIOD OF UTAMARO

1. Yeishi—2. Utamaro—3. Toyokuni.

1. Yeishi.—When towards the year 1790 Kiyonaga retired from the scene, he bequeathed his heritage to three masters, who had already perfected their powers during the eighties, took the lead during the nineties, and continued to hold it until the beginning of the nineteenth century. These three were Yeishi, Utamaro, and Toyokuni. They represent, no longer indeed the greatest strength and richness, yet the extremest refinement of Japanese wood-engraving, more especially Utamaro. Yeishi, as well as Utamaro, introduced a new element into this art of the people, as they both proceeded from the aristocratic Kano school which had been trained on Chinese models. In the place of the charming daintiness with which Harunobu, the heir of the primitives, endowed his women, and the healthy fulness that distinguished Kiyonaga's simple figures, we now meet with a refinement in stature, carriage, and expression which bears witness to a general change in manners and increased demands on life, resulting in a modification of the ideal of beauty. Woman, though she be often only the simple woman of the people or the courtesan, continues henceforth to play, as generally in the Japanese art of the eighteenth century, and in infinitely heightened measure at the end of this period, the chief part in pictorial representations. She always appears as a princess, tall and slender of figure, of queenly carriage and a

graciousness all the more captivating for being shy and reserved. To be sure, this tendency soon degenerated into exaggeration, but in its beginnings it undoubtedly served to enrich the scope of art.

Yei-榮 shi 之

Hosoi Yeishi was a pupil of the court painter, Kano Yeisen, of Yedo.[1] His family name was Hosoda, his name in art Tomisamburo, and also Chobunsai (Hayashi Catalogue). It was at the beginning of the eighties that he started on his career, which lasted until the beginning of the nineteenth century. Being then outstripped in popular favour by Utamaro and Toyokuni, he devoted himself from about 1805 to 1815 chiefly to painting, and presented the beauties of the day in numerous pictures of rapid but always distinguished brush-work. His activity unfolded itself almost parallel with that of Shunman, whose tender grey tones he further developed independently, with a stronger accentuation of colour. Like Shunman he inclined toward Kiyonaga's quiet narrative manner and broad composition; but in comparison with the former he enlarged the scope of his representations, not contenting himself with the designing of pleasing groups, but studying actual life in all its phases in the different classes and callings of the people, and thereby offering us a faithful, varied, and animated picture of his times. His woodcuts of the eighties are especially famous (Tokio Catalogue, p. 88). One of 1783 is cited in the Hayashi Catalogue (No. 966), as is an illustrated book of 1788 (No. 1677). It was probably Yeishi who popularised the combination of yellow, carmine, and black.

Towards the beginning of the tenth decade he had fully perfected his style, which found its chief satisfaction in the composition of large triptychs; Fenollosa (*Outline*, pl. xiv.)

[1] Fenollosa Cat., Nos. 284–299; Anderson, *Japanese Wood-Engraving;* Bing Cat., No. 331 ff; Goncourt Cat. The Gillot Cat. mentions as his teacher Michinobu, of the Kano school.

illustrates a print by him in which he makes use of the dull tints of Toyokuni, which remained in fashion to the first decade of the nineteenth century. Towards the end of the century he, too, was unable to withstand the mannerism which had crept in, in consequence of altered tastes, and which about 1800 reached its extreme point in the elongation of the figures and the mask-like, expressionless character of the faces. At the same time, notwithstanding his arbitrary rendering of form, Yeishi always retained an uncommon mastery of drawing.

He is particularly distinguished for his triptychs, restricted mostly to a few sober colours, as the following:—

The interior of a house in the Yoshiwara (about 1792 according to Fenollosa, No. 294, who designates it as one of his most beautiful works).

The visit of a lady to a young man.

A young man surrounded by women near a garden well.

Young women on a verandah on the sea-shore.

Four young women on a verandah, overlooking a river full of boats.

Fishing party in a boat.

Women playing on musical instruments beneath an umbrella in a pleasure-boat built in the form of a peacock.

A pathway leading past rice-fields (according to Fenollosa, No. 288, about 1788).

A lady resting near her carriage under blossoming trees.

Pentaptych: a youth of rank playing the flute, accompanied by three female musicians.

Among the single sheets there are series of courtesans in outdoor costume; in one of these series, saké-cups are used as a distinguishing mark; in another, rabbits. A series distinguished by flowers depicts young women as representatives of art.

In the book *Onna sanjiurokkasen*, of 1798, for which Hokusai drew the title-page, Yeishi depicted thirty-six young poetesses of Yedo.

His principal pupil was Yeisho, who was active until the end of the eighteenth century, and who developed a graceful and distinctively decorative talent.[1] His artistic name was Chokusai. He, too, devoted himself principally to the production of triptychs, among them the following:—

Yei- 榮
sho 昌

Three women in the interior of a house sitting in front of a screen decorated with a huge Howo bird.
A young nobleman waited upon by women.
Young women at a banquet.
Young girls gathering iris in a garden.
Under the cherry trees.

An illustrated book of 1798 is mentioned in the Hayashi Catalogue.

Yeisui, whose artistic name was Ichirakute, worked in the first decade of the nineteenth century.[2] Bing's Catalogue cites by him a young man with a falcon. Of Yeiri, Fenollosa cites (Catalogue, No. 392) a painting which he places about the year 1803. His name in art was Rekisentai. According to the Tokio Catalogue (p. 107) he was a pupil of Yeishi, and later, after about 1800, came under the influence of Hokusai.

The Hayashi Catalogue (No. 1002, with illustration) mentions as his pupil Rekisentai Sarin.

Further pupils of Yeishi were: Gokio (Hayashi Catalogue, No. 996: but the Gillot Catalogue calls him a pupil of Sekiyen); Choyensai Yeishin (Hayashi Catalogue, No. 997); Yeiju (*ibid.*, No. 998).

Akin to Yeishi are the following: Soraku, who was also a poet (*ibid.*, No. 999); Tamagawa Shuncho, who is perhaps connected with Buncho: according to Kurth (*Utamaro*, p. 148), his work is wholly in the direction of Utamaro; Kyritera, by whom there is a print in the Straus-Negbaur Collection in Frankfort, a geisha with two attendants amid blossoming trees, with a hedge in the background.

[1] Fenollosa Cat., No. 300 f.; Bing Cat., No. 350 ff. [2] Fenollosa Cat., No. 302.

UTÁMARO

GIRLS UNDER CHERRY-TREES

BRITISH MUSEUM

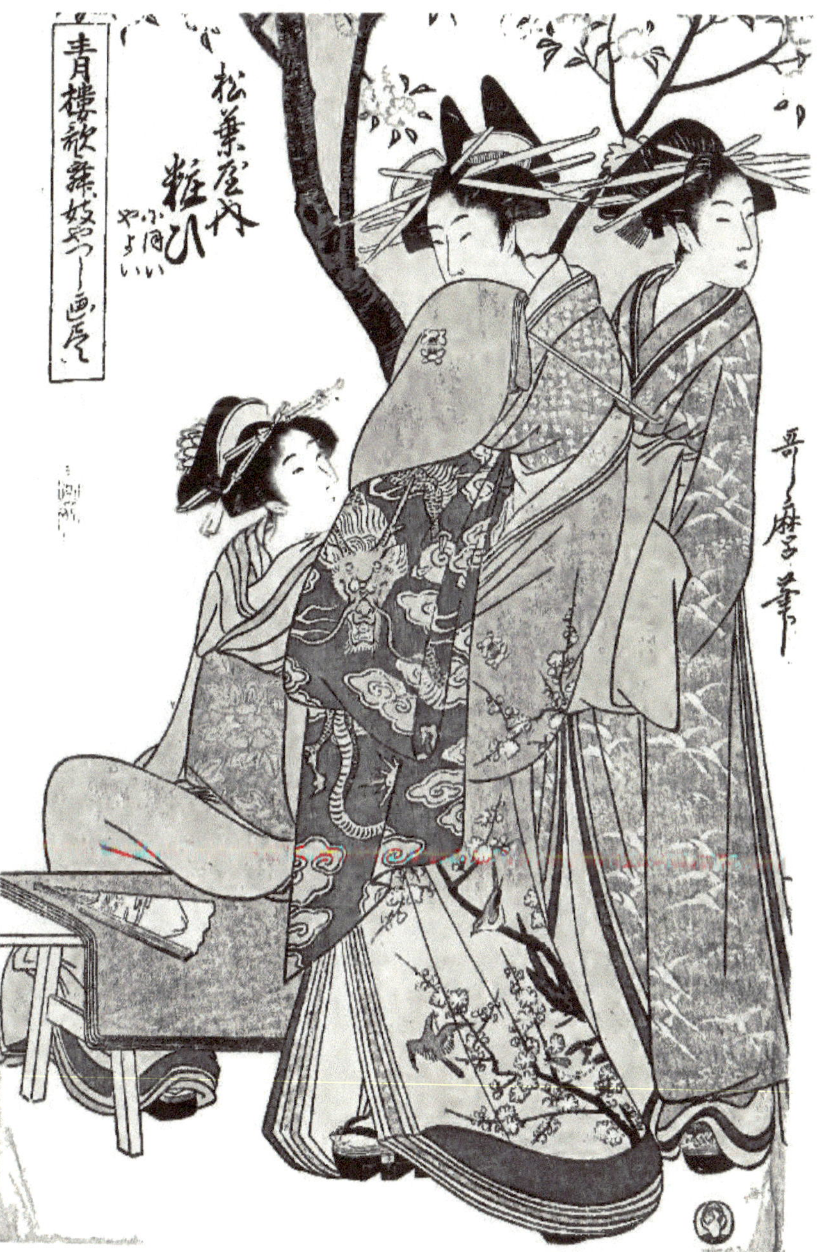
青楼歌舞妓やつし画尽
松葉屋内
粧ひ
哥麿筆

2. UTAMARO.— Utamaro is the Japanese artist who, after Hokusai, is best known to us. Although the elongated heads of the women with their narrow slits of eyes, hardly perceptible mouths, and huge coiffure which towers upward and broadens out at each side, can give us absolutely no idea of the real artistic ability of the man, since they belong to the time of the complete decay and degeneration of his art into mannerism, nevertheless these pictures, produced by him in hundreds and therefore so widely circulated, must be regarded as characteristic examples of the style and taste which prevailed in Japan about the close of the eighteenth century, and which were mainly due to the influence of Utamaro himself. Art, at that time, had passed during a hundred years through all its various stages, from the powerful-heroic by way of the graceful-delicate to the classically simple beauty of Kiyonaga, the most perfect master of Japan and the immediate predecessor of Utamaro, and was now, at the beginning of the last decade of the eighteenth century, fallen into a state of feverish excitement, which has not unjustly been compared to the close of the nineteenth century in Europe, in its search for new and unheard-of effects. Health and naïveté had been lost, and their places taken by morbid susceptibility which nothing but the extreme of subtlety and refinement could satisfy, even to the dissolution of all natural principles and, in art, the abrogation of all fidelity to nature. As with us, the causes of this phenomenon are not to be sought for primarily in the exigencies of art as such, but in a general change, under stress from without, of the modes of life and thought. In the sphere of art Utamaro now appeared in Japan as the man of destiny, who should actualise all the new powers that were in the air and demanded concrete embodiment. Woman had always played a prominent part in the popular art of the country, but now Utamaro placed one type of the sex in the absolute centre of all attention, the type, namely, of the courtesan initiated into

all the refinements of mental culture as well as of bodily enchantment, and then playing in the life of Japan such a part as she must have played in Hellas during the golden age of Greek civilisation. For expressing the inexpressible, the simple rendering of nature did not suffice; the figures must needs be lengthened to give the impression of supernatural beings; they must have a pliancy enabling them to express vividly the tenderest as well as the most intense emotions of the soul; lastly, they must be endowed with a wholly peculiar and therefore affected language for uttering the wholly peculiar sensations that filled them. Utamaro possessed the courage still further to exaggerate these effects even beyond the limits of the possible, until the point was reached when he could go no further, and a gradual relaxation imposed itself as an obvious necessity.

This time of extreme mannerism did not last longer than a decade, from about 1795 to 1805, and was at its height about 1800. Whether we should seek for its causes, with Fenollosa, in a tightening of the reins of government by the Shoguns, the all-powerful rulers of the country, and explain these fantastic excesses as the reaction of free thought against police interference, or whether, as is more probable, the causes of this movement are deeper and more general: at all events, on the artistic side, Utamaro constituted the truest expression of this remarkable era. It does not suffice to compare him, as did Gonse, with the masters of the school of Fontainebleau in the sixteenth century: it is true that the Ricci, Abbate, and Primaticcio drew figures of impossible length, but these had no other than a decorative significance, and were not intended to personify certain recondite thoughts and feelings. On the other hand we should not be far wrong in calling him a decadent, the Parisian of his day; and it is significant that Goncourt, that finely sensitive explorer of the phenomena of decadence in our times, should begin precisely with this artist his series of bio-

VEVER COLLECTION, PARIS

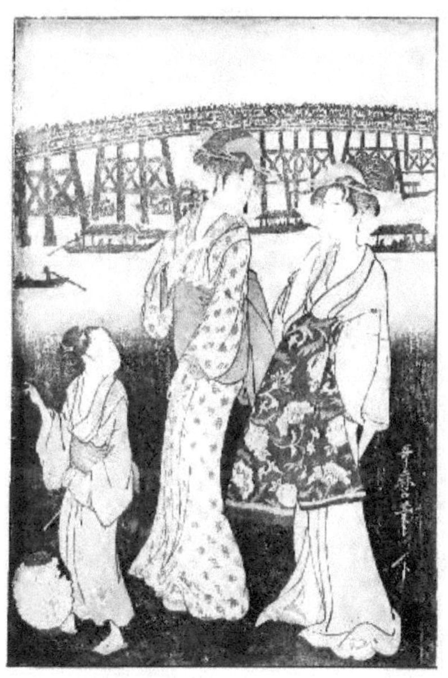

UTÁMARO: NIGHT FESTIVAL ON THE SUMIDA RIVER, YEDO. In the background the bridge Riogóku. Part of a triptych, the left side of which is lost.

R. WAGNER, BERLIN

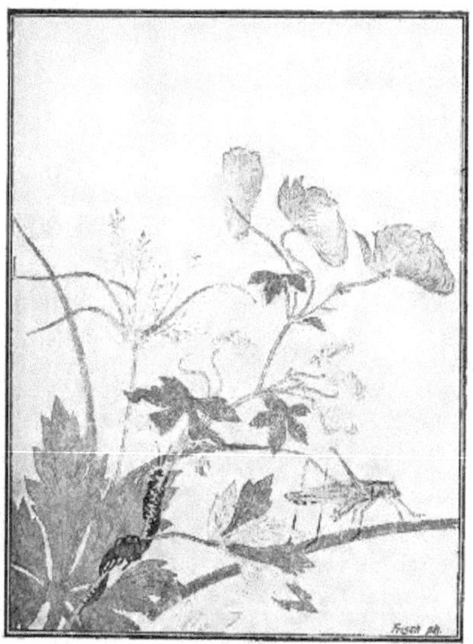

UTÁMARO: GRASSHOPPER AND CATERPILLAR. From the "Plant and Insect Book."

graphies of Japanese artists (*Outamaro;* Paris, 1891). However, we must not omit to notice, in considering the entire sphere of Utamaro's activity, that, over and above his significance for the history of civilisation, he possessed also an artistic significance of unusual importance, manifested for the most part in those productions which appeared before the time of his degeneracy, but sometimes even those of his already thoroughly mannered period. This significance indeed belongs to him not merely as an isolated phenomenon, but, on the contrary, he also plays a great part in the development of Japanese art, both as its guide to new stages, and as fructifier of the whole subsequent period.

鳥 Tori- 山 yama 石 Seki- 燕 yen

Utamaro's teacher, Toriyama Sekiyen, also called Toyofusa (1712–1788), who had issued from the old Kano school of painting, which held fast to Chinese traditions, seems to have had but slight influence upon him.[1] Judging from the illustrated books which he published in the seventies, Sekiyen still belonged entirely to the generation of popular artists influenced by Harunobu and Shunsho. Fenollosa, who calls him an excellent painter, believes him to have studied together with Toyoharu under Ishikawa Toyonobu. His works are the following:—

Toriyama Sekiyen gwafu, large sketch-book in several tints, of 1774.
Gwajikihen, illustrated legends. 1777.
Hiakki yagio, the hundred monsters of the night (spirits), in black and grey, 1779; also in a reprint.

Besides Utamaro, Sekiyen had the following pupils: Hokujin Fujo (Hayashi Catalogue, No. 922) and Sekijo (*ibid.*, No. 952), who, according to Kurth, were later on both influenced by Utamaro; finally Nagayoshi (Choki), his most important pupil, who will be discussed further on. Kurth (*Utamaro*, p. 48) also mentions Koikawa Shuncho, who is here placed among Utamaro's pupils as a pupil of Sekiyen.

Only in one of six sheets by Utamaro relating to poems

[1] Fenollosa Cat., No. 305; Goncourt, *Outamaro*, p. 4; Anderson Cat., p. 344.

about snow (the *Silver World*), a landscape printed in imitation of a Chinese drawing in ink, does Goncourt recognise the direct influence of Sekiyen (*Outamaro*, p. 4, note). Out of love for his master, Utamaro took at first the cognomen Toyoaki. After having exercised himself sufficiently in painting after the manner of the Kano school, he turned all the more decisively to the national Japanese style, the Ukiyo-ye, which had been brought to its highest perfection by Kiyonaga; from this time dates his independent activity.

Kita 北 gawa 川 Uta- 歌 maro 麿

Kitagawa Utamaro, whose real name was Yusuke, was born in 1753 in Kawagoye (not in Yedo), in the province of Musashi, but came to Yedo in early youth.[1] Having served his apprenticeship with Sekiyen and afterwards embraced the style of Kiyonaga, he lived there uninterruptedly with his publisher, Tsutaya Juzaburo until the latter's death in 1797, at first near the principal entrance of the Yoshiwara, the tea-house quarter, where he found the chief inspiration for his creations, then in the centre of the city. He signed himself Toyakira, Yentaisai, Yentoku, and also Murasaki Utamaro. His first productions date from the seventies, and show him still under the influence of Shunsho. He began his career with book-illustrations in black and white. The statement that he refused proudly to produce actor prints, then very popular, refers only to the time of his full development; in the beginning he produced several sheets of this kind of medium size; in fact, Goncourt (page 10, note) refers to a long design in the surimono style representing a play-scene with seventeen actors. In this early time his compositions are still executed in broad liquid brush-work.

After having, as it seems, occupied himself chiefly with painting until about 1780, he turned, in the first half of the ninth

[1] Goncourt, *Outamaro*, 1891; Bing in the *Studio*, 1895; Fenollosa Cat., Nos. 305-336; Anderson Cat., p. 345; Cat. Burty, p. 219 ff.; Bing Cat., No. 362 ff.; Cat. Goncourt. The year of birth has been corrected as against Goncourt (1754).

decade, to the illustration of those small works of popular fiction which, from their yellow covers, are called Kibiyoshi (yellow books). From as early as 1785 on, two pupils collaborated with him, Mitimaro and Yukimaro. All these illustrations were printed in black and white. In the year 1786 his first book of erotic contents was produced in collaboration with Rantokusai, in which he still signs with his own name. From 1787 onward he published, still always in black and white, a series of books of larger size, and at the same time, in 1788, the splendid book of insects, printed in colours, for which his teacher Sekiyen wrote an epilogue attesting his touching love for his pupil and taking, remarkably enough, the form of a eulogy upon the naturalism reintroduced into art by Utamaro. Here, he says, are the first pictures painted with the heart. About this time, which marks his nearest approximation to Kiyonaga, he probably produced the book of shells, finely drawn and coloured with all the subtlety of the later surimono, in which the figures at beginning and end remind us strongly of that master. Kurth (*Utamaro*, p. 41) assigns it to the period around 1780 (see also his pl. vi.). The third of his books of natural history, the *Hundred Screamers* (birds), the finest of all his work, probably did not appear until the nineties. Kurth (*ibid.*, p. 76) assigns it to so early a period as about 1789. Utamaro had also announced the publication of a book of mammals and a book of fishes, but these were never executed. In the year 1788 further appeared *The Poem to the Pillow*, with colour illustrations, the finest of his erotic works; lastly, in 1789, *Verses to the Moon*, and an erotic volume.

His illustrated books continued in the nineties, but dates more rarely appear. Of those printed in polychrome, except the *Testing of the Pines*, of 1795; the *Flowers of the Four Seasons*, of 1801; the *Fallen Blossoms*, of 1802; and the *Green Houses*, of 1804, only the *Promenade at the Time of the Cherry*

Blossom and the *Silver World* bear a date, in both cases 1790. The *Silver World* is one of his finest works. About this time also he published two series of six sheets each: six children disguised as poets, and the six signboards of the most celebrated saké (rice wine) houses, represented by women, one of his most beautiful creations.

When Kiyonaga, at the beginning of the tenth decade, withdrew from the field, there sprang up between his successors, Shuncho, Yeishi, Utamaro, and Toyokuni, a rivalry for the precedence. Fenollosa names the year 1792 as the acutest period of this strife, from which Utamaro emerged victorious, and thereafter, through more than a decade, bore uncontested sway. While Shuncho and Yeishi, though gifted with strong personalities, were only able to continue the style of the master, and that in a weakened form, and Toyokuni, the youngest of them, with all his talent for colour and elegance, did not possess enough creative power to lead art to higher levels, Utamaro was able to add a new element to what had already been achieved, by further development in the direction of a keenly observant naturalism; landscape especially, which thus far, despite all progress since the primitives, had nevertheless stopped short at more or less carefully executed suggestions, was first fully co-ordinated by him, and thereby attained an independent significance within the design as a whole. In this he showed himself the natural successor of Toyoharu, the pupil of Shigemasa. At the same time he began to be noted as the painter of woman, whom he studied devotedly in every condition, as mother, as maiden, as courtesan, so that his achievements in this province are his most lasting title to fame.

He created an absolutely new type of female beauty. At first he was content to draw the head in normal proportions and quite definitely round in shape; only the neck on which this head was poised was already notably slender. This is the style

Vever Collection, Paris

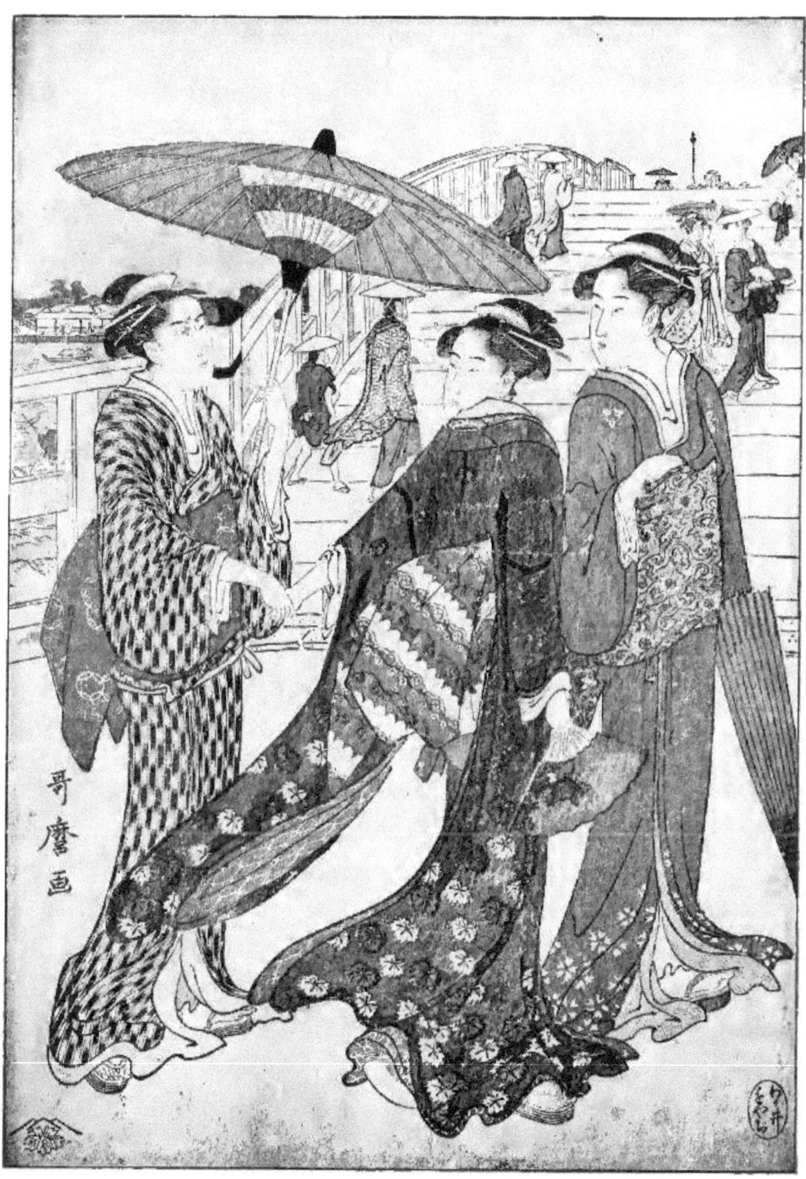

UTÁMARO : Two Ladies, one of whom is being held back by a Girl.
Centre of a triptych.

of the beautiful half-length figures on a mica ground which appeared in and after 1790 in several series and are now among the most coveted creations of the master. They show him in close connection with his fellow-pupil, Nagayoshi (Choki), whose work first came before the public about this time. If finally we take into consideration the actor pictures of Sharaku, we are in a position to visualise the salient features of the phase into which Japanese art had passed in 1790, a phase of unique interest, truly aristocratic alike in its draughtsmanship and in its opulent yet delicately graded colouring—a transition phase between the classic figures of Kiyonaga and the exaggerated proportions of the later Utamaro, according to which he is usually judged.

It is true that soon after he yielded to the general tendency of his age, elongated his figures, imparting to them an ethereal, supple, and fragile nature, and gradually insisted on these attributes to exaggeration, even to impossibility, while his fame of having been the first to give such morbid inclinations completely satisfactory and therefore unsurpassable expression is a title of somewhat doubtful value, even if in any case a high historical significance cannot be denied it. Nevertheless we must not forget that within this domain of the hyper-æsthetic, Utamaro was the creator of a most original and individual style. Nay, if we could only admit the morbid and exaggerated to be as fit subject-matter for art as the healthy and sane, we must grant that this style is one of altogether enchanting originality, and that, however dangerous might be its immediate influence upon the spectator and particularly upon possible successors, it does none the less lift us beyond the cramping limits of reality and is therefore not wanting in idealism of a kind.

Towards the middle of the tenth decade these exaggerated proportions of the body had reached such an extreme that the heads were twice as long as they were broad, set upon slim long necks, which in turn swayed upon very narrow shoulders; the upper coiffure bulged out to such a degree that it almost surpassed the head itself in extent; the eyes were indicated by short slits and were separated by an inordinately long nose from an infinitesimally small mouth; the soft robes hung loosely about figures of an almost unearthly thinness. Finally, about the year 1800, Utamaro's tendency toward the bizarre had reached such a height that his heads were three times as long as broad and his figures more than eight times longer than the heads, thus considerably exceeding the normal ratio. In this period were produced the majority of his large female heads, which have spread his name so far abroad, by no means to the advantage of his artistic reputation.

But these exaggerations soon ceased and Utamaro returned to approximately natural proportions of the body. Thus his *Chronicle of the Yoshiwara*, of 1804, in two volumes, the work which justly made him so celebrated, is in no way peculiar in this respect. In the triptychs again, which he produced in greater number than any other artist of his country, these unnatural proportions appear but seldom. Probably, therefore, these sheets were produced for the most part before or after the period of delirium, and the endless file of his single sheets and series representing women during it. One of these triptychs, wherein the dissolute life of the reigning Shogun (Generalissimo and real monarch of Japan), Iyenari, is ridiculed under the figure of the Taiko, an historic personage of olden times, drew down on Utamaro a term of imprisonment which broke his bodily strength. Still, in 1805, he created the beautiful triptych in which a group of children impersonating the Seven Gods of Fortune are drawn by women in a car which has the form of a ship.[1] In the following year, 1806, the

[1] Compare the New Year's Procession, or Carnival of Marduk, among the recently excavated Ai-ibar-shabu of Babylon. A. H. D.

Vever Collection, Paris

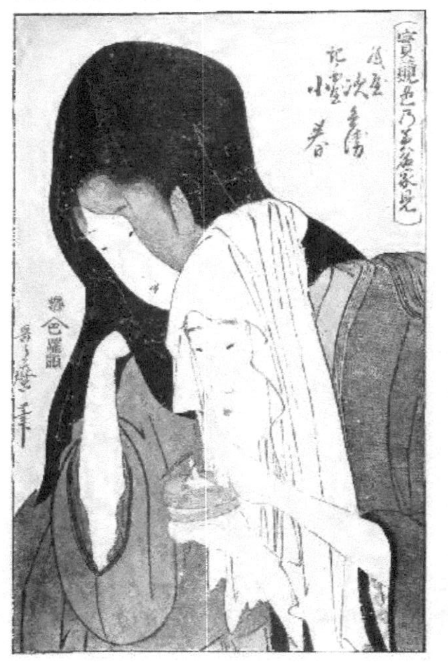

UTÁMARO: An Elopement Scene. The paper-dealer Jihéi, his handkerchief over his head, extinguishing a paper lantern: and the singer Kohárn in a black veil. *Grey ground.* Medium size.

Vever Collection, Paris

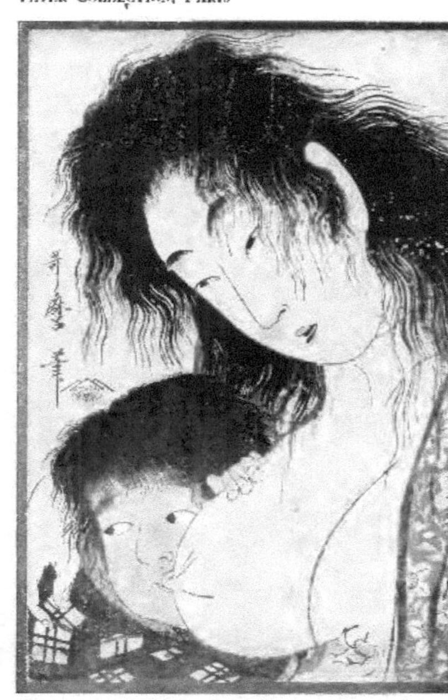

UTÁMARO: Kintoki suckled by the Mountain-woman. Medium size.

Vever Collection, Paris

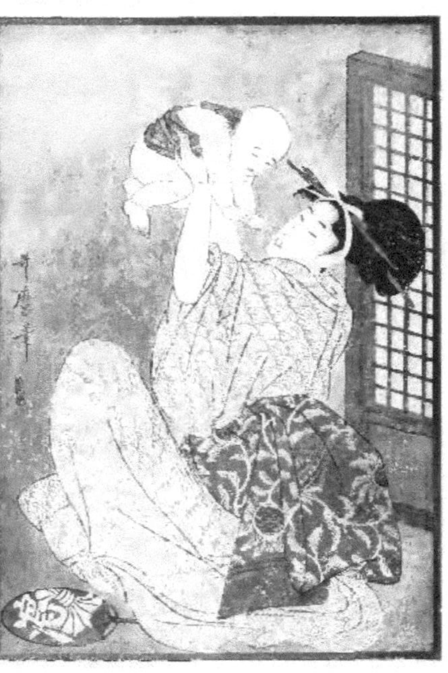

UTÂMARO: Mother and Child (La Gimblette). Green robe, with wave pattern (*seigainámi*); red sash. *Grey background.*

artist died. His works probably continued for some time afterwards to be imitated, even with misuse of his name, but were never equalled, much less surpassed.

Utamaro has glorified the Japanese woman with an enthusiasm unexcelled in any other age or nation. It is true that he consecrated his worship to a class of woman that stands outside the pale of society and, despite the splendour that surrounds her, is one of the most unfortunate of all creatures; but he did not depict her as she appears in reality, but formed of her an ideal of nobility and loveliness that stamps her as a goddess. It was not until the age declined to complete degeneracy that he degraded this ideal into caricature. Then it was, too, that in contrast to the usual custom he added those vulgar, burlesque masculine figures which were intended to serve as a foil to their beauty, but which brutally destroy the sweet illusion. The women are represented in the most various occupations. One is painting, another composing poems, a third preparing tea; others again are arranging flowers, smoking out of little silver pipes, playing with a mouse; still others at their toilet, colouring their lips, removing hairs from their faces with a strigil, tying their girdles—at the back when an honourable woman, in front when a courtesan—while sometimes holding with their chins a book in which they have just been reading. The artist is in particular inexhaustible in the depiction of the joys of motherhood. The gorgeous robes in which he clothes them are well in keeping with these queenly figures, and their rich patterns illustrate the entire animal and plant kingdoms. But when necessary he well knew how to keep the ornamentation as simple as possible. Certain patterns, says Goncourt, look as though the beauty had returned from a walk under blossoming trees and had brushed off with her sleeve or shoulder some of the petals.

His eye, incomparably sharpened by the study of nature,

K

enables him to render the hair of women, especially when hanging loosely down during the toilet, with a combined precision and softness within the deep black never elsewhere attained. Particular care was necessary in the printing of his blocks owing to the fineness of the detail, and for the same reason he attached the utmost importance to their colouring. No other Japanese artist understands so well as he how to attain an extremely harmonious and yet rich effect with a few colours, such as grey, light brown, and dark green. Where more lively colours are employed they are modified or combined with each other by a skilful application of green spaces, or else they run gradually into lighter tones and even dissolve into another colour. By quite imperceptibly delicate tinting he contrives to bring out the background or the flesh tones; in his large heads he is fond of using for the background the so-called mica, or dust of mother-of-pearl, which still further enhances the silky gloss of good Japanese paper. In short, he may fitly be called the first colourist of his nation.

Among his compositions, the large representations in several divisions play an important part. Among them is one of eight sheets:—

A popular festival.

Also one of seven sheets:—

The procession of the Korean ambassador, represented on the day of the Niwaka (carnival) by geishas with peaked green hats; executed before 1790, according to Kurth, who gives a reproduction of it (pl. 12).

One of six sheets:—

A wedding and celebrations after the wedding (Hamburg).

Some of five sheets:—

The boys' festival, with the picture of Shoki, the destroyer of demons and the guardian spirit of boys, on a kakemono.

The New Year's fair, a boy in the throng holding up a little pagoda.

SHARÁKU

ACTOR READING ANNOUNCEMENTS FROM A SCROLL BEFORE A PERFORMANCE

BRITISH MUSEUM

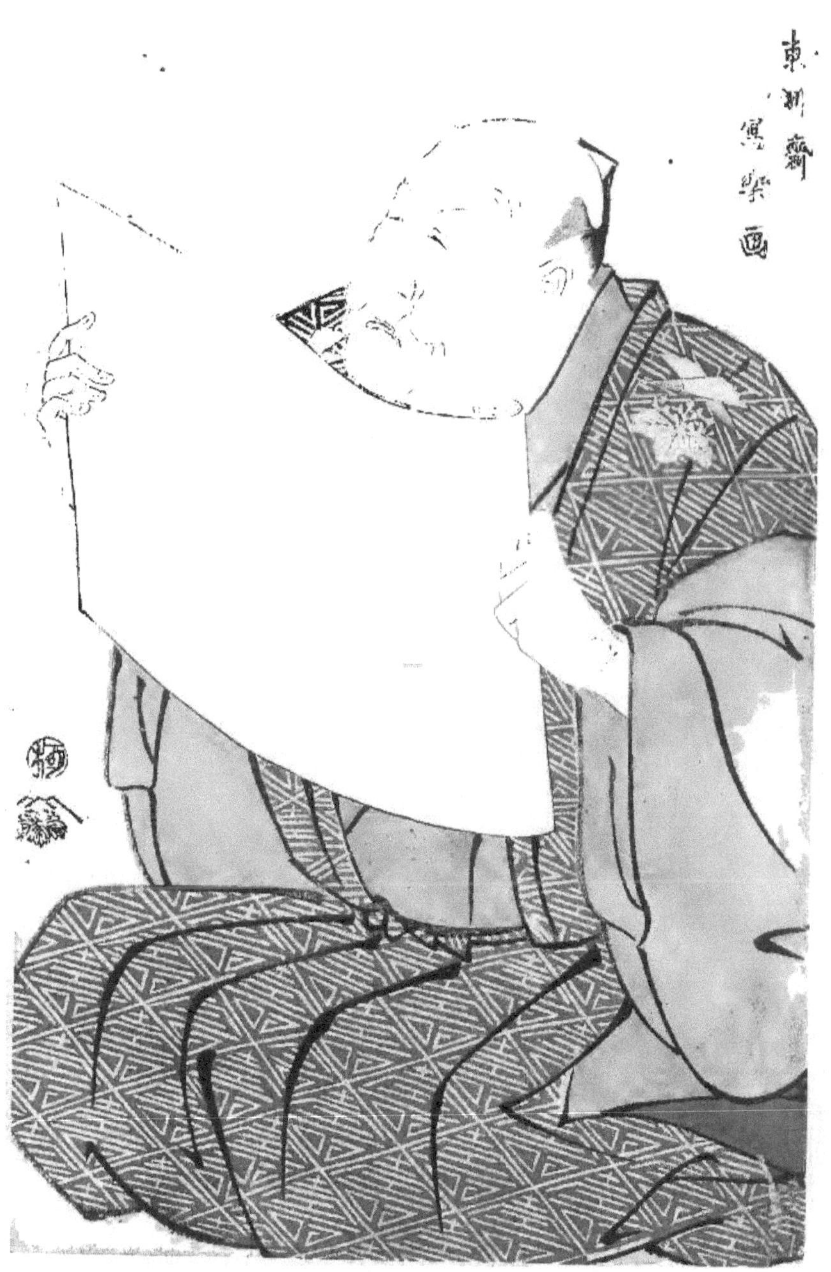
東洲齋寫樂画

Rain shower, in the middle a pair of lovers under an umbrella.
Cleaning of a "Green House."

Of three sheets:—

The dance of a geisha in a nobleman's palace (according to Fenollosa, No. 316, who places it at about 1792, his most beautiful composition).
Taigo Hideyoshi, the conqueror of Korea, with his five wives; an allusion to the ruling Shogun Iyenari, on account of which Utamaro was thrown into prison.
A fashionable wedding, in front of the bride three saké-cups.
Saké, seven kinds of drunkenness depicted by women.
New Year's day, a woman holding out to other women a skein of thread.
Daikoku, god of wealth, painting his own likeness, surrounded by women.
The various processes of wood-engraving.
Three groups under cherry trees (cited by Fenollosa, No. 344, as characteristic of his latest period).
Women on a journey, three of them under a mosquito net.
Gathering kaki (persimmons), very rich and life-like, drawn broadly.
A prince with basket of shell-fish among salt-carriers.
The Riogoku Bridge over the Sumida River, with nine women on it.
Night festival on the Sumida, women and children on the banks are seen against the dark water.
Women chasing fireflies.
Snow, moon, and flower, represented by women.
Women representing the Seven Gods of Fortune, in a boat of which the prow has the shape of a dragon.
Similar representation, the prow of the boat in the figure of the bird Howo: 1805.
Children dressed up as the Seven Gods of Fortune on a boat-shaped car drawn by women.
Spring occupations, in allusion to the Seven Gods of Fortune.
The pilgrimage to Ise, women wading through the water on the seashore facing the double cliff Meotoiwa.
The cranes of the Shogun Yoritomo (1190).
The awabi (shell-fish) girls (diving girls); a print for which 1050 francs was paid at the Burty sale, 1871, and 1300 francs at the Goncourt sale, 1897. In the centre is a woman nursing a child;

on the left a woman half undressed, her foot playing in the water with fish swimming about it; behind her a woman standing; to the right is one wringing water out of her clothes, and beside her a companion kneeling by a basket. The half-clad figures, which Goncourt rightly calls *un peu mannequinées*, are drawn with uncommon precision; the outlines of the nude are printed in a dark reddish brown.

Female divers in junks.

Utamaro also published a countless number of series, of which the following may be mentioned :—

Geishas celebrating the Niwaka Festival, 6 sheets (dating from the seventies ?).

Signboards of the most celebrated saké-houses, represented by women who have at their feet purple mats and stand out against the yellow background; 6 sheets, about 1790.

The Kamuros of the Yoshiwara, 6 sheets, also a continuation in 7 sheets.

Courtesans and geishas compared with flowers.

The five festal days.

The six arms of the Tamagawa River, women on undulating ground; at the top views on fans.

The six views of the Tamagawa River, women promenading.

Women compared with landscapes in the vicinity of the Yoshiwara, 8 sheets.

The six poetesses.

Courtesans compared with the six poets.

The story of the fair Osomi and the clerk Hisamatsu.

Examples of beautiful women typifying the seven-fold fortune, the gods of fortune each represented by a female figure in a circular frame.

Half-length figures on a mica ground, two series of ten leaves each (illustrated in Kurth, pl. 17, a girl before a mirror).

Half-length figures of women in pairs, several series; among them one representing the four seasons, and another of the same kind representing the twelve hours of the day.

Large heads, more than a hundred sheets.

Bijin ichisai goyusan tsugi, the fifty-three stations of the Tokaido represented by women, half-length figures, each with a circular landscape in the upper right-hand corner, 55 sheets.

Seiro Junitoki, the twelve hours of the Yoshiwara (named after animals and corresponding to the twenty-four European hours), each represented by two women, twelve pictures in large folio; probably the most graceful series by this artist, the garments very tasteful and the delicate colours harmonised by a great variety of greys.

Joshoku kaiko tewagagusa, sericulture, 12 sheets, each depicting about three women, very simple in colour (a description of the process in Goncourt, page 48). Kurth (No. 264) places this series after 1790, and adds that an earlier edition was printed in yellow, green, and violet.

Komei bijin mitate chushingura, the history of the faithful Ronins represented by the most beautiful women, 12 sheets (on the last sheet a portrait of Utamaro himself); also two other similar sets.

The four sleepers, with parodies of celebrated old pictures.

The fortunate dreams, 12 sheets, each representing the head of a dreamer; also of dreaming animals, *e.g.*, an old cat.

Kintoki, the child of the wilderness, with his mother Yamauba (for this story, dating from about 1000 A.D., see Goncourt, page 58 ff.). Several sheets, which are among the most admirable work of this artist; Kintoki riding on the back of his mother; at his mother's breast; the woman with the chestnut, &c. Kurth (pl. 20) illustrates Kintoki with his hobby-horse; see in Kurth (p. 224 *seqq.*) the list of these various subjects.

Tose kodomo rokkasen, children dressed as the six poets, 1790, in subdued colours.

Parental exhortations, on every sheet a pair of eye-glasses.

Some series of small prints, representing full-length or half-length figures of women, very simple in colour, rank among his most attractive work in virtue of their graceful draughtsmanship and the delicacy of their cutting. As they can scarcely be said to show any trace of mannerism, they were probably produced before 1790. A considerable number came up at the Gillot sale.

Here belong also his sheets in surimono style :—

The play scene with seventeen actors.

Five sheets of a series (Gonse Coll. in Paris, see Goncourt, p. 257) and two sheets of the same series (Bing Coll. in Paris).

Three sheets in narrow vertical form, but not kakemono-ye (Coll. Gillot in Paris, see Goncourt, p. 259).

Of the kakomeno-ye may be mentioned :—

A woman standing, leaning against a lattice, at her feet crouches another, playing with a casket (Coll. Gillot).

A woman bending down towards a young girl and carrying a child on her back (Coll. Bing).

A woman fishing, below a young man in a boat (Bing).

A young man carrying a young woman on his back.

Two girls playing the game of Makura-hiki, oblong.

Of single sheets, we may name the following :—

A young woman crouching allows a white mouse to run over her arm, while another, looking on, holds in her arms a child playing with a wooden horse.

A woman nursing her child under a mosquito net.

A mother and child reflected in a basin of water.

A mother tossing her child in the air (*la gimblette*).

The maid of the inn, front and back view, on two sheets made to fit over each other exactly ; a magnificent facsimile of this is in Kurth (pl. 24).

The stationer Jihei abducting Koharu, the singing girl, half-length (*la sortie nocturne*).

Benten, the goddess of fortune, appearing to Utamaro (illustrated in Kurth, pl. 11).

Books in black and white :—

Four prints with songs from plays date from 1776–77, and are signed Kitagawa Toyokira (Hayashi Catalogue, No. 1649). His earliest book is the Hundred Ronins, 20 sheets : Yedo, 1777.

I. Kibiyoshi (yellow books of small size) from 1780 to 1784, then from 1788 to 1790 (see Goncourt, p. 171 ff.); the earliest is the 800 Lies of Mampachi, 29 sheets: Yedo, 1780.

II. Books in Mangwa size, 1787–90 (Goncourt, p. 174). Also a book of 1802.

III. Books of erotic contents, beginning with the Yehon mina mezane (All the World Awakens) of 1786, in collaboration with Rantokusai (Shundo), with delicate half-tones (see Goncourt, p. 263); the Yehon Tamakushige of 1789, printed with especial care.

According to a personal communication from Kurth, Rantokusai signs together with Utamaro on the last print but two, and alone on the sixth, while Utamaro signs alone on the last.

Books in polychrome :—

Yehon ginsekai, the Silver World, poems on snow, 5 double sheets with figures, of very great charm, with little gradation in the colours, important for the landscape, 1790.

Yehon kiogetsubo, poems on the moon, 5 double sheets, landscape compositions with a few figures, 1789.

Yehon waka yebisu, New Year's Day Customs, 5 double sheets with very spirited figures, exceptionally delicate in colour and very finely cut, 1786 (Kurth, pl. 8).

Yehon hananokumo, poems on the cherry blossoms (lit. flowers of the clouds).

Yehon matsu no shirabe, the Testing of the Pines, 1795, several volumes. In this he signs himself Karamaro, *i.e.* the Chinese Maro.

Yehon shikinohama, flowers of the four seasons, in 2 vols., 1801; therein an interior during a thunderstorm (Kurth, pl. 37).

Fugenzo, promenades during the cherry-blossom season, 5 double sheets, 1790.

Occupations of women according to rank, 16 small sheets (Coll. Duret in Paris).

His principal work is :—

Seiro yehon nen ju gioji, the events of the year in the Green Houses (Yoshiwara), with the addition: Umpire of the lists for one year;

printed in 2 vols., 8vo, for New Year's Day, 1804, one vol. of 12, one of 11 sheets, rich in figures and full of life, but somewhat sombre in colour. Some copies are printed in black and white; as the impressions in these appear much more delicate, Kurth (*Utamaro*, p. 124) conjectures that the black and white prints formed the first edition, the later issue being coloured to disguise the defects in the blocks. The work was executed with the aid of his pupils, Kikumaro, Hidemaro, and Takimaro. Text by Jippensha Ichiku. The title of the first volume, with a border of an apple twig in blossom and a red camellia, contains the verses of Sandarahoshi: "O pealing bell of morning dawn, didst thou feel the sadness of parting, gladly wouldst thou lie rather than re-echo the six strokes." The title-page of the second volume likewise depicts flowers. The border of the index represents the outer gate of the Yoshiwara. For the description of the single sheets, see Goncourt, page 72 ff. Reproductions in Bing's Catalogue.[1]

Books pertaining to natural history:—

Momochidori kioka awase, the hundred little screamers (birds), the first edition (dating from the tenth decade?) with 8 double sheets; the second in two volumes with fifteen illustrations. One of the most beautiful polychrome books; blind printing is put to excellent use, *e.g.*, in case of the parts of the bodies of animals that are in water. The ducks, pigeons, cranes, and herons are excellent.

Mushiyerabi, selected insects, 2 vols., with 15 double plates and a title-page, 1788 (illustrated in Gonse, p. 265). With an epilogue by his teacher, Sekiyen. The contours are not black, but in the colours of the objects represented.

Shiohi no tsuto, memento of the ebb-tide (poems on shell-fish), 8

[1] Yoshiwara, the courtesan quarter of Yedo, was founded in 1600 by Shoji Jinyemon near the palace of the Shoguns. After the great fire of 1657, it was changed to its present site in the northern part of the city and surrounded by moats. A single gateway forms the entrance to this quarter, which is divided into many parts by intersecting streets. The tea-houses are situated along the main thoroughfare. In the "Green Houses" lived the courtesans, who had received the most perfect education, like princesses, and spoke a peculiar, old-fashioned language. Each one of these Oirans had two young attendants, Kamuros; as soon as these reached a certain age, they, too, were promoted to the rank of Oiran. The Geishas (playing and singing girls) formed an entirely different class and were obliged to live an honourable life.

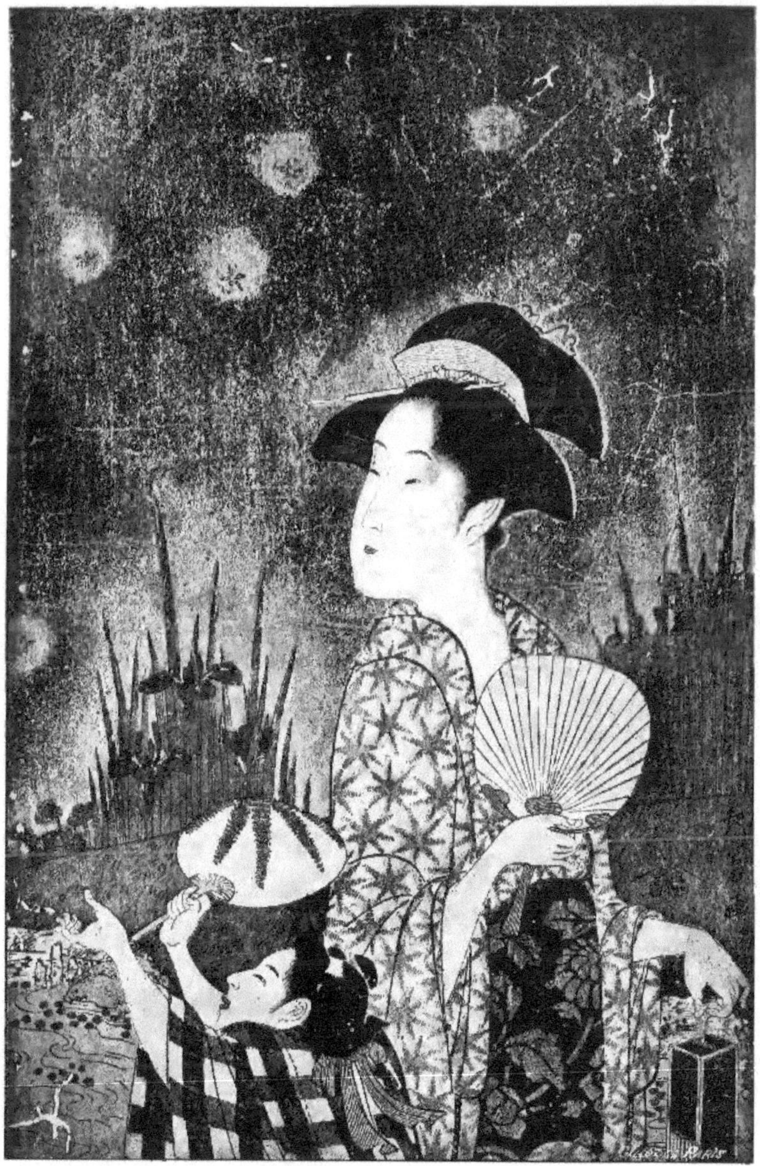

NAGAYOSHI: CHASING FIREFLIES ON A SUMMER EVENING. The woman, in a blue figured dress and a black sash figured with dark green, holds an insect-trap. The child in violet. *Dark mica ground.* Medium size.

double sheets (of the ninth decade), beginning with a stroll on the beach, ending with a game of Kaiawase, with girls crouching round a circle formed of shell-fish.

Representations of foreign birds, 10 sheets (Coll. Gonse in Paris).

To a book of larger size belong probably: a falcon on a blossoming plum-tree (Coll. Gonse) and a crane by his nest on a pine branch (Coll. Bing).

Seven sheets with bouquets of flowers belong to a book printed in black and white (Coll. Gillot).

Two single sheets (Coll. Bing); two crabs with some sea-weed; a chrysanthemum stem and rice straw.

To a series belong: 1, two flower-boxes; 2, a toad with a lotus-flower in its mouth; 3, a tortoise with the same; 4, a deity holding a flower-vase.

Books of erotic contents:—

Utamakura, the Poem of the Pillow, 1788; on the first page a goddess of the sea. His most beautiful work of this kind.

Yenipon hanafubuki, fallen blossoms, 3 vols., 1802.

For the rest, the reader may be referred to the catalogue of Utamaro's works in Kurth, *Utamaro*, which runs to 530 numbers, as against 285 in Goncourt.

Together with Shunyei he published a series of wrestlers, in which the pairs of female spectators are done by Utamaro. Goncourt (page 186) refers to three works of other artists (Hokusai, Toyokuni, &c.), to which Utamaro contributed single sheets.

Strange reproduces, on page 42, a female figure in half-length, and in pl. iv. a similar one in the form of a celebrated poetess. Fenollosa (*Outline*, pl. xv.) reproduces a not very characteristic print. Other reproductions in Bing's essay in the *Studio* of 1895.

His pupil, Koikawa Shuncho, married his widow, took his name, and under it continued his master's activity from 1808 to 1820 with the same publishing firm; after 1820 he signed himself Kitagawa Tetsugoro.[1] But his only real successor and pupil is said to be Shikimaro, of whom we have the work—

> Zensei tagu no kurabe (?), a concourse of women in the flower of their beauty.

He, however, is not nearly so refined, nor so delicate in his colour as Utamaro (Goncourt, page 153); he is the author of the series of three prints, each representing an oiran in her out-of-door dress (Hayashi Catalogue, No. 944). His pupils, Mitemaro and Yukimaro, worked with him after 1785 on the yellow books; on the Yoshiwara, from 1804, his pupils, Kikumaro, Hidemaro, and Takimaro. Kikumaro died in 1829; about 1796 he employed the name Tsukimaro; a book by him appeared at Yedo in 1805 (Hayashi Catalogue, No. 1676). Strange, page 44, gives us a reproduction from him of a woman seated, preparing tea. Other illustrations in Hayashi Catalogue, Nos. 936 and 938. This Catalogue has been followed in making both names apply to one artist, whereas in the first edition they appeared as those of two men, on the authority of Anderson (Catalogue, p. 363).

The Hayashi Catalogue mentions the following further pupils of Utamaro: Isomaro (No. 945); Hiakusai Hisanobu (No. 954); Chikanobu (No. 955) and Shintoku (No. 956). Kurth (*Utamaro*, p. 146) follows Strange in adding Kyosai Chikamaro, who appears to have worked in the manner of Hiroshige.

The following were influenced by Utamaro: Bunro, perhaps derived from Buncho (Hayashi Catalogue, No. 946); Hayami Shungiosai (Riukoku) (*ibid.*, No. 947), a book by whom is mentioned in Duret; and finally Banki (*ibid,*, No. 951).

Naga- 長 yoshi 喜

In immediate connection with Utamaro must be mentioned Nagayoshi, an excellent and very rare artist, who worked toward the end of the eighteenth century.[2] He is usually called Choki,

[1] Strange, p. 44; Kurth, *Utamaro*, p. 49.
[2] Fenollosa Cat., No. 303; Kurth, *Utamaro*, p. 84 *seqq*.

VEVER COLLECTION, PARIS

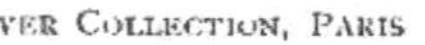

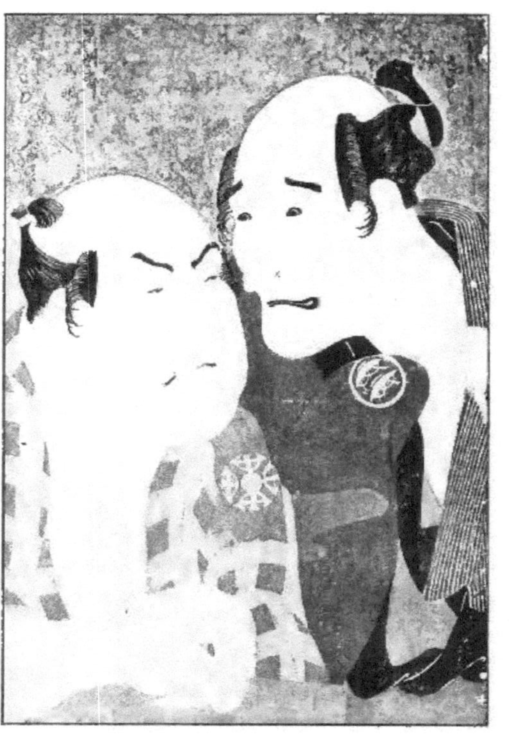

SHARÂKU : TWO ACTORS. The stouter one in grey and green, the other in brown. *Silver ground.* Medium size.

ROYAL PRINT ROOM, DRESDEN

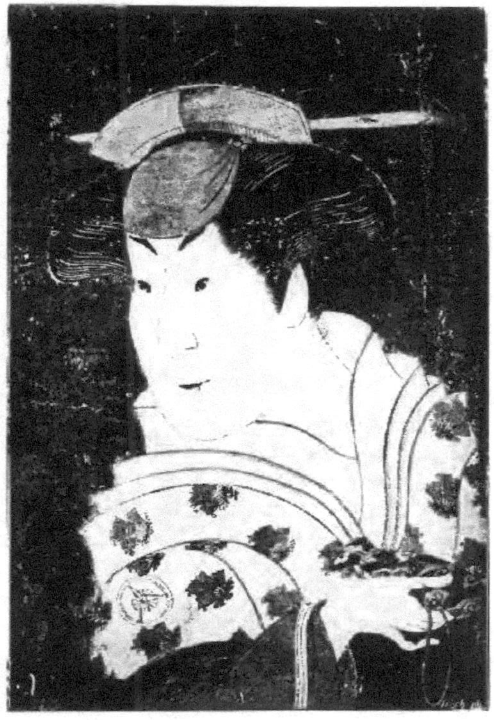

SHARÂKU : ACTOR IN A FEMALE PART, HOLDING A BAG. *Silver ground.* Medium size.

according to the Chinese reading (*on*). He is said to have been Utamaro's fellow-pupil under Sekiyen, but he was probably influenced by Kiyonaga, so that it is not impossible that he was the latter's pupil. At first he also signed himself Shiko and sometimes, later, Yeishosai. About 1790 he came forward with fully developed powers and so closely approached Utamaro in the types which the latter was then employing that it is possible sometimes to confuse him with Utamaro. His slenderly proportioned but always graceful figures are characterised by especial refinement. He gives us pictures of beautiful women in full length, half-length, and head-and-shoulders, on mica backgrounds, and he is in addition remarkable for the beauty and tastefulness of his colouring. It is significant of his connection with Sharaku that he represents on one of his prints a girl with a palm-leaf fan, which contains a likeness of Sharaku (Hayashi Catalogue, No. 923). Later on, as his powers declined, he attached himself to Yeishi. His series entitled *Seiro niwaka zensei asobi*, Entertainments of the Blossom of the Green Houses, on metal ground, has a reputation. An illustrated book by him appeared at Yedo in 1795 (new edition in 1803). Illustrations in Hayashi Catalogue (Nos. 931, 925).

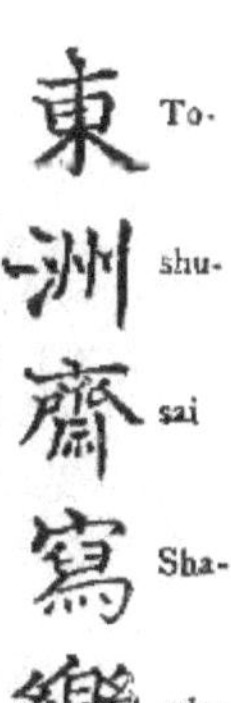

Toshusai Sharaku demands a place to himself at this time. He is an artist who is said to have worked but for a few years, and who produced in this short period a number of quarter-length and full-length figures of actors, mostly in large size and in very peculiar, grotesque, but exceedingly delicate drawing, and especially in altogether unique colour-tones and harmonies.[1] In regard to his estimate of this artist, Fenollosa stands in complete opposition to the French collectors. He agrees with Anderson, who held that Sharaku drew less correctly than any of his contemporaries, in describing him as vulgar and repulsive, and in recognising in his degraded types a proof that Kiyonaga, had his

[1] Anderson Cat., p. 345 ; Fenollosa Cat., No. 357 ; Bing Cat., No. 311 ff.

activity been longer continued, would have sunk into an unhealthy atmosphere. If we consider with what wonderful completeness precisely this artist is represented in the Paris collections, and especially in that of Count Camondo, we cannot suppress the suspicion that something like jealousy sounds out of Fenollosa's words. The exaggeration of facial expression has certainly gone to greater lengths in Sharaku than in any other artist. But we cannot deny that these distorted features bespeak a most superior mind that grips the observer, as well as does the greatness of his drawing, down to the patterns of the costumes, and the extraordinary sureness of taste which succeeds in harmonising deep, opaque colours that are found nowhere else. In representing whole figures he usually groups two of them on one design; the flesh is usually left uncoloured, as it is sufficiently clearly brought out by the contrast with the mica background.

Kurth (*Utamaro*, p. 82) states that his name was Saito Inrobei Kabukido Toshusai Yenkyo Sharaku (Hayashi Catalogue), that he began by being a No-dancer to the lord of the southern province of Awa, and that he published several series of actor pictures with the firm of Juzabro in 1790, but was forced to discontinue his work, owing to the indignation caused by his realism.

Uta- 歌 gawa 川 Toyo- 豊 kuni 國

3. Toyokuni.—Utagawa Toyokuni, whose real name was Kumakichi, also called Ichiyosai, and who lived from 1769–1825, began his activity about the middle of the ninth decade, and continued it until about 1810. He became, towards the end of Utamaro's career, his most notable rival. While he did not possess the strength and boldness of Yeishi and Utamaro, he yet commanded a wholly individual and well-considered style. He won a special significance for the further development of the nineteenth century by his having trained Kunisada, who later called himself Toyokuni II., and Kuniyoshi, both of whom

HÓKUSAI

THE WATERFALL OF YORO

(One of the eight Waterfalls)

BRITISH MUSEUM

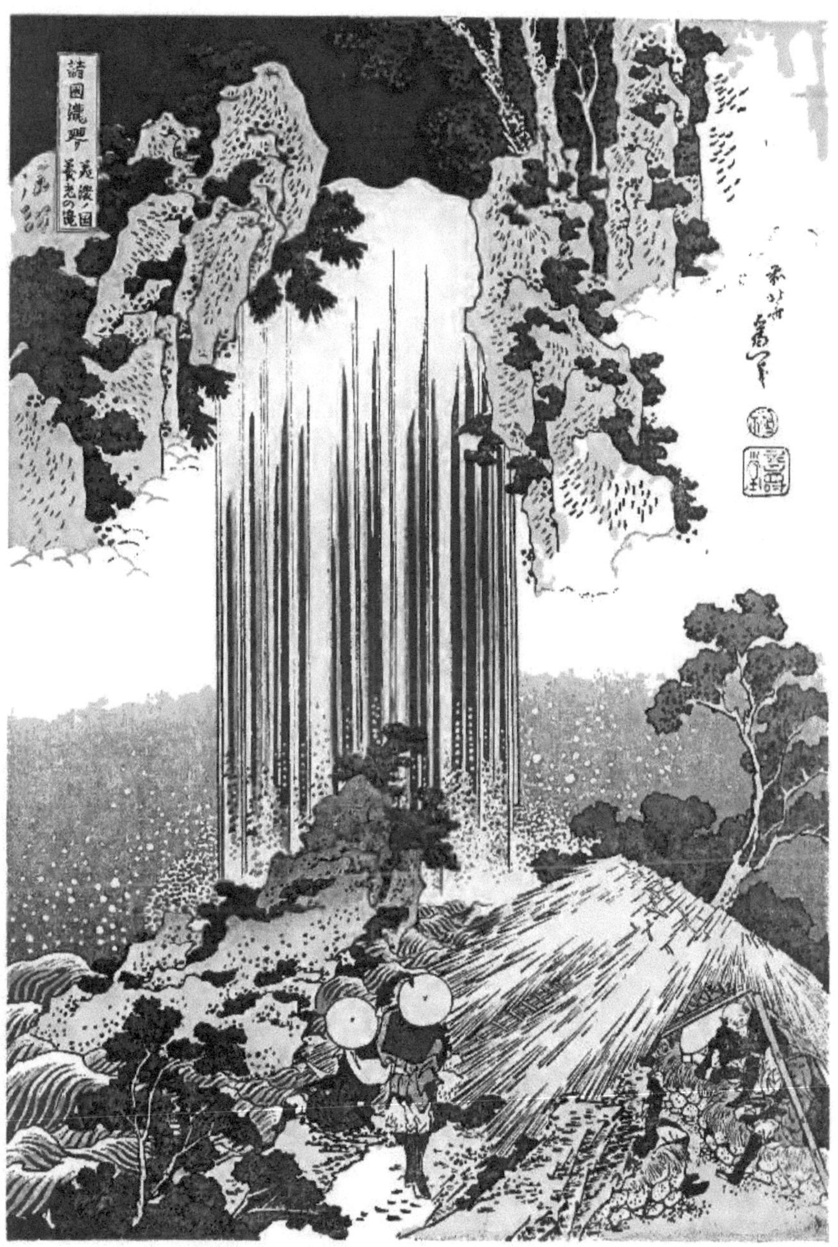
諸國瀧廻り
美濃ノ国
養老の滝

dominated art until the middle of the century, and gave it its essential stamp.

Toyokuni was the son of Kurabashi Gorobei, a Buddhist image-carver in Yedo; he first studied the style of Hanabusa Itcho and Giokusan, but went over to Toyoharu and formed his name by taking part of that of the old Toyonobu, as Fenollosa assumes.[1] Unlike Yeishi and Utamaro, therefore, he had no need to familiarise himself with the popular style, but was from the start educated in a conception not over far removed from that of the still dominant Kiyonaga. Toyokuni was without doubt Toyoharu's greatest pupil. He understood how to dispose his mostly very quiet figures in graceful groupings; although his colouring lacks a special originality, yet it was strong and in good taste. After Kiyonaga had given up actor representations, Toyokuni took over this field; he began to depict actors off the stage, in land and water picnics, or in the company of beautiful women; but as he treated these subjects carelessly, this branch of art fell into a temporary decay until his pupils took it up again with renewed energy. Towards the end of the ninth decade he developed his full strength and independence, in a style reminding us of Kiyonaga. The European influence, which had already become noticeable in Toyoharu, his teacher, may be clearly traced in his work also. From the middle of the nineties he began to approach more nearly the style of Utamaro. About 1800 his figures also reached an impossible length, and his faces rounded into a long-drawn oval. He then developed, in rivalry with Utamaro, a peculiar angular style, which reached its height in 1804, and displays him, even in comparison with his former model, Kiyonaga, as a wholly independent artist of a peculiar and austere grace. Except for the time when he, too,

[1] Anderson Cat., p. 348; Strange, p. 47; Fenollosa Cat., Nos. 337-356; Bing Cat., No. 199 ff.; Cat. Goncourt, No. 1283 ff.; Cat. Burty, No. 258; Goncourt, *Outamaro*, pp. 187, 103 ff. The biographical dates are corrected according to the Hayashi Cat.

was unable to withstand the universal taste for the exaggerated, he retained always a relatively high degree of naturalness; and where he appears unnatural, it is generally to be explained by the affected attitudes of the actors of the time. Later on, however, his works become coarser. He and Kiyonaga were probably the first to make use of the bluish red which introduced a staring tint hitherto unknown to Japanese wood-engraving. There can be no suggestion of their having employed aniline dyes, as these were not put on the market by Perkins until 1856 and probably did not reach Japan until the sixties. Still, we cannot but feel the extreme gaudiness of the general effect, which appears towards the end of the eighteenth century to be a foreign element and a falling off, perhaps under the influence of China, from the older Japanese seriousness of purpose. It is only because this delicate and bright colour-scheme, which correspondingly modifies the yellows and blues as well, has preserved its original freshness in but very few copies, that we do not recognise it more immediately as a characteristic feature of precisely this period.

Immediately after Toyokuni retired from the field, his pupil, Kunisada, about 1810, continued the activity of his master, at first under his own name; about 1844, however, long after his master's death, that is, he assumed Toyokuni's name. A likeness of Toyokuni is found in Kuniyoshi's *Fuzoku komeidan*, Anecdotes of Celebrated People, two small volumes, in black and white (Kioto, 1840), on the last page.[1]

Like Hokusai, whose first period he lived through, Toyokuni illustrated tales of Kioden, Bakin, and others. With Kunimasa he published, at the beginning of the nineties, a series of actor pictures, for which Utamaro drew the title; in 1801, he published alone a collection of actor pictures of small size, which may be considered about his best work; in 1802, there

[1] Reproduced in Burty's Cat., No. 65.

BING COLLECTION, PARIS

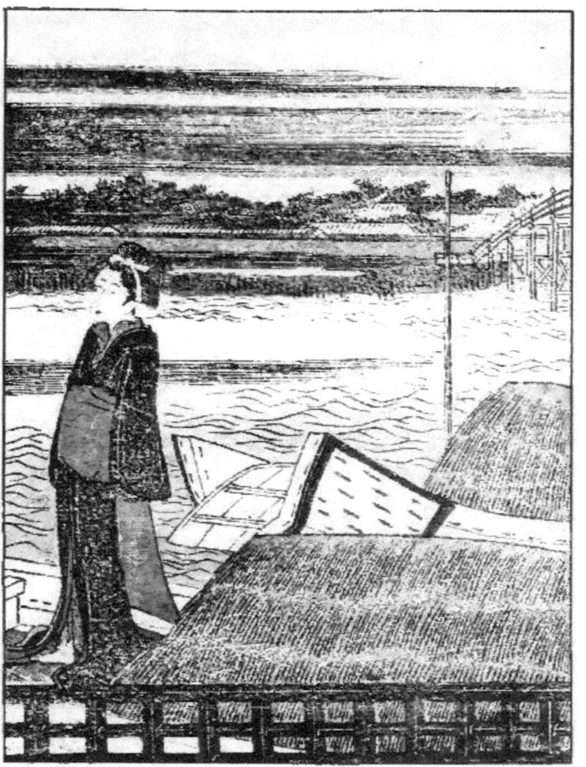

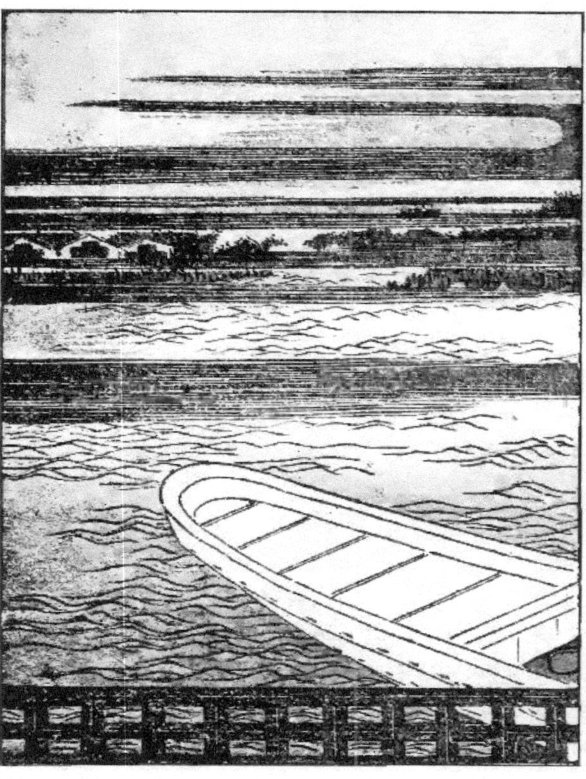

TOYÓKUNI: WOMAN IN HER BOAT. Last illustration in the second volume of the "Yehon imayo sūgata" of 1802.

followed the representations of women of all classes. Besides his numerous triptychs, the pleasing picture, in ten small sheets meant to be pasted side by side, of a rain shower driving a throng of people of every trade to seek shelter under a gigantic outspread tree, is particularly celebrated. His landscapes are rare. He also rendered flowers on a large oblong surimono. Illustrations in Strange: plate v., a garden scene, early; on page 48, an actor; on the same, a woman floating a little boat, reminding us of Utamaro. Gonse, i., p. 42: courtesans in a boat (part of a triptych). Fenollosa (*Outline*, pl. xvi.) reproduces a print of his decline.

Of his triptychs the following may be cited:—

Snow scene, a lady of rank with her little daughter making snowballs; dated by Fenollosa (No. 348) about 1798; perhaps his most beautiful work of the kind.

A lady of rank on horseback with attendants, Fuji in background; a very beautiful composition, in subdued colours: yellow, violet, black, and a little green.

The ford, a lady of rank carried in a palanquin by eight men.

The gust of wind.

Women as gods of fortune in a ship, the prow of which has the shape of a white cock.

Actors and women in a boat on the river; dated by Fenollosa (No. 353) about 1805.

Washerwomen at the whirlpool.

Haul of fish on the shore.

The bath; according to Fenollosa (Nos. 351, 352) about 1803.

The banks of the Sumida River at the bridge of Riogoku.

A fan shop, in front a boy playing with five puppies; dated by Fenollosa (No. 338) about 1789; one of the best of his early period.

The rat-dream; according to Fenollosa, about 1794.

Three actors (Catalogue Duret, No. 91).

Scene in a temple garden, dated by Fenollosa (No. 342) about 1800. In collaboration with his pupil Toyohiro.

Pentaptych: main street of the Yoshiwara in cherry blossom time; dated by Fenollosa (No. 341) about 1792.

Series of sheets:—

The rain shower, 10 small sheets; among those seeking shelter under the giant tree in the middle of the long design are a young nobleman with a falcon, a young girl trying to cover his hair, a washerwoman, a man with a monkey, a faggot carrier, and several blind people,-who have fallen down in their haste (Bing Catalogue, No. 208).

Views of the environs of Yedo, 8 sheets, quarto, dating from the beginning of the century (Catalogue Leroux).

The six Tamagawa rivers, in circles, only slightly coloured.

The six celebrated poets, in pairs.

Courtesans in the likeness of Komachi, 7 sheets, medium size.

Illustrated books:—

Haiyu raku richutsu (?), pictures of Yedo actors, in collaboration with Kunimasa, beginning of tenth decade; the title by Utamaro, representing the implements of the No-dance; by the same is an actor seated, smoking and watching three women leaving the theatre.

Yakusha konotegashiwa, collection of celebrated actors, 2 small vols., Yedo, 1801; perhaps his best work.

Yehon imayo sugata, the manners of the present time, women of all classes, 2 vols., coloured, 1802; in the first volume respectable women, in the second, those of the Yoshiwara, &c.

Toyokuni toshidamafude, reminding one of Hokusai's Mangwa.

Yehon Yedo no mizu, Yedo, 3 vols., black and white.

Yobo shashin sangai kio, Recreations of Actors, Yedo, 1801, 2 vols.; excellent in colour.

Bakino, Comparison of the Theatres with Famous Places, 1800, 2 vols.; humorous.

History of Princess Sakura, a romance by Kyoden, Yedo, 1806, 5 vols.

Yakusha awase kagami, Actors, Yedo, 1804.

In collaboration with Shunyei he published a work at Yedo in 1806; in collaboration with Toyohiro: Otagi Kanoko, 12 coloured pictures, Yedo, 1803.

His best pupil was his brother, Toyohiro, who developed a peculiar manner, and later had the privilege of training the great landscape painter Hiroshige. Of Toyokuni's pupils, Kunisada (later Toyokuni II.), and Kuniyoshi, both of whom will be

Royal Print Room, Dresden

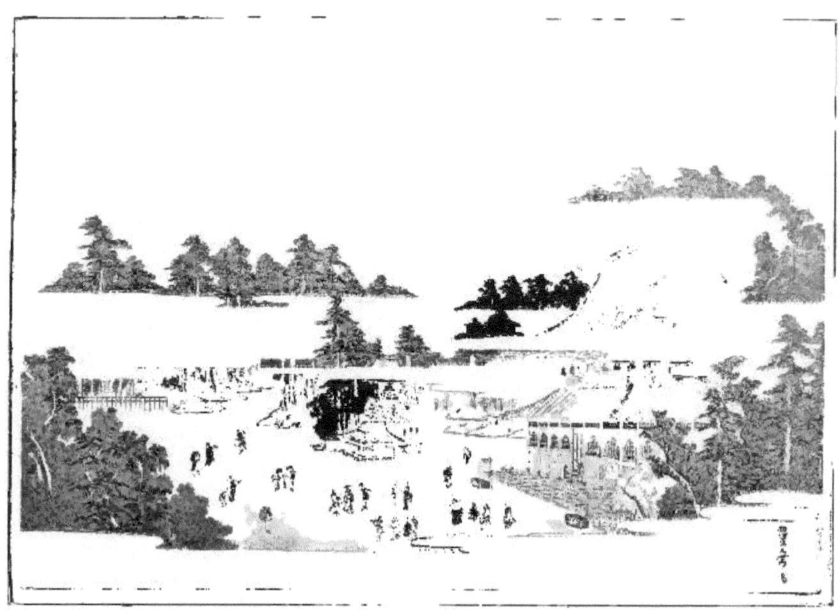

TOYOHIRO: The Evening Bells of Uyeno (Park containing the Tombs of the Shoguns) at Yedo. Streaks of mist. From the eight *Hakkei* (views) of Yedo. Medium size.

mentioned later, attained the widest celebrity. Pupils of his early period were Kunimasa (see above) and Kuniyasu (Hayashi Catalogue, No. 1092), who produced especially actor prints, but whose works are rare. Kunimasa lived from 1773 to 1810; he also signed himself Ichiyusai. Illustrated in Hayashi Catalogue, No. 1088; Duret (No. 267) mentions one book. His son, Naajiro, was also his pupil; he first took the name Toyoshige, but later adopted his father's name, so that he must be carefully distinguished from Toyokuni II.; sometimes he signs himself Gosotei Toyokuni. His style is reminiscent rather of Yeisen than of his father.

Utagawa Toyohiro, also called Ichiriusai, the brother of Toyokuni, was his pupil, but also studied as the pupil of Toyoharu.[1] He was born in 1773; his ordinary name was Okajima Tojiro (Hayashi Catalogue, No. 1051). He began his career about the middle of the tenth decade, reminding us at first of Shunsho, then, in 1800, collaborating with Toyokuni. In the first two decades of the nineteenth century he illustrated many books, in which to a certain extent he approached the style of Hokusai. He died in 1828. His pupil was Hiroshige, who likewise called himself Ichiriusai.

歌 Uta-
川 gawa
豊 Toyo-
廣 hiro

Toyohiro's chief single sheets are :—

The abduction of Otoku by Fukusuke; medium size.

A young girl in the snow; dated by Fenollosa (No. 350) about 1801; his most beautiful and characteristic work.

An actor in the rôle of a Kashira, with a large umbrella.

A branch of blossoms in wicker basket on lacquer stand.

Triptychs :—

Gathering persimmons in the presence of a young prince; dark tones.

The crossing in a ferry-boat, containing several blind people.

Supper on a terrace facing the river.

---

[1] Anderson Cat., p. 347; *id.*, *Japanese Wood-Engraving;* Fenollosa Cat., Nos. 344a, 350; Cat. Burty, No. 182 ff.; Bing Cat., No. 183 ff.

L

Illustrated books :—

Kengu irigomi sento shinwa (?), 1802, black and white.
Fuku nezumi Shiriwo no Futozawo, the lucky rat, 1804, in colour.
Sunden jitsujitsuke (?), romance by Bakin, 1805, 5 vols., black and white.
Katakiuchi sembonzakura, fantastic stories, 1809, black and white.
Tosei shoriu ika bonedzu, bouquets, excellent in draughtsmanship and colour (Berlin Kunstgewerbemuseum). Duret (No. 219 *seqq.*) mentions works of 1793 and 1807.

Reproductions :—Anderson, *Japanese Wood-Engraving*, No. 22 ; Strange at p. 46.

Further pupils of Toyokuni are mentioned by the Hayashi Catalogue : Kuninaga (No. 1090) ; Kunimitsu (No. 1091) ; Kuninao (No. 1093) ; Utagawa Yoshimaru (No. 1096).

Utagawa Toyomaru is mentioned as having done actor pictures about the year 1800 (Bing Catalogue, No. 233). A book illustrated by him appeared at Yedo in 1798. Illustration in Hayashi Catalogue (No. 1052). Sekko (Gillot Catalogue) and Raisen (Gillot Catalogue, print with two dates) worked at the same time as Toyomaru.

Bing Collection, Paris

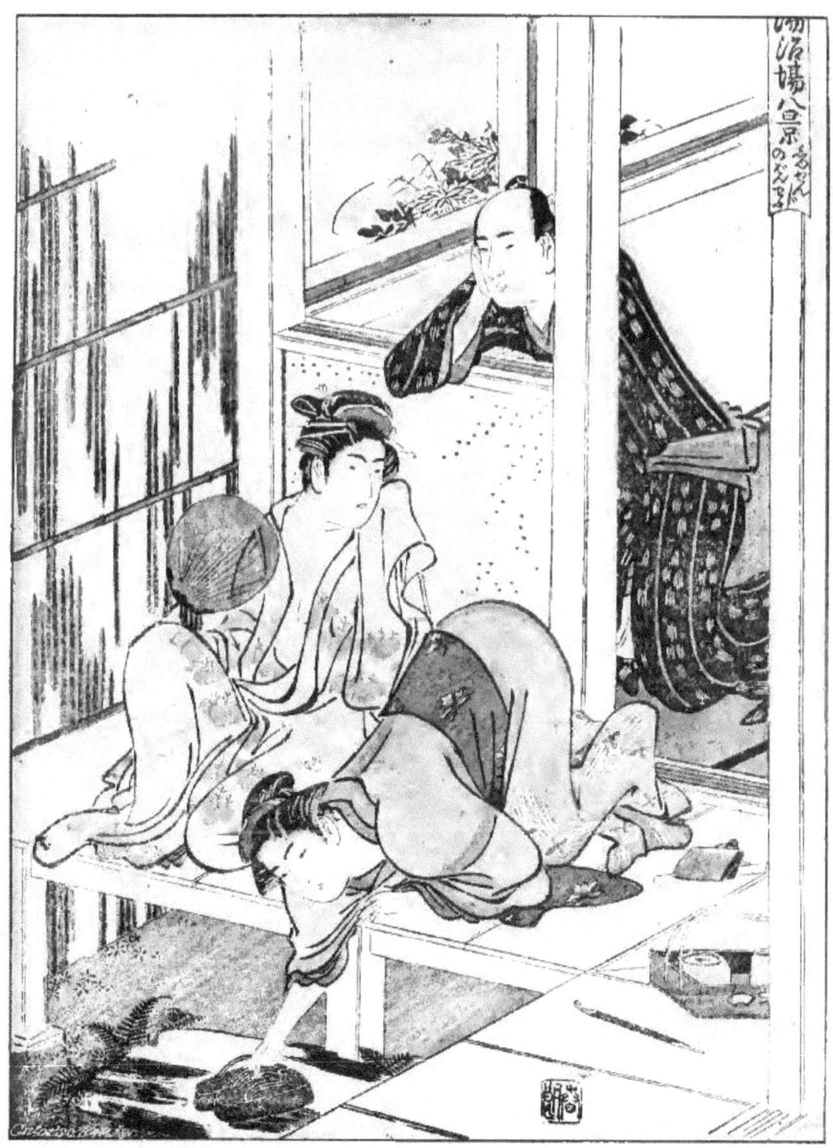

SHUNRŌ (HÓKUSAI): Courtesan in a Bath-gown, with her Servant, who is arranging a Pair of Shoes. A young man in the background. *Yellow and pink tones.*

CHAPTER VIII

HOKUSAI

HOKUSAI is in Europe the most popular of all Japanese artists; for a long time indeed Europeans were inclined to regard him as the greatest. He plays an important part in the history of Japanese wood-engraving, by virtue both of the peculiarity of his talent and of the influence that he exerted during a long and laborious life; nevertheless, to the masters of the eighteenth century he does not attain. It is just those peculiarities which are new in him and his work, and which make it appear so familiar, indeed almost akin, to the European eye—namely, realism without style or subordination of the observation of nature to any higher artistic conception—it is just these that brought upon him in his own country the disregard under which he had to suffer during his lifetime. We, for our part, have no desire to join in either panegyric or condemnation. Looked at from the European point of view, Hokusai certainly displays a richness of invention, a keenness of observation, and a sureness of touch which we could find but little to match; and even from the Japanese point of view, we must admit that during the first decades of his activity, from about 1790 to 1805, he stands worthily beside Yeishi, Utamaro, and Toyokuni, producing graceful work of an individual stamp; what he created later during his best period, from about 1815 to 1835, in the field of landscape, animal representation, and still life, surpasses anything of the kind that has been produced in Japan in the nineteenth century. To speak truth, however, he never adventured himself on representations of a great and noble style, on high art proper, and that of itself suffices to assign a subordinate rank to the artist in the judgment of the Japanese, who find no compensation in wit and humour for defects of formal beauty. Literary culture also seems never to have been his forte; and as his success was mainly due to his native talent, so he remained to the last an artisan.[1]

During an activity of more than sixty years—he died in the year 1849, at the age of ninety—he is reputed to have produced some 30,000 sketches and to have illustrated about 500 volumes.

Katsu-shika Hoku-sai Shun-ro 葛飾北齋春朗

Katsushika Hokusai was born in Yedo on 5th March 1760, and was adopted in early youth by Nakajima Ise, looking-glass maker to the Tokugawa clan, who lived in the garden-suburb Honjo, on the farther side of the Sumida River, in the district of Katsushika.[2] At the age of twelve he was apprenticed to a bookseller; then from the age of fourteen he studied the art of wood-engraving, and became in 1779 a pupil of Katsukawa Shunsho, as such adopting the name of Katsukawa Shunro. He painted actors and theatrical scenes, illustrated from 1781 many of the small popular books, called Kibiyoshi, from their yellow colour, but was obliged to leave his master in 1786. According to Bing, he then went to Kano Yusen, whom likewise he was soon obliged to leave. In the years 1786–88 he employed the name Gummatei. From 1789, he himself composed many popular

[1] See the just, but in the main unfavourable, judgment of Binyon (p. 247).

[2] Edmond de Goncourt, *Hokousaï:* Paris, 1896, containing the artist's biography taken from the *Ukiyo-ye ruiko*, p. ix. ff., which, however, needs frequent correction; S. Bing, "La jeunesse de Hok'saï," *La Revue blanche*, x. 310 ff. (No. 68, 1 April 1896); wherein is related that Iijima Hanjuro printed in Japan his materials collected on Bing's commission, from which Hayashi made translations in Paris for Goncourt. Anderson Cat., pp. 350, 357 ff.; Fenollosa Cat., Nos. 358–388; Strange, p. 60 ff.; Brinckmann, pp. 241–272; Duret, *Critique d'avant-garde*, pp. 191–209; and elsewhere. The year of birth is taken from Revon. Fenollosa (*Outline*, p. 45) gives a good appreciation of the artist.

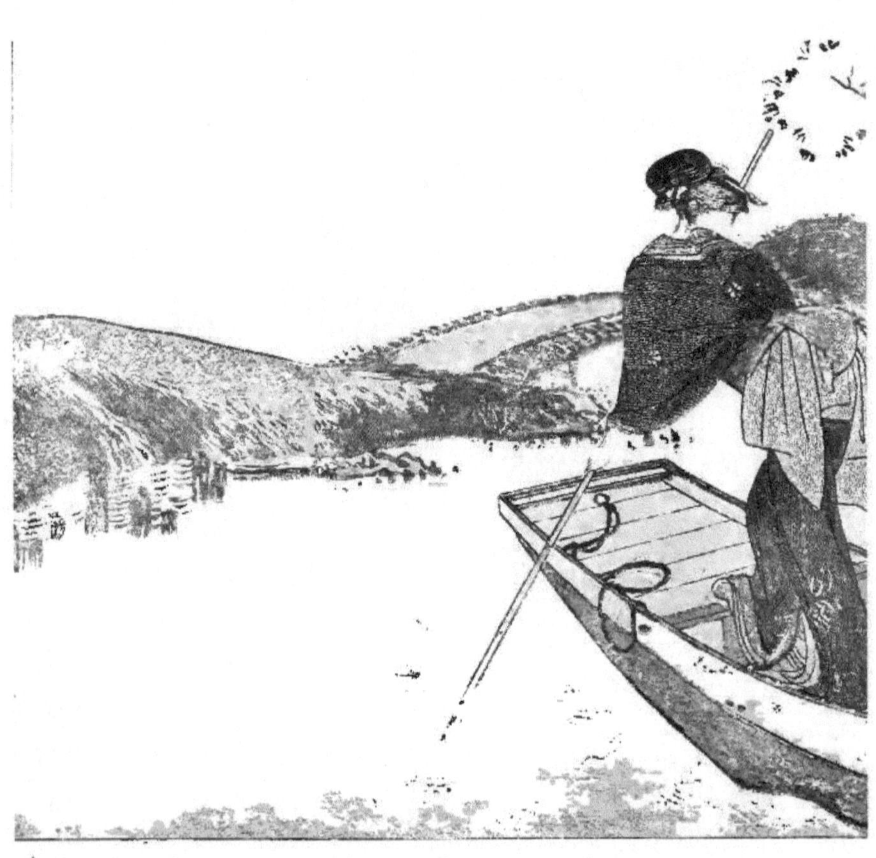

HÓKUSAI: THREE GIRLS BOATING AT THE SEASON OF CHERRY-BLOSSOM. *Green, grey, brown, and yellow.* Diptych. Medium size. About 1800.

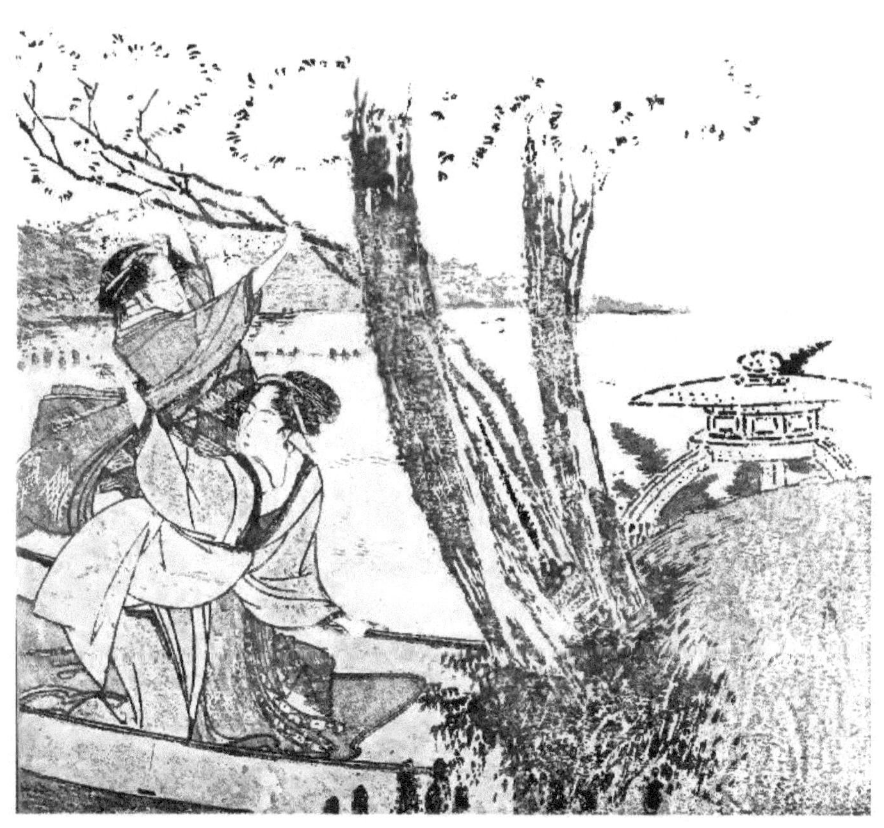

tales and novels, which he illustrated at the same time. He is also said to have been an adept at the popular forms of poetry. In 1792 he illustrated the story of the "Tongue-cut Sparrow," still signing himself Shunro, but not Katsukawa. In the following year he styles himself alternately Mugura (instead of Katsukawa) Shunro, Toshu formerly Shunro (as pupil of a certain Torin, according to Bing), Tokitaro Kako (in two books of about 1798–1801 (Duret, Nos. 287, 283) and on the "Eight Views of Lake Omi," which are represented by female figures), and Sori, as pupil of the painter Tawaraya Sori, whom he had succeeded about 1795; this name he later gave up to his pupil, Soji. He signed himself Tawaraya Sori, Hiakurin Sori, and Hokusai Sori (Tokio Catalogue, p. 101), and under this name published a book in 1803 (Hayashi Catalogue, No. 1771), and a series of fine landscapes in large oblong *format*.[1] His publisher at that time was Yeirakuya Toshiro, of Nagoya, who had a branch establishment in Yedo. Before the end of the century he had already used the name Tokimasa Taito (not Tatsumasa Raito, as Anderson states in his Catalogue), which he assumed again later on, as is proved by a *Santei gwafu* of 1816 and the *Hokusai gwashiki* of 1818.[2] In the year 1797 he illustrated books together with Yeishi, Shigemasa, and others; in 1798 he brought out with them and Utamaro a work: *Dantoka* (?) "Dancing Songs for Men." In the s e year is dated the foreword to the work *Onna niobo*

菱 Hishi-
川 kawa
宗 So-
理 ri

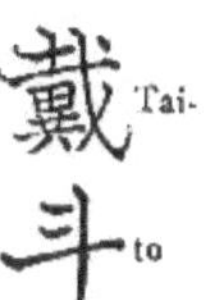

[1] Fenollosa Cat., No. 359, cites a certain *Hishikawa Sori*, but leaves it doubtful whether this be, as Fenollosa inclines to believe, a distinct painter or only one of the many metamorphoses of Hokusai. Of this Hishikawa Sori there survive some very delicately conceived and beautifully coloured illustrations of Poems on Artisans, 30 sheets, small folio. As the prints signed Sori are as fine as any of Hokusai's work, there seems no need for denying them to him, as the Hayashi Cat. does (No. 1205).

[2] A certain Katsushika Taito, several of whose prints are mentioned by the Hayashi Cat. (No. 1240 *seqq.*), and who is the author of an illustrated work: *Flowers and Birds*, that appeared in two volumes at Osaka, 1848–49 (*ibid.*, No. 1785), was probably a late pupil of Hokusai (but see also under Shigenobu).

sanjiurokkasen, the Thirty-six Poetesses, printed in 1801, for which Hokusai designed the title and Yeishi the other sheets. Here he already uses the name *Hokusai*, which he is supposed to have taken as a token of his great reverence for the god Hokushin Mioken, and which first occurs in 1790 in the *Mitate shushingura*; Anderson's Catalogue, however, traces this name back to his "northern studio," as the artist presumably designated his dwelling from its situation. He generally called himself Katsushika Hokusai, from the precinct of that name, in which he grew up; from 1800 he often signed himself Gwakiojin Hokusai, meaning "Hokusai Dote-on-drawing." After having, about 1820, given up his surname Taito to his son-in-law, Shigenobu (or a pupil by name of Kameya Kisaburo), he often signed himself Iitsu (which read in Japanese is sounded like Tamekazu).

I- 為
itsu 一

During his activity in the last two decades of the eighteenth century, Hokusai underwent the influence of the most diverse masters. Under the influence of Shunsho he produced, as early as the latter seventies, a succession of actor pictures; then he imitated the warriors of Shunyei and the landscapes of Toyoharu; Shigemasa, too, had some effect upon him. Bing, however, emphasises especially the influence of Kiyonaga, the greatest master of that period; in the style of Kiyonaga he executed a picture of Kintoki embracing a bear while an eagle is perched on his shoulder, as well as a triptych with scenes from the history of the Ronin. His representations of wrestlers date from the beginning of the tenth decade. He early learned from Shiba Gokan the rules of perspective, which he occasionally, but not always, applied; a series of twelve landscapes, 1796, already bear a horizontal signature in the European manner; a contemporaneous set of eight views of Lake Biwa likewise shows European influence. Besides his numerous book-illustrations, he produced, toward the end of the century, four sets of the Stations of the

R. WAGNER, BERLIN

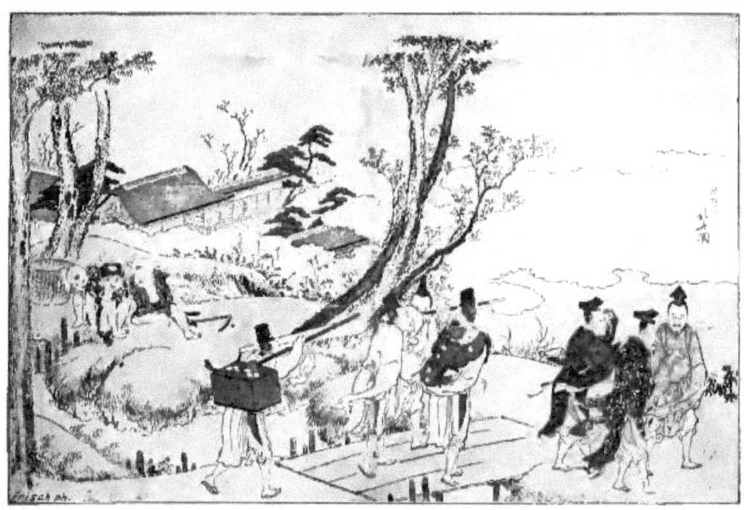

HÓKUSAI: A TRAVELLING COMPANY. Among them a little prince, carried on the back of one of the men. In the foreground an arist cratic house. From the "Onno Sanju rokkasen" of 1798. Signed: Gwakiyojin Hókusai (Hókusai Dote-on-drawing). Diptych.

ROYAL PRINT ROOM, DRESDEN

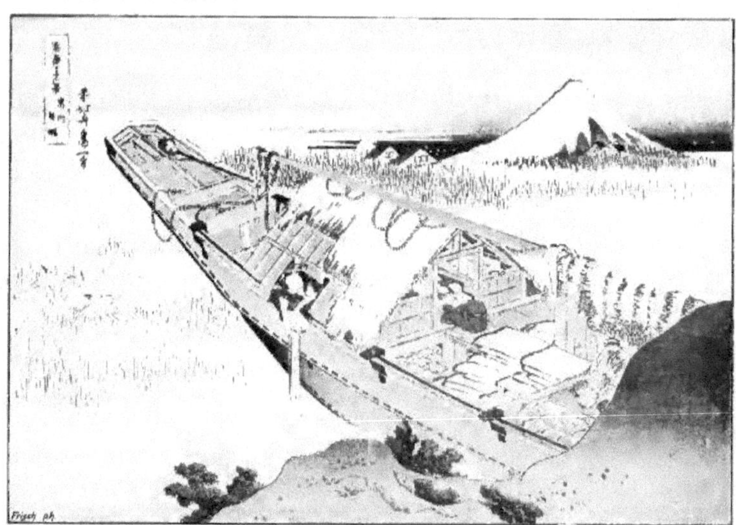

HÓKUSAI: A BOAT LADEN WITH MATS AND MELONS. View of Fuji from Ushibori, in the Hitache province. From the "Thirty-six Views of Fujiyama." Diptych.

Tokaido, followed by a fifth in 1801; the finest of these is that in the form of small oblong surimonos, no less beautiful an upright one produced at the same time: further, several series treating of the history of the Ronin, one in lateral form, 1798 (illustrated in Strange, p. 64); a second series of eleven sheets in lateral form, also two series, each of twelve sheets, in vertical form. The beautiful large oblong sheet, the Ferry-Boat, is placed by Fenollosa (No. 363) about the year 1798, when Utamaro's influence on him was very noticeable, especially as regards the extreme slenderness of the figures. But he was distinguished favourably from his contemporaries by a healthy breadth of treatment, which he afterwards lost.

The period of his prime was that about 1800. He had mastered perfectly both landscape and figure drawing; his slender, elegant figures move with consummate grace and ease in idyllic spots about the banks of Yedo's many streams, at all seasons and times of day; his colouring is serious, simple, and almost sombre, with a predominance of dark green, dark violet or blue, yellow and grey, similar to Yeishi. The year 1800 was for him particularly fruitful in surimonos, the first of which he had executed about 1793 under the name Mugura Shunro; his output in this field went on increasing until about 1804. Besides the two small volumes *Itakobushi*, or *Chorui zekku*, love-songs, of 1801, and the *Yehon Chushingura*, the history of the Ronin, of 1802, in two volumes, this period witnessed the production of those series of views of Yedo which brought him fully into popular favour: the *Yehon Azuma asobi* of 1799 (in colours, 1802), the *Toto meisho ichiran* of 1800 (in the second edition of the same year *Toto shokei ichiran*), and the *Sumidagawa riogan ichiran* of 1804. At this time also he drew the unusually broad sheet which shows the two banks of the Sumida as seen from one of the connecting bridges. In 1804 there further appeared one of his most beautiful works: the three-volume

Yama mata yama, "Mountains and yet again Mountains," views taken from Yedo bay.

From 1805 to 1817 he devoted himself chiefly to the illustration of novels, especially those of his friend Bakin, with whom he had a disagreement later. The year 1807 was particularly fertile in this respect; during it appeared the first instalment, comprising ten volumes, of the ninety-volume *Shimpen Suikogwaden*, or New Illustrated *Suiko Den*, tales of robbers, the text of which was written at first by Bakin and afterwards (for the last eighty volumes) by Ranzan. Hokusai resumed his activity as an illustrator toward the close of his life, from 1845 onwards.

The chief turning-point in the life of Hokusai occurred in the year 1812, which saw the production of the first volume of his celebrated *Mangwa*, the "Fancy Sketches," followed in succeeding years by thirteen others. In these rapid sketches, which comprise the whole circle of daily life, of legend and of history, as well as of nature, executed with the greatest brilliancy, and exhibiting an extraordinary mastery of anatomy, Hokusai created a work which departed widely from all previous efforts of the Japanese, and pursued an aim similar to that of the art of Europe. An infinite abundance of observation is stored up in these sketches, but comparatively little has been done towards co-ordinating it. However much fresh suggestion they might offer to Europeans, the art of Japan, which seeks to progress only through strength and individuality of style, could draw from it but little inspiration. But the tireless ingenuity, the inexhaustible creative power, and the imperturbable good humour of the artist constantly arouses our admiration anew. Madsen, page 117, cites as a characteristic example the dancer in the third volume of the *Mangwa*, who is presented in thirty different postures without his head once becoming visible.[1] In the first

[1] For a detailed description of the contents of the fourteen volumes, see Brinckmann, p. 244 ff.

VEVER COLLECTION, PARIS

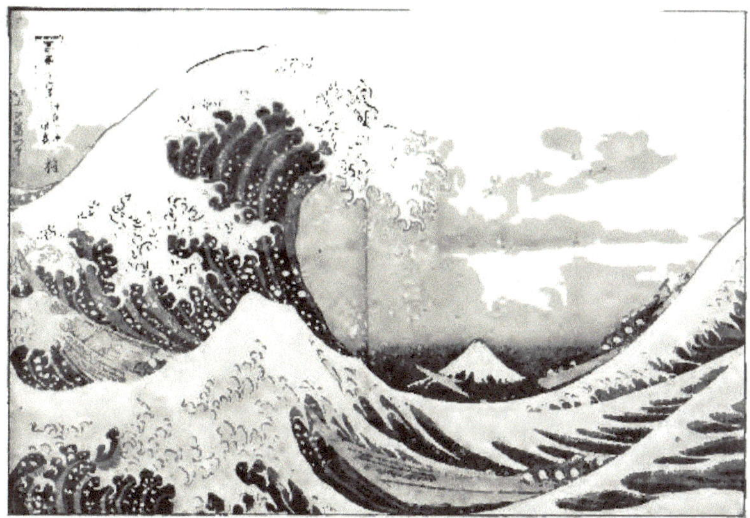

HOKUSAI: THE WAVE. From the "Thirty-six Views of Fuji." Diptych.

KOECHLIN COLLECTION, PARIS

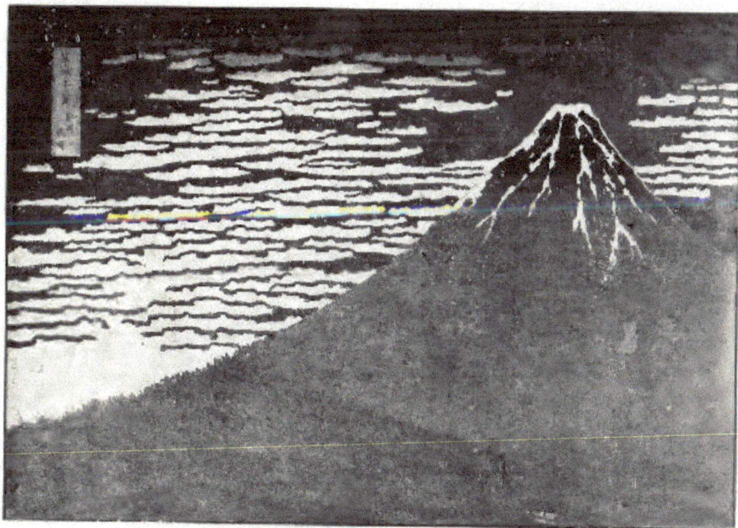

HOKUSAI: FUJI IN FINE WEATHER FROM THE SOUTH. The red mountain, with its snow-capped peak, melts gradually into the green of the lower part. The blue sky, against which the white clouds are relieved, is darkest at the top. From the "Thirty-six Views of Fuji." Diptych.

edition these sheets, toned in black, grey, and light red, are of extraordinary sharpness; there are said to be also some pulls in black or in red only.

With this work Hokusai began the series of publications that relate to instruction in drawing; it is probable, therefore, that about this time he attained a special reputation as a teacher; until the year 1823 there followed in quick succession various works of this class. In the year 1812 itself there appeared the first volume of the *Riakugwa hayashinan*, "Rapid Lessons in Abbreviated Drawing," which was followed in 1814 by the second; a third appeared undated. In the first all objects are reproduced by segments of circles, and also partly by squares; in the second Hokusai depicts himself holding brushes in both hands, in his mouth, and with both feet (illustrated by Goncourt in the *Gazette des Beaux-Arts*, pér. iii. t. xiv. [1895], p. 441); in the third the drawings are brought into the form of idiographs. In 1813 appeared his studies of nature, *Shashin gwafu*, fifteen polychrome sheets of various content, coloured, of medium lateral *format*, usually collected in two albums, one of his best works (illustrated in Perzynski, No. 20).[1] From 1816 dates the *Santai gwafu*, the album of the three different kinds of drawing (in the strong, the withered, and the dead style), signed Taito, in two colours, medium size. From 1817–19 there appeared in two volumes the *Yehon hayabiki*, "Rapid Review of the Art of Drawing," on every sheet some fifty or sixty human figures in outline, the heads generally indicated only by an oval, to prove that a face can be drawn without features. In 1813, the *Hokusai gwakio*, "the Mirror of Hokusai's Drawings," large (in the second edition called *Denshin gwakio*), with the *Shashin gwafu* of 1814, the principal work of this kind. 1818, *Hokusai gwashiki*, "Hokusai's

[1] Described by Goncourt, p. 136 ff. Siebold is said to have brought back four copies now to be found in the libraries of Paris, Vienna, and the Hague, and in the Gonse Collection.

Method of Drawing," signed Taito, published with the assistance of his pupils. In this work Hirata, the author of the text, remarks: "Hokusai is incomparable. While all his predecessors were more or less the slaves of classical traditions and acquired rules, he alone emancipated his brush from all such fetters, and drew according to the dictates of his heart. Whatever it be that his eyes, devoted to nature, absorb into themselves, he works it out with severity and precision." 1820, *Hokusai sogwa* "Rough Drawings," Yedo, in black and white. Lastly, 1823, the *Ippitsu gwafu*, sketches with a single stroke of the brush, slight colouring, medium size. He also produced a series of extremely vivacious caricatures, in a small oblong *format*, which are printed in two different greys and a flesh tint, and therefore probably belong to the same period as the *Hundred Views of Fuji*. His deep blue prints are especially delicate. In 1848 there appeared the *Yehon Saishikitsui*, a treatise on colouring, in two volumes; Hokusai promised a third, but was not able to finish it.

To the time of his chief activity as a teacher probably belong his gigantic paintings, which he was in the habit of executing to astonish his admirers. In the celebrated epilogue to the first volume of his *Hundred Views of Fuji*, 1834, he speaks of his own artistic development, saying that as early as his sixth year he felt the impulse to draw the forms of things; when he was about fifty years old he had already published innumerable sketches, but was dissatisfied with all that he produced before his seventieth year (1830). It was not until the age of seventy-three that he began to comprehend approximately the true form and nature of birds, fishes, and plants; consequently he hoped to make great progress after the age of eighty, and at the age of ninety to penetrate into the essential being of all things. Then with one hundred years he would surely attain to a higher and indescribable state, and when he should have reached the age of one hundred and

HÓKUSAI

ONE OF THE SMALL FLOWER SET

BRITISH MUSEUM

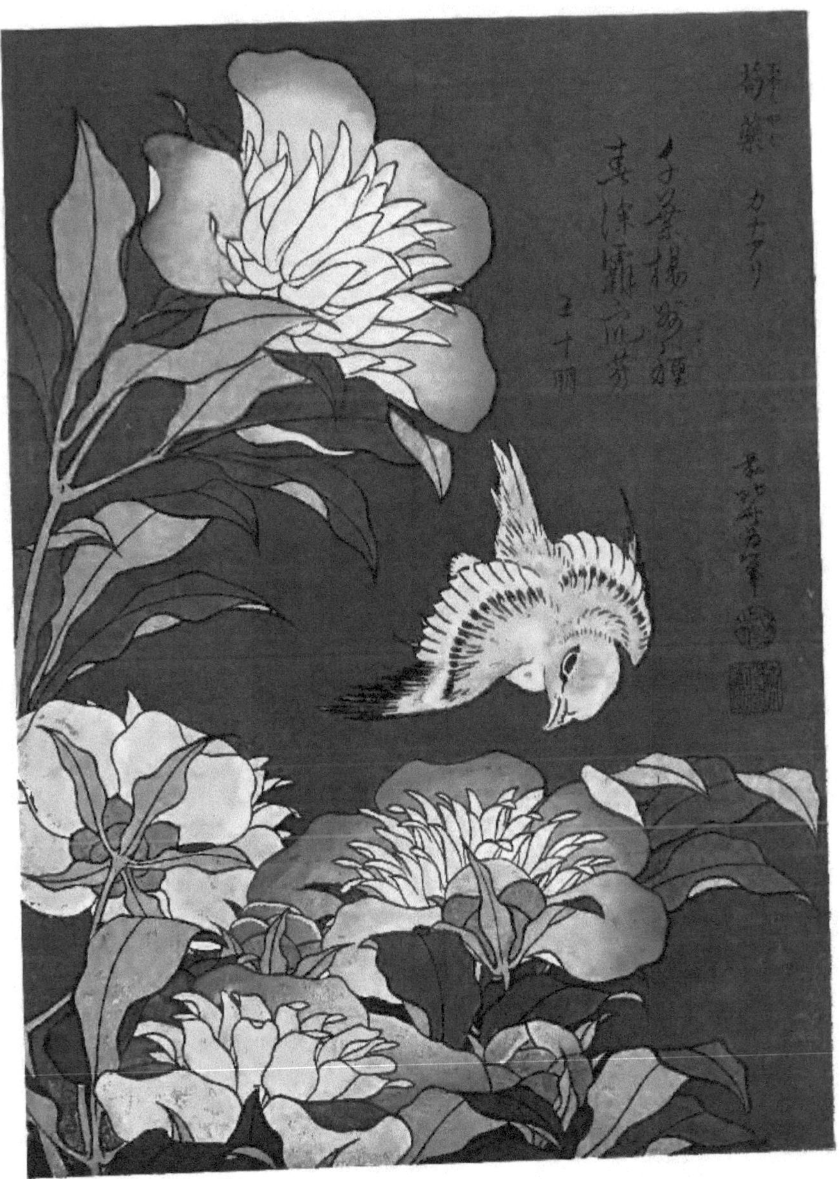
カナアリ

ten, everything, every dot and every line, would be alive.[1] From his eightieth year he signed his age on his paintings. About 1820 he had already trained a considerable number of pupils, many of whom made a name for themselves, and, like Gakutei and Hokkei, reacted in turn upon their master's style; a proof of this may be found in the surimonos, the production of which he resumed about that time, and which he rendered particularly rich and varied by employing innumerable metallic pigments.

As Hokusai—although without ever reaching his great predecessors in style—developed further that sense for natural life in the plant and animal world which had already begun in the last quarter of the eighteenth century and was cultivated more especially by Utamaro, so he also gave proof of his susceptibility to the tendencies of the times in the numerous landscapes which he produced, more especially since the twenties. Together with Hiroshige and Kunisada he forms the artistic constellation which proclaims the revival at this time of a feeling for nature and represents a last characteristic uplift in Japanese art. After the landscape with the hundred bridges, a very large sheet of 1823, there appeared until 1829 the celebrated *Thirty-six Views of Fuji*, the volcano, 3729 metres high, which lies to the west of Yedo, and which may be regarded as a landmark of the country. In this set, which was printed mainly in blue, green, and brown, and gradually increased to forty-six sheets, of medium size and oblong form, he exhibited the mighty mountain now near, now afar, in the reflection of varying hours and seasons. The ever-changing foreground, which differs in each print, in itself awakens our interest; but though sometimes the mountain appears only as a vanishing point, yet it is always indispensable to the total impression.[2]

[1] Brinckmann, p. 203.

[2] See the description of the single sheets, Goncourt, p. 162 ff. Fenollosa (No. 382) mentions the picture with the Boat as perhaps the most original and impressive. Colour-reproductions in Perzynski (pp. 16, 64, 80), black and white, *ibid.* (Nos. 52–61); see also *ibid.*, p. 77, *seqq.*

About 1827 appeared the waterfalls, *Shokoku takimeguri*, eight sheets, vertical, and 1827–30, the bridges, *Shokoku meiko kiran*, eleven sheets, oblong, similar in execution to the thirty-six views of Fuji. Lastly, in 1834–35, he published his *Hundred Views of Fuji*, the smaller work printed in black and white (in the second edition a light blue tone is added), which, while it is inferior in creative power to the thirty-six views produced ten years earlier, contributed by its amazing wealth of invention almost as much to the popularity of the master as did the *Mangwa*.[1] He also executed some landscapes in the "Dutch" (European) taste.

Toward the close of the twenties he returned with fresh vigour to book-illustration. We have of this time an excellently printed erotic work: *Kinoye no Komatsu*, the Young Pines, in three medium-sized volumes; then the *Yehin teikinorai*, Illustrated Correspondence about the Family Garden, an educational system, in three medium-sized volumes, one of his most beautiful works, 1828; further, the five thrilling sheets of apparitions, entitled *Hiaku monogatari*, the Hundred Tales, of 1830; of about the same time, the ten large sheets, *Shika shashinkio*, Pictures of Poets, excellent and very rare (Goncourt, p. 185 ff.); five sheets of animals, signed Hokusai Iitsu (Goncourt, p. 188), the ten large flower pictures, in oblong form, excellent in style (Goncourt, p. 190), ten somewhat smaller sheets with flowers; further the cock, hen, and chickens, one of the largest known colour-prints, 45 cm. in height and 60 cm. in breadth (in Bing's Coll.), and in similar style the No-dance (Vever Coll.), 40 cm. by 51 cm., and the kakemono with the pyramidally arranged street-dancers (in the same collection).

In his best style is his *Toshisen Yehon* of 1833 (and 1836), the illustrated poems of the Tang period, in black and white; from 1835 dates the *Yehon Kokio*, Filial Love, two medium-sized

[1] Madsen, p. 129 ff.; Brinckmann, p. 258 ff.; Goncourt, p. 208 ff.

Vever Collection, Paris

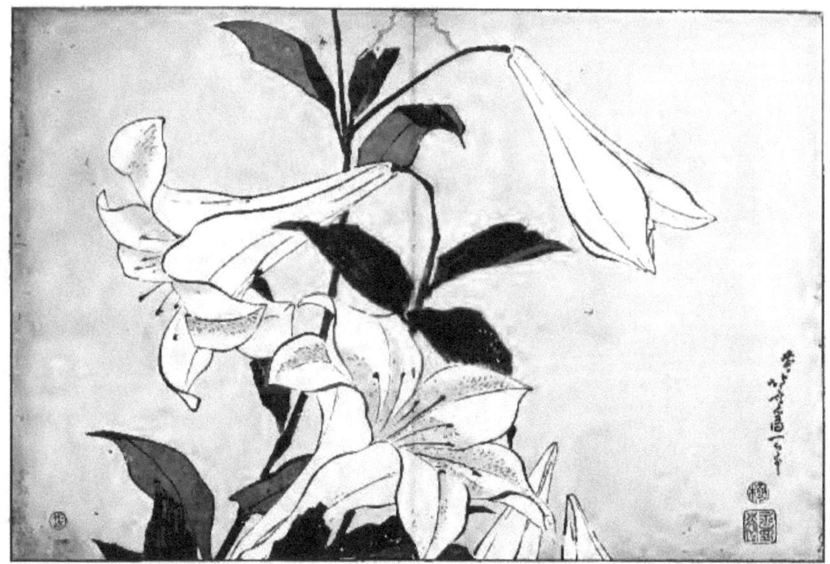

HOKUSAI: Lilies. *Bluish ground.* Medium size.

Vever Collection, Paris

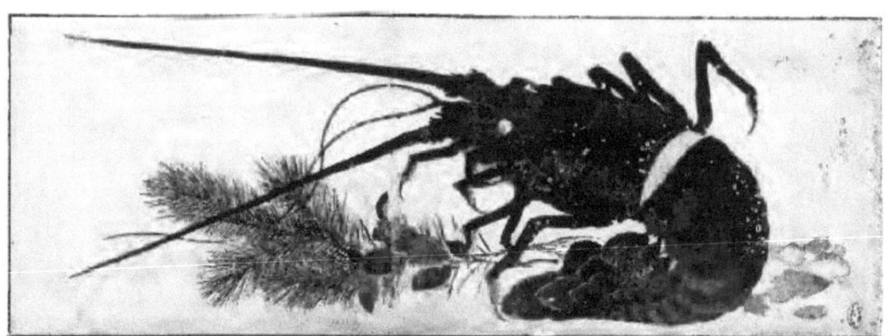

HOKUSAI: Lobster and Pine-branch. Large.

volumes, in which is also the well-known large signature which Brinckmann (p. 199) reproduces; to show his extraordinary versatility it suffices to point to his models for combs and pipes, *Imayo Shikken hinagata*, of 1822–23, the 10,000 drawings for industrial workers, *Banshoku zuka*, 1835, five volumes, tinted, signed Taito (*cf.* Brinckmann, p. 266 ff.), and the architectural drawings, *Shin hinagata*, of 1836.

Of the three daughters of the artist, the youngest (Oyei?) became a very clever painter; she married a certain Minamizawa, but was later divorced. Another of his daughters, Oteru (Omiyo?), married his pupil, Yanagawa Shigenobu. Their son caused his grandfather much anxiety, forcing the old artist, in order to escape his grandson's creditors, to live during the years 1834–39 in the little village of Uraga, in the province of Sagami; indeed, he was probably the cause of Hokusai's restless manner of life—it is said that the artist never spent more than one or two months in any one place. When, in 1839, a famine broke out, and as a last calamity Hokusai's house with all his drawings was burned down, the old man was obliged to live from the sale of albums that he drew. In the same year he brought out twenty-seven of the projected hundred sheets of the *Hiakkuninisshu ubagayetoki*, one hundred Poems explained for Nurses (Goncourt, p. 238 ff.); to these succeeded a series of three sheets, snow, moon, and flowers. In this last period of his life, he repeatedly collaborated with Toyokuni II. (Kunisada), Kuniyoshi, his son-in-law Shigenobu, and Yeisen, in illustrating books. In 1843 appeared his small *Mangwa*.

In 1849 the master died, at the age of ninety years. A list of his paintings and drawings is given by Goncourt, pages 269–332. No other artist has so often changed his name as Hokusai; Gonse, i. 275, mentions nine different signatures. The number of pupils trained by him is very large; the most prominent of them we shall mention later. A likeness of

Hokusai may be found in Kuniyoshi's *Tatsugawa*, the hundred celebrated poets (reproduced in Burty's Catalogue, p. 130). A portrait of him in his eightieth year, by his daughter Oyei, is reproduced by Goncourt in colours at the beginning of his book. We find reproductions of his works in Gonse, i. 94, 95 (landscapes of about 1790), i. 274, and ii. 338 (of the year 1802), and in Anderson's *Japanese Wood-Engraving*, ill. 24 (interior view in perspective from a work of 1826), as well as in numerous other places. Fenollosa (*Outline*, pl. xvii.) reproduces one of his paintings.

After a thorough training in youth, Hokusai had risen, about the year 1800, to the first rank of artists; by his subsequent activity, which always exhibited great ability and imagination, and an effort to expand the sphere of representation, he retarded the inevitable decline of Japanese art for decades, but as he was lacking in culture and sterling personality, and remained fast-bound among externals, he was neither able to lead art back to its former height nor to create a new and great style.

In addition to the data previously given concerning his individual works, we may here add the following.

Single sheets :—

Actors, in yellow and a little pink, about 1778 (?).

Kintoki between a monkey and a dog that is carrying his trunk; early.

The same, with a bear and an eagle, black and white, medium size (Berlin Kunstgewerbemuseum).

A fisherman caught by a cuttle-fish, near by a youth laughing.

Representations of wrestlers, about 1793.

Triptych with scenes from the story of the Ronins; under the influence of Kiyonaga.

A boat with the gods of fortune fishing; dating from the nineties.

Kintoki embracing a bear, with an eagle perched on his shoulder, signed Shunro; under the influence of Kiyonaga.

Dakki, the mistress of a Chinese tyrant, looking out from a window at a hangman holding up a child.

The sun-goddess in her cave.

View of the two banks of the Sumida, seen from a bridge; very broad sheet, about 1800.

The Landscape with the 100 Bridges; very large.

Fujiyama across the water. 1802, unsigned.

The Fifty-three Stations of the Tokaido as a Sugoroku-game; large.

Surveyor at work, 1848; large oblong.

Representations of animals: eagle on perch beside a cherry-branch in blossom; two storks on a pine-branch under snow; two carp swimming up a waterfall; horses grazing; tortoises at the bottom of the sea.

Series:—

The six Tamagawa; somewhat brutal.

The same, with medallions.

3 sheets, evening landscapes with women promenading; small.

Shika Shashinkio, poems, 10 large sheets, with excellent landscapes and figures.

The Liukiu Islands, 8 sheets.

27 (?) sheets, the Hundred Poems; oblong, signed Hokusai Manji.

Surimonos:—

A young merchant, 1793; on the back the programme of a summer concert.

The Twelve Months typified by female figures.

The Childhood of Characters in History.

Large size: lobster and pine-branch, 1802; another without the branch; tea-house by the river, 1804; plum-branch in blossom, 1806; sempstresses, 1809; series of five sheets of shells, signed Gechi Rojin Jitsu.

Book-illustrations:—

Yellow books (kibiyoshi), size 17 by 12½ cm., from 1780 to 1811 (see Goncourt, page 347 ff.). Among them the story of the Tongue-cut Sparrow, 1792, and the Paths of Riches and Poverty, 1793.

His earliest work was the Meguron o hiaku zuka (Yedo, 1780), 2 vols., with twenty pictures.

Yehon onaga mochi, the Box of Various Contents. Yedo, 1784.

Mitate chushingura, Contemporaries compared with the Forty-seven Ronin. 1790. Signed Hokusai.

Aa shinkiro, 1804 (men with shells in place of heads).

Onna niobo sanjiurokkasen, the Thirty-six Poetesses, 1801; with a preface of 1797. The first page is by him, the rest is by Yeishi.

Yehon Azuma asobi, the Promenade of the East (that is, in Yedo, the capital of the East); large. 1799, black and white in one vol.; 1802, coloured in three vols. Not so good as the following. Illustrated in Gonse, i. p. 274; ii. p. 338; Strange, p. 66.

Toto meisho ichiran, Views of Yedo, 2 vols.; large. 1800. Very various in style, with a number of small figures in the landscape. In the second edition of same year called Toto shokei ichiran.

Sumidagawa riogan ichiran, View of the two Banks of the Sumida, 3 vols.; large. 1804. Beginning with spring and ending with winter (reproduction in Strange, pl. vii.).

Later editions of all three above-mentioned works, 1815, with the addition of a blue tone; also still good.

Yehon chushingura, History of the Ronin, 2 vols.; medium size. 1802.

Shimpen suikogwaden, New illustrated Suiko den, in nine sets of ten vols. The first, 1807, with text by Bakin; the others with text by Ranzan; second set, 1829; the third and remaining ones not until later. Every volume contains some three double sheets.

Mangwa: I., 1812; II., 1814; III., 1815; IV. (especially mythological) and V., 1816; VI. (gymnastic, &c.) and VII. (landscapes, &c.), 1817; VIII., 1818; IX. and X., 1819; XI. and XII., 1834; XIII., 1849; XIV., 1875; XV., 1879. Reprints 1844–1848, and 1875. According to Duret, Hokusai was assisted in the completion of the ninth volume by his pupils Bokusen, Hokun, Hokkei, Hokusen, Utamasa. The first edition of the twelfth volume is printed in black and white, without the flesh-tint block. For the contents of the volumes, see Perzynski (p. 59 *seqq.*). Ill. *ibid.* (Nos. 11–17).

Dochu gwafu, the Tokaido, in 2 vols.; medium size. 1836. New impression in 1881.

In the Kwacho gaden are very fine representations of animals, which are among his best work of the kind (illustrated in Perzynski, Nos. 37–42).

The Hundred Tales (see Perzynski, p. 84 *seqq.*; ill. *ibid.*, Nos. 67–70).

The blocks of the Yehon Toshisen gogon zekku, 110 pictures, were not discovered until 1880 and were then printed at Tokio in 2 vols. (Gillot Catalogue).

The Hundred Views of Fuji: first ed. with falcon's feather on cover; vol. i., 1834; vol. ii., 1835; vol. iii., unknown in this edition. Printed in black and white. Second edition soon after, with overprint of a bluish tone. Reprint of 1880, much darker than first edition. Illustrated in Perzynski (Nos. 73–86; see *ibid.*, p. 87 *seqq.*).

About twenty artists are specified as Hokusai's pupils. We mention here the following:—

Teisai Hokuba worked during the first three decades of the nineteenth century, and therefore ranks along with Hokkei as the oldest of these pupils.[1] Fenollosa mentions a painting by him which he places about the year 1800. Of his illustrated works, the following are mentioned:—

北 Hoku-
馬 ba

Toshitsu yogen kwairoku, Lights and Shadows of the Night's Constellations, 28 vols., 8vo, black and white. 1809.

Denka chawa, 5 vols. 1829.

In his later years, from about 1830 onwards, he followed the style of Kunisada and of Hiroshige, and finally attached himself to Kuniyoshi. According to the Tokio Catalogue (p. 108) he did not adopt the name Teisai until about 1830. He produced good surimonos. Reproduction of a spirited composition in Strange, page 74.

Uwoya Hokkei, Hokusai's best pupil, was born in 1780 and

北 Hoku-
溪 kei

[1] Anderson Cat., p. 367; Burty Cat., No. 671 ff.; Fenollosa Cat., No. 391; Strange, p. 73.

M

died in the period of Ansei (1854–59).[1] Before he came to Hokusai, he is supposed to have studied under Kano Yeisen. According to the Hayashi Catalogue (No. 1229) he also signed himself Todoya, Kiosai, Kiyen, &c. He excelled in his surimonos, one of which is illustrated by Fenollosa (*Outline*, pl. xix.). Of his illustrated books the best known is the

Mangwa (1814) 2 vols., 8vo.

Besides this the following are mentioned:—

Fujin gwazoshu, Japanese Poetesses, 8vo, black and white. 1806.
Sinsen kioka gojunin isshu, Fifty Poets, 8vo, black and white. 1819.
Kioka foso meisho zuye, Celebrated Places, 3 vols., 8vo, coloured. 1824.
Suiko Den, 108 Heroes, 8vo, coloured. 1828.
Hokuri junitoki (Yedo, about 1820), Views of the Yoshiwara, black and white.
Shokoku meisho, Celebrated Places.
Yoshiwara junitoki, the Twelve Hours of the Yoshiwara.
Hokkei zuko, sketches, 2 vols., 8vo, in 3 tones.
Poems to the Moon, 8vo, black and white.
Haikai hiakkachu, 100 hokku (poems of seventeen syllables), and portraits of poets, 8vo, black and white. 1848.
One of his most important prints is the large suspension-bridge in the snow.

Among his pupils were, besides Gakutei, Keiju (Hayashi Catalogue, No. 1252) and Keise (*ibid.*, No. 1253).

Gaku- 岳
tei 亭

Gakutei, who worked in the first third of the nineteenth century, is supposed to have been originally an author, then to have studied with Shunsho, and later with Hokusai (or according to the Hayashi Catalogue, No. 1249, with Hokkei).[2] He also was celebrated for his surimonos, as *e.g.* the series of

[1] Anderson Cat., p. 367; Cat. Burty, No. 675 ff.; Goncourt, *Hokousaï*, p. 339; Fenollosa Cat., No. 389.
[2] Anderson Cat., p. 343; Strange, pp. 32, 74; Goncourt, *Hokousaï*, p. 341.

the Seven Gods of Fortune represented by beautiful women in gorgeous robes. Gonse, i. 144, gives a reproduction from him of the year 1822. Of his works may be mentioned :—

Ichiro gwafu, drawings of an old man. Yedo, 1823.
The thirty-six poets, double sheets, 1826.
Riakugwa shokunin zukushi, the craftsmen, 46 sheets, 8vo.
Illustrations of poems, mostly landscapes, 11 double sheets.
Landscapes, 40 sheets, 8vo ; not very good.
Dancing girls in the light of a red lamp; a series of five small sheets (Gillot Catalogue).
The Ko-Shoguns, five surimonos (Hamburg).

Yanagawa Shigenobu, 1787–1842, married Hokusai's daughter Omiyo, who later obtained a divorce from him ; after this he imitated Kunisada's style.[1] From his father-in-law he had received, about 1820, the name Taito. Of his works the following may be named :—

Satomi Hakken den, illustrated in collaboration with Sadahide and Keisai Yeisen.
Yanagawa gwacho, album with various representations, in black and red, 8vo. Owari, 1821.
Yanagawa gwafu, the same, 1821.
Landscapes, 20 double sheets, 8vo ; not very good.
Kioka meisho zuye, 1826, tinted.
Sansui gwajo, 1835, landscapes.

Yanagawa Shigeyama was his pupil ; he produced the *Yehon Fujibakama*, famous women, Yedo, 1823 ; new edition 1836, 2 vols.

Katsushika Isai counts among the later pupils of the master.[2] Of his work may be mentioned :—

Kwannonkio riakuzukai, a Buddhist tract. 1851.
Nichiren Shonin ichidaizuye, the life of Nichiren, 6 vols. 1858.

---

[1] Anderson Cat., p. 368 ; Goncourt, *Hokousaï*, p. 344 ; Cat. Burty, No. 687.
[2] Anderson Cat., p. 370; Cat. Burty, No. 726 f. ; Duret, No. 417.

Isai gwashiki, sketches, 2 vols., black and white. 1864.
Kwachosansui zushiki, 5 vols., small oblong, black and white. 1865-68.
Mangwa hayabiki, four series. 1867.

Shotei Hokuju published a drawing-book, *Hokuju gwafu*, also landscapes in European style, which are much sought after; they are remarkable for their indigo-blue with pine-green and manganese violet and for their masses of light cloud, and mostly represent views of rivers. Duret (No. 384) mentions a book of 1813. Fenollosa assigns a print of his to about 1835.[1]

Hokuun, at first an architect, brought out a *Mangwa*, 8vo, in black and white, which is closely akin to Hokusai.[2] The Hayashi Catalogue (No. 1775) mentions a book by him, *Nagoya*, of about 1818.

Shofu Kiosai, the youngest of Hokusai's pupils, born in 1831, imitated his master with faithfulness and spirit. By him are:—

Kiosai gwafu, sketches, about 1860.
Yehon takakagami, 5 vols., about 1870.
Mangwa, 1881 (from which Brinckmann reproduces an illustration p. 214).

Other pupils of Hokusai are as follows: Rinsai Soji (Hayashi Catalogue, No. 1214). Isai Hokutai (*ibid.*, No. 1235), a book of 1803 by him: Yedo. Hotei Gosa Hokuga (*ibid.*, No. 1238), a book of 1820 by him: Yedo. Katsushika Hokuga, surimonos. Taigaku (*ibid.*, No. 1244). Hokute Joren, about 1840 (*ibid.*, No. 1245). Yanagawa Shigeyama, a book of 1823 by him (Duret, No. 390). Hokusu, a book of 1808 by him: Yedo (Hayashi Catalogue, No. 1773).

[1] Anderson Cat., p. 367; Goncourt, *Hokousaï*, p. 343; Fenollosa Cat., No. 390.
[2] Anderson Cat., p. 367; Goncourt, *Hokousaï*, p. 343; Burty Cat., No. 688.

CHAPTER IX

THE REMAINING ARTISTS OF THE NINETEENTH CENTURY

1. Artists of the beginning of the century—2. Kunisada—3. Hiroshige

1. Artists of the Beginning of the Century.—While Hokusai, from the second decade on, held the field as sole ruler after Yeishi, Utamaro, and Toyokuni had retired from the scene, a small number of artists whose style was rooted in the eighteenth century were still at work. The first to be mentioned are the two pupils of Shunyei, Shunsen, and Shuntei, the last artists of the Katsukawa clan of painters, both of whom were active in the two first decades of the century.

Katsukawa Shunsen studied first with Torin, a master of the Chinese school; later with Shunyei.[1] According to the Hayashi Catalogue (No. 620) he was a pupil of Shunsho. Besides book-illustrations, we may mention as by him :—

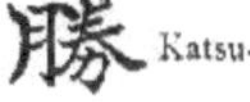

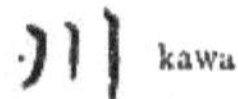

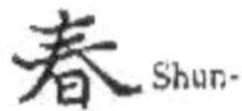

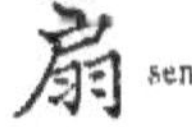

> A set of eight landscapes with figures in the foreground; rose and yellow predominate, the water indicated by blind printing.
> Shell-gathering at sunset.
> The banks of the Sumida in winter.

A reproduction in Strange p. 80.

Afterwards, under the name of Shunko II., he devoted himself exclusively to faïence painting.

There exists a book of Singing-Birds by Tsutsumi Torin, Toshimitsu and Rinsho, published in 1795 (Duret, No. 148).

[1] Anderson Cat., p. 364; Strange, p. 80; Cat. Bing, No. 289 f.

Other pupils of Torin were as follows: Sawa Sekkio (Hayashi Catalogue, No. 1007); Umpo (*ibid.*, No. 1011); Riusai Masazumi (*ibid.*, No. 1015).

Katsu- 勝 kawa 川 Shun- 春 tei 亭

Katsukawa Shuntei produced, besides actor scenes and pictures of celebrated wrestlers, some very dramatic compositions from history and legend, mostly in grey, green, and yellow, but owing to ill-health his output was small; the early impressions of his works are especially rare.[1] According to the Hayashi Catalogue (No. 785) he was a pupil of Shunyei. He is to be looked upon as a forerunner of the historic school that arose about 1830. Of his works the following are cited:—

Kuraiyama homare no yokozuna, a tale. 1812.
Nanko seichu gwaden, the history of the faithful Kusunoki Masashige, 4 vols. 1815.
Itogoromo Tengu Baikai (?), a tale, 6 vols. About 1815.
Most celebrated in his two-volume work, the Game of the Young Prince.
The seven gods of fortune, surimonos.
The contest of a hero with a monstrous serpent (illustrated in Strange, page 38).

Shinsai, who is mentioned as an early pupil of Hokusai (about 1800–10), would be better classed with Shumman.[2] Eight views of Lake Omi in the "Dutch" style are by him; he also worked at surimonos; one with two crabs is reproduced by Gillot.

Bokusen, in Owari, was Hokusai's contemporary; in his house, in 1812, the plan for the *Mangwa* first originated; he himself, in 1815, brought out a similar collection of sketches, *Bokusen sogwa*, 8vo, in polychrome.[3] Duret mentions a peculiar book by him: *Kiyogwayan*, the Garden of Caricatures (Uagoya, 1815).

[1] Anderson Cat., p. 363; Strange, p. 38; Cat. Bing, No. 292 ff.
[2] Anderson Cat., p. 366; Goncourt, *Hokousaï*, p. 342; Cat. Bing, No. 329.
[3] Anderson Cat., p. 369.

The only real rival of Hokusai between 1810 and 1820 was Kikugawa Yeizan, whose real name was Giokusai Mangoro, a son of the painter Kano Yeiji, in Yedo.[1] At first he worked at making artificial flowers, then studied the style of Utamaro, later that of Hokusai, entered into friendly relations with Hokkei, and, lastly, imitated Kunisada.

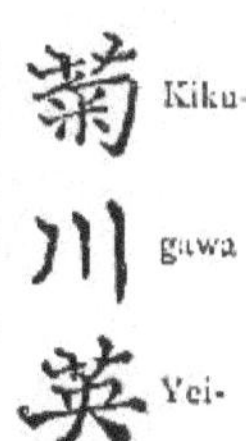

Of his works may be mentioned :—

A series of the twelve months.
Snow, moon, and flowers, 3 sheets.
Series of large figures in half length.

From the year 1829 he began to compose his own texts, which he then illustrated. Strange reproduces, at page 58, a woman with an umbrella. A pupil of his was Keisai Yeisen, of whom we shall speak later.

Closely related to Utamaro is also Shiko, a painter of the Ganku school; Strange, who is almost inclined to prefer him to Utamaro, reproduces a kakemono-ye by him at page 60.[2] Some of his prints remind one of Hokusai's best period.

Of other artists the following may be mentioned :—

Mori Shunkei, with his *Gwafu*, representations of flowers, birds, and insects in polychrome, after Chinese models, 1820 (Anderson Catalogue, p. 364).

Kawamura Bumpo, a pupil of Ganku. He began to illustrate books as early as 1800 (Duret, No. 468). *Bumpo Gwafu*, in the Chinese style, appeared at Kioto in 1813 (Gillot Catalogue). Books of reproductions after his work, containing landscapes and *genre* pictures, appeared in the years 1809–24 (Burty Catalogue, No. 136 ff.; Anderson Catalogue, p. 449).

Oishi Matora (1792–1833), a celebrated illustrator of *meishos* (books of travel). By him appeared caricatures in

[1] Anderson Cat., p. 363; Fenollosa Cat., No. 393; Strange, p. 57.
[2] Anderson Cat., p. 449; Strange, p. 58.

colour (Osaka, 1828, and 1833), 2 vols., 8vo (Burty Catalogue, No. 712).

Hasegawa Settan in Yedo also illustrated *meishos*, which appeared from 1832–39. The *Yedo meisho* of 1836, 20 vols., in black and white, is the finest of its kind (Anderson Catalogue, p. 364; Burty Catalogue, No. 438).

Other humorous illustrators of the school of Kioto are, according to Duret (Nos. 462–516): Kanyosai (Mokio), who lived from 1712–74 (see chap. iii., end). Kyaro, works by him of 1798 and 1799; Kuro (Kino Baitei) is the author of *Kuro Gwafu*, Kioto, 1797. Shimo Kawahe Jiusui followed Sukenobu's style; by him is *Kummo zuye*, an encyclopædic work in 21 vols. (Kioto, 1789).

To the nineteenth century belong: Nichosai (*Kotsijukai*, Osaka, 1802, 2 vols.). Sato Sui Saki (work of 1814). Kishi (*Aoi Sokiju*).

2. Kunisada.—Besides Hokusai and his school, the first halr of the nineteenth century was dominated by the school of Utagawa, which was called into being by Toyokuni. Its chief representative during the whole of this long period was Kunisada, who, perhaps even more than Hokusai himself, may be regarded as the typical master upon whose works was based the generally accepted European view of Japanese art. In his violently agitated figures, their big faces filled with exaggerated expression, in his variegated colouring, and his composition that is loth to leave the smallest corner unfilled, Europe thought to recognise the distinguishing characteristics of the art of Japan. It is true that, if we shut our eyes to all the clumsiness, crudeness, and exaggeration in his work, there still shine through it glimpses of the old grand style to which Hokusai had not been in equal measure unfaithful; but the falling-off is nevertheless so great that we can only call this new tendency, which entirely dominated Kunisada, the evidence of a rapid

and uncontrollable decay. Although some of these works may offer so much that is artistic that, comparing them with the other products of the nineteenth century, we may look up to them with admiration as models that in some respects we have not yet equalled, particularly in regard to decorative power and the keen observation of nature; yet from a Japanese standpoint, and measured by the works of the past, they are unable to engage our interest. Only the landscapes of Hiroshige, with whom this survey concludes, form an exception to this statement.

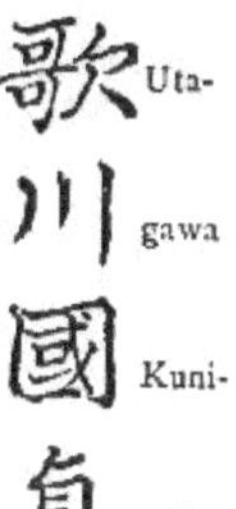

Utagawa Kunisada, often erroneously called simply Toyokuni, like his teacher, though he did not assume the surname Toyokuni II. until the last quarter of his long career, was born in 1787 in Bushu, but spent his life in Yedo.[1] In the beginning, from about 1805, he worked entirely in the style of his teacher Toyokuni. He is first supposed to have achieved celebrity by the likeness of a celebrated actor, and later he became one of the most fertile of actor painters. In collaboration with his master he represented the actor Ishikawa Hakuyen in his principal parts, in a series of some hundred and fifty sheets. In 1808 there appeared the first of his illustrated books. Afterwards, about the middle of the twenties, following the tendency of the times, he included landscape in the scope of his representations; not until about 1830 did he attain his full maturity, and thenceforward he ruled Japanese art side by side with Hokusai and Hiroshige. Duret (Nos. 195, 200) mentions illustrated books by him of the years 1828 to 1833. In collaboration with Hiroshige he illustrated the *Tokaido*. From the time of his assuming the surname Toyokuni II.—in the year 1844—his style became more careless and his colouring gayer and cruder. It is he who naturalised the discordant glaring colours usual in

[1] Anderson Cat., p. 366; Strange, pp. 50, 114; Fenollosa Cat., Nos. 394–400, 444–447; Cat. Burty, No. 233 ff., 262 ff.; Bing. Cat., No. 693 ff.

Japanese wood-engravings of our own times. His most celebrated work is the fifty-four folio sheets illustrating the novel *Genji Monogatari*, which in the year 1857 was followed by a smaller series on the same subject. He also, together with his younger classmate Kuniyoshi, illustrated the *Tokaido* and other works. He died in 1865, at the age of seventy-eight years. Fenollosa (*Outline*, pl. xviii.) reproduces a triptych by him.

Of his works the following are mentioned :—

Triptych : a young girl on the seashore (about 1806, according to Fenollosa, No. 394).

Pentaptych : the great Sumida bridge.

Series :—

The actor Icchosai in his chief comic parts, 48 sheets, fol.

Actor prints, above each an orchestra of five musicians, fol.

Actors in half length, 8vo.

The courtesans, 118 sheets, fol.

Genji Monogatari, at the top of every sheet a fan with various designs, 54 sheets, fol. 1828.

Azuma Genji, 54 pictures of women, with variants on Genji Monogatari, 8vo.

Miyomato Mansashi, ghost pictures and others, 124 sheets, fol.

Joso sanju rokukisen, occupations of women, fol.

Hana no sugatami, more than 60 theatrical scenes, 12mo, with the names of the different provinces where the scenes take place.

Anderson's Catalogue cites several works of the years 1827–32. Strange reproduces, at page 50, three of his sheets; Gonse, i. page 98, a surimono.

Kiku- 菊 chi 池 Yo- 容 sai 齋

Kunisada's contemporary, Kikuchi Yosai, also called Takiyasu, endeavoured, although he belonged to the naturalistic Shijo school, to arrest the decay of art by approaching to the old Tosa style.[1] Born in Kioto in 1787, he first studied under a

[1] Anderson Cat., p. 419; *idem.*, *Japanese Wood-Engraving*, p. 58; Strange, p. 102; Madsen, p. 137; Brinckmann, p. 211; Cat. Burty, No. 135.

Kano master and then turned to the Shijo school. His principal work is the *Zenken Kojitsu*, the illustrated biography of the great men of the past, a work of 20 vols., 8vo, with prints in black and white, which appeared in 1836; to this, three supplementary volumes were added. Some have been disposed to rank him even above Hokusai, whose vigour, however, in spite of all his good taste, he was not able to reach. Reproductions in Anderson, *Japanese Wood-Engraving*, fig. 29; Brinckmann, page 212 f. He died in 1878, at the age of ninety-one.

More unassuming, but at the same time of more ability and of greater significance for his time, was Keisai Yeisen, also called Ikada, Yeizan's best pupil. Born in 1792 in Yedo, the son of a Kano painter, he lived to see the last phase of the great evolution, and then from about 1820–40 developed an independent activity, particularly in the field of landscape, as well as in delicate and tasteful surimonos. In his landscapes he achieves a very clear effect with a few broad strokes of the brush (reproduction in Gonse, i. 296). He died in 1848.[1]

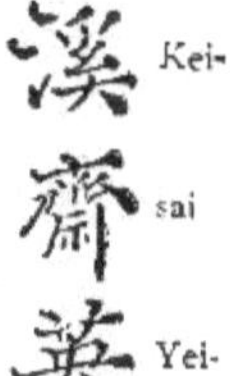

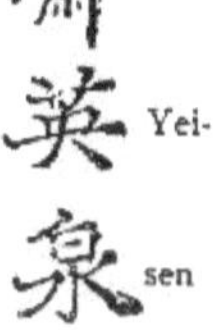

Of his single sheets the following may be cited:—

A temple in Yedo; large.
Laden cows led in the rain; large.
Snow landscape with pines; large.
A carp leaping up a waterfall; very large (according to Fenollosa, No. 410, about 1840).
A cat watching goldfish.
A series of waterfalls.
12 sheets, the history of the Ronin, obl. fol., his best work.

Anderson cites from him, among other works, the following:—

Jingi Andon, sketches, in collaboration with other artists, 5 vols. 8vo, about 1825.

---

[1] Anderson Cat., p. 365; Strange, pp. 76, 113; Madsen, p. 137; Fenollosa Cat., Nos. 405–411; Cat. Burty, No. 699; Bing Cat., No. 668 ff.

Nishikino Fukuro, sketches in style of Mangwa. 1829.
Keisai sogwa, 5 vols. 1832.
Keisai ukiyo gwafu, in collaboration with Hiroshige, 3 vols., about 1836, his principal work of the kind.

Uta- 歌 gawa 川 Kuni- 國 yoshi 芳

Kuniyasu and Kuniyoshi were, like Kunisada, pupils of Toyokuni. Kuniyasu (illustrated in Strange at page 54) died in 1840, aged thirty years. Utagawa Kuniyoshi, born at Yedo in the year 1800, began his activity about the middle of the second decade.[1] Following a path exactly parallel with Kunisada's, he nevertheless developed in the domain of landscape a strength and grandeur of style that gives him a place perhaps even higher than Hiroshige. He died in 1861, at the age of sixty-one.

The following are mentioned as his principal works:—

View of Lake Biwa with Fuji in the distance; dated by Fenollosa (Catalogue, No. 404) about 1840.
The priest Nichiren in the snow; signed Ichiyosai.
A series illustrating the history of the Ronin, 47 folio sheets, a celebrated work.
Tatsutagawa, the hundred famous poets; also celebrated.
Genji Monogatari, 54 sheets. 1844.
The stations of the Tokaido, with representations of legends referring to the places concerned, in collaboration with Kunisada, 70 sheets (?).
The rainbow: three people climbing a hill.
Japanese heroes, over 50 sheets.
Views of the waterfall of Benten.
Siukoden, the 108 Chinese heroes.
Examples of Chinese filial love, 14 double sheets.
Fuzokuko meiden, celebrated persons, 2 vols., 8vo. Kioto, 1840. In black and white.

Anderson cites some illustrated works from the period 1831 to 1856. Strange (plate vi.) gives a reproduction.

[1] Anderson Cat., p. 367; *idem., Japanese Wood-Engraving;* Strange, p. 52; Fenollosa Cat., Nos. 401–404; Cat. Burty, No. 299 ff., 242; Bing. Cat., No. 672 ff.

HIRÓSHIGE

BRIDGE IN RAIN

(One of the Hundred Views of Yedo)

BRITISH MUSEUM

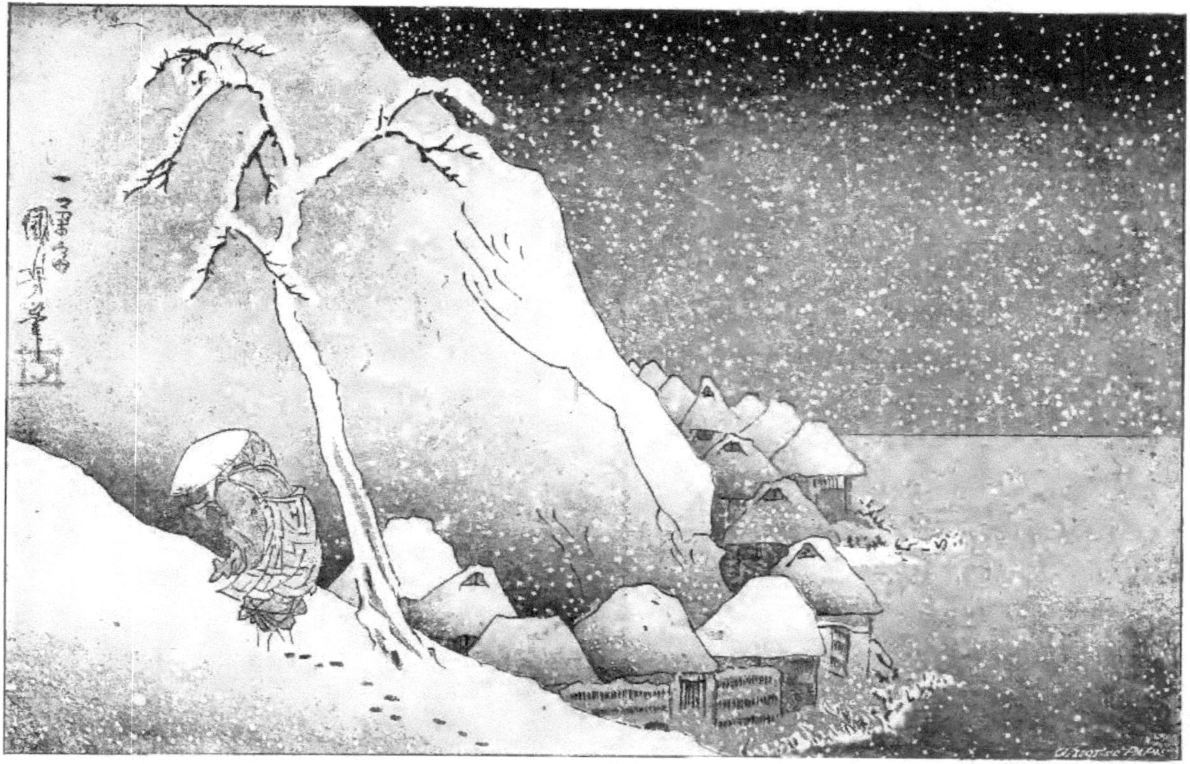

KUNIYOSHI: THE PRIEST NICHIRÉN, FOUNDER OF THE BUDDHIST SECT HÔKKA (THIRTEENTH CENTURY), IN THE SNOW. Pink dress, blackish-grey sky. Medium size.

3. Hiroshige.—Japanese wood-engraving, after it had advanced in the course of 150 years' development from the ornamental to the idealistic and then to the fantastic method of representation, dropped anchor in the haven of naturalism at the end of the first quarter of the nineteenth century. Landscape, which up to then had played but a minor part, now attained an independent significance; at the same time the representation of animals was also perfected. It is true that these efforts were no longer able to put fresh life into the national art, as the general conditions of the country had already assumed too unfavourable an aspect; but for us at all events, this closing era of Japanese wood-engraving has a particular interest on account of its close connection with more recent tendencies in Europe. In the centre of the development of landscape stands Hiroshige, side by side with his older contemporary Hokusai and his younger Kuniyoshi; he himself being probably the creator and in any case the perfecter of this new branch of art. What brings this last great master of Japan especially close to us is, besides this naturalism, the fact that he approaches more nearly to the European method than any other of his countrymen; in fact, he must have studied it extensively, though he does not go so far as to assimilate it completely. In his works the rules of perspective are to a certain extent observed; he aspires to correct composition, with the proper adjustment of foreground and background, and chooses his standpoint accordingly; more particularly, each of his designs has both inner unity and outward finality, in contrast with the Chinese style, which floats as it were in the air. Despite this close approach to European method of representation, however, he still remains completely Japanese; he sees nature with his own eyes, and by virtue of his poetic feeling and largeness of conception he discovers qualities in her which we had failed to appreciate: effects produced by the simplest means, a stretch of flat country, a few

tall tree-trunks, a steep mountain-slope, a glimpse of the coast-line far below our feet, or of a broad whirlpool, and the like. Not line in itself, not the contour of a mountain or tree, not the idyllic or heroic character of a locality; but the *mood* of a landscape seen in a certain light and from a certain point of view—this it is that moves the artist to fix it with his brush. It is in this sense, and not in regard to technique, which, on the contrary, is always of quite architectural precision, that one may speak of impressionism in the landscapes of Hiroshige and his contemporaries; and it is accordingly Hiroshige who, as he himself learnt from Europe, so in turn contributed most of any Japanese artist to the further development of European art.

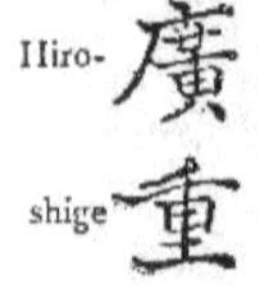

Hiroshige, also called Ichiriusai, was born in the year 1797 and died of cholera in 1858, at the age of sixty-one.[1] Having begun life as a member of the fire-brigade, he served his apprenticeship under Toyohiro and seems to have started his artistic career about 1820. His *Thirty-six Views of Fuji* are assigned to this year. At first he also produced representations of actors, of women, &c., as did the other artists; and he illustrated various books even into the thirties. From the middle of the twenties he doubtless devoted himself particularly to landscape, while also working zealously at animal renderings, principally birds and fishes. It is not certain when he produced his principal work in landscape, the *Fifty-three Stations of the Tokaido*, in oblong folio; but as we may rightly assume that his earliest landscapes are also his best, and these undoubtedly belong to his best, we shall certainly not go far wrong in dating them about 1830, remembering Hokusai's landscape work of the same time. He produced several similar sets of the *Tokaido*, particularly a small one, also one for which Kunisada drew the figures, &c. About the same time as the large *Tokaido* there

[1] Anderson Cat., p. 369; Strange, pp. 83, 110–112; Fenollosa Cat., Nos. 412–447; Bing Cat., No. 617 ff.; Cat. Burty, No. 379 ff., 705; Cat. Goncourt.

ROYAL PRINT ROOM, DRESDEN

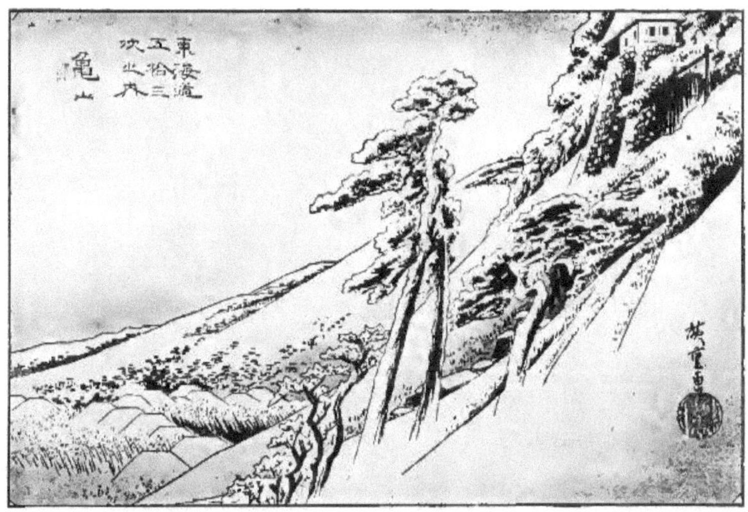

HIRÓSHIGE: TRAVELLERS ASCENDING A MOUNTAIN IN THE SNOW
Neighbourhood of Kameyáma from the Tokaidó. Medium size.

ROYAL PRINT ROOM, DRESDEN

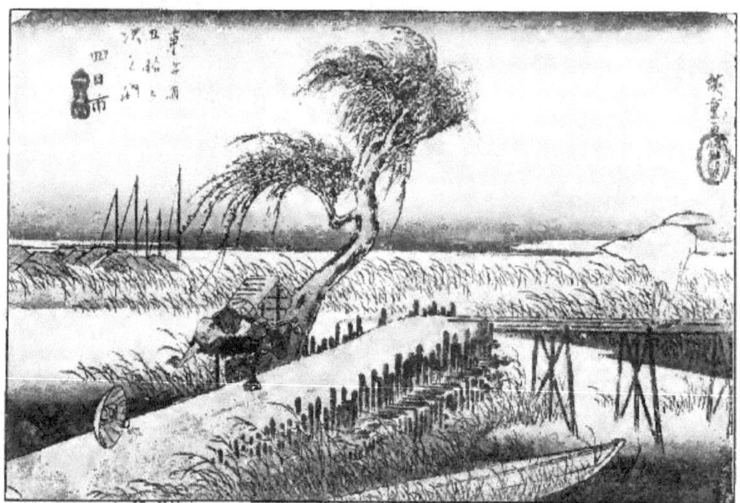

HIRÓSHIGE: THE HURRICANE. Travellers on a bridge. Neighbourhood of Yokkaičhi from the Tokaidó. Medium size.

probably appeared the *Kisokaido*, the sixty-nine stations of the inland road. As in all these sheets the localities are rendered with great conscientiousness, so the figures also, if somewhat summarily drawn, are still very correct and characteristic in their movements. Peculiar to Hiroshige are the landscapes of triptych form and compositions of very large kakemono-ye *format*.

Hiroshige is supposed to have lived in Yedo from 1846 to 1849, and in the fifties he acquired a special reputation for his views of this city. The change in his style, the transition from the broad and powerful manner of his earlier work to the sharper and more delicate drawing of his later years, but especially the change in his signature, from the Japanese cursive to the Chinese square style, has led some to suppose that there were two artists of the same name, a Hiroshige I. and a Hiroshige II., which latter did not become an artist until late in life, and sojourned in Yedo during the years above mentioned. Quite apart from the fact that Strange's statement of this view suffers from obscurity and contradictions, there is no need whatever for such a supposition, if we consider how gradually and through what intermediate stages the change in the artist's signature was made. Moreover, the change in Hiroshige's style is sufficiently explained both by his increasing age and the progress of the times.[1]

Although Hiroshige was never concerned, even in the good impressions of his works, to reproduce in colour the more delicate charms of nature and the multiplicity of her tones, yet he always strove by a few well-blended colours to effect a monumental impression. In the ordinary prints, on the contrary, the very ones that have found widest circulation, the complete decay of Japanese wood-engraving is already evident in the repellent effect of the crude and harsh aniline dyes employed. Repro-

[1] The discovery that there was actually a Hiroshige II. has been definitely made by Mr. J. S. Happer, but this younger Hiroshige is of very minor importance.

duction in Gonse, i. 88 (snow-scene), p. 108 (the same), and p. 298 (bridge in rain).

Single sheets:—

A girl awaking, large, about 1822, according to Fenollosa, No. 412.
Yoshitsune and the tengus (monsters with beaks like a bird's).
Dragon flying up into the air.
Parrot on tree, large, about 1840, according to Fenollosa, No. 429.
A hawk on a pine-branch, very large, about 1842.
Storks and rice-fields, large, about 1848.
White heron among the reeds.
White stork flying over iris.
Travellers on the highroad, large, about 1825, according to Fenollosa, No. 413.
Mountain landscape in snow, very large, 2 sheets, about 1843.
Yedo by night, large, about 1848.
The fox-fire, *i.e.* will-o'-the-wisps represented by foxes that are gathered by night around a large solitary tree; medium size, late.

Triptychs:—

Naruto rapids, near Kioto, 1846.
Beach in moonlight.
Mountains in snow, about 1850, excellent.
A gentleman in a plum orchard, in collaboration with Kunisada, beautiful, about 1850.

Illustrated works and series:—

The history of the 47 Ronin, 11 double sheets.
Kwannon reigenku, the 100 wonders of the Kwannon, 34 sheets, fol., in the upper part of each sheet a sanctuary of the Kwannon, in the lower a miracle; the latter by Kunisada.
Kioka hiaku ninitsishu, comic verses of the 100 poets, 8vo, light brush drawings in two tones.
Keisai ukiyo gwafu, 3 vols., 8vo, the two first by Keisai, the third by Hiroshige, in several tones.
Sohitsu gwafu, 3 small vols. of sketches.
A series of birds, 12 sheets.
A series of the fishes, oblong folio.

Vever Collection, Paris

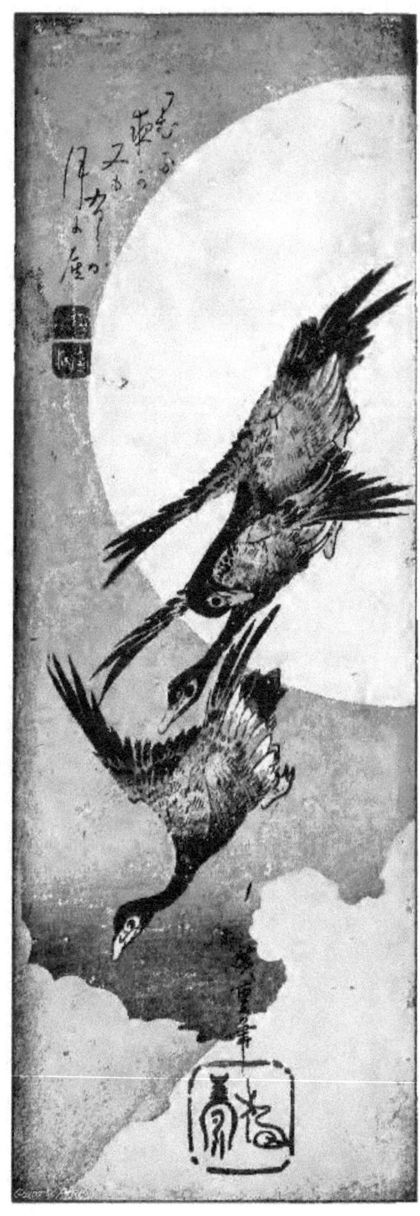

HIRÓSHIGE: Wild Geese at Full Moon. *Black and yellow.* Blue sky, melting into grey. Medium size.

Eight celebrated localities of the Omi province.
Eight views of Lake Biwa.
Eight views of Kanazawa.
Fuji no hiakuzu, 36 views of Fuji, 1820, mostly only in blue and green.
Tokaido fukei sogwa, views of the 53 stations of the Tokaido, 55 sheets, oblong folio.[1]
Tokaido, small, 1851 ?
Kinka shu, "Collection of beautiful flowers," views of Tokaido, 1858.
Kisokaido, views of the 69 stations of the mountain road from Kioto to Yedo in the interior, oblong folio.
Yehon Yedo miyage, "Souvenir of Yedo," scenes from Yedo, ten small volumes, about 1850. A hundred views of Yedo, 1856. Yamato jinbutsu, types and scenes from the streets of Yedo, 4 vols. 8vo, according to the four seasons. Yedo meisho hiakkei, the environs of Yedo, 120 sheets folio, one of his most beautiful series, 1820, 2 vols.
Kioto meisho.

Beside and after Hiroshige there remain but few masters to be mentioned. Yoshitoshi, the pupil of Kuniyoshi, is the last artist mentioned by Fenollosa (Catalogue, No. 447). Among his work is a hermit sitting in the snow under a roof of foliage, oblong. Kwa Setsu's well-known book of silhouettes, 33 sheets in folio (Burty, No. 716), dates from about 1840. Sugakudo distinguished himself by his representations of birds and flowers, the *Shiki no Kwacho*, Seasons of Birds and Flowers, which appeared in 1861 in folio (Burty Catalogue, No. 522). Lastly, Shofu Kiosai, the pupil of Hokusai, born in 1831, deserves to be mentioned on account of his humorous animal representations (see above p. 180; for a detailed account of him, see Brinckmann, 208 ff.). Anderson's *Japanese Wood-Engraving* (fig. 33) gives a reproduction from him. Shibata Zeshin is

[1] The ancient coast road from Kioto to Yedo, through Kanazawa, Odawara, Hakone, Nunazu, Shizuoka, Kakegawa, Hamamatsu, Okasaki, Miya, Minakuchi, &c.

N

also to be mentioned (Brinckmann, p. 212 f.). Renzan is the author of a large oblong surimono with a good and spirited representation of a tiger, about 1860.

Since the opening up of Japan to Europeans and the spread of anti-national views, the art of the country has entirely receded, and has preserved only a thin thread of purely technical tradition. It is not from petrifaction, as in China, but owing to the unfavourable conditions, the dissolution of the relationship which binds the artist to his public, that Japanese art has perished. There was no lack of talent that could have advanced art, just as well as in the eighteenth century; tentative steps had been taken toward new formations, towards extending the circle of representation and opening up new modes of conception. The public, however, which alone could have furthered such tendencies, was wanting. It contented itself with bad actor-likenesses and was amused by indifferent illustrations. Therefore it received the art that it deserved.

If we should ask, in conclusion, whether it is conceivable that the Japanese will ever again attain a characteristic and important art on the basis of the ancient traditions, the answer, it would seem, must be in the negative. Ancient culture and modern civilisation are mutually exclusive notions. Japan has chosen the latter path and indeed was probably bound to choose it, if she did not wish to be crushed out of existence in the strife of the nations. That choice, however, compelled her to renounce her past completely, more completely even than Europe, which has been spared such an abrupt transition. A new Japanese art would of necessity have to be founded on an entirely new basis, which could certainly not be that of European art.

BIBLIOGRAPHY

Adams, F. O. History of Japan. London, 1875.

Adeline, Jules. Le Chat d'après les Japonais. Rouen, 1893, 8vo. Deux eauxfortes et croquis lithographies (pp. 10 *et seq.*, Colour-prints).

Alcock, Sir Rutherford. Art and Art Industries in Japan (chaps. v. and vii.). London, 1878, 8vo, with illustrations.

Anderson, W. A History of Japanese Art. In Transactions of the Asiatic Society of Japan, vol. vii. (1879), pp. 339 *et seq.* See also Satow and Hawet.

Anderson, W. The Pictorial Arts of Japan, with a brief historical sketch of the associated arts, and some remarks upon the pictorial art of the Chinese and Koreans. London, 1886, 2 vols. large 4to, with illustrations.

Anderson, W. Descriptive and Historical Catalogue of a Collection of Japanese and Chinese Paintings in the British Museum. London, 1886, large 8vo, with illustrations.

Anderson, W. See Catalogue, Burlington Fine Arts Club.

Anderson, W. Japanese Wood Engraving. The Portfolio, No. 17, May 1895, with illustrations.

Appert, G., avec la collaboration de H. Kinoshita. Ancien Japon. Tokio, 1886, 16mo, with map (pp. 141 *et seq.*, List of Japanese Painters).

Audsley (George Ashdown). The Ornamental Arts of Japan. London, 1882, 2 vols. fol., with many illustrations (vol. i. pp. 36–41, Woodcutting and Wood-printing).

Bigelow, see Catalogue.

Bing, S. Le Japon Artistique. Documents d'art et d'industrie réunis par S. Bing. Paris, 1889–1891. 36 numbers, large 4to. Illustrations with explanatory text. Also in English.

Bing, see Catalogue, Exposition 1890.

Bing, S. The Art of Utamaro. In The Studio, iv. (1895), with illustrations.

Bing, S. La Vie et l'Œuvre de Hok'sai.—L'Art Japonais avant Hok'sai.—La Jeunesse de Hok'sai, Shunro. In La Revue Blanche, x. (1896), with illustrations.

Bing, S. La Gravure Japonaise. In L'Estampe et l'Affiche, April 15, 1897.

Binyon, R. Laurence. Painting in the Far East (chap. xvii. on Colour-Printing). London, 1908.

Bowes, James Lord. Japanese Marks and Seals. London, 1882, 8vo (pp. 219–270, Illuminated Manuscripts and Printed Books).

Bramsen, W. Japanese Chronological Tables (645–1873). With an introductory essay on Japanese Chronology and Calendars. Tokio, 1880. Small qu. fol.

Brinckmann, Justus. Kunst und Handwerk in Japan, vol. i. Berlin, 1889, 8vo (pp. 161 *et seq.*, Painting; pp. 215 *et seq.*, Printed Books and Reproduction).

Brinkley, Frank. The Art of Japan, 2 vols., with illustrations. Boston, Mass., 1901.

Burty, see Catalogue.

Catalogue, Burty Collection. Peintures et Estampes Japonaises. (Sale, March 16–20, 1891, Hôtel Drouot.) Paris, E. Leroux, 1891, large 8vo, with an introduction by E. Leroux.

Catalogue of the Exhibition of Works by Hokusai, from the collection of Dr. Bigelow, in the Boston Art Museum, with an introduction by Prof. Fenollosa.

Catalogue by W. Anderson, of Prints and Books illustrating the History of Engraving in Japan, exhibited in 1888 at the Burlington Fine Arts Club. London, 1888, 4to.

Catalogue de l'Exposition de la Gravure Japonaise à l'Ecole des Beaux Arts en 1890. Paris, large 8vo, with illustrations. Introduction by S. Bing.

Catalogue de la Collection d'Estampes Japonaises, pièces de choix provenant du cabinet de M. Théodore Duret. Vente à l'Hôtel Drouot, le 15 févr. 1897, 8vo.

Catalogue de Peintures et d'Estampes japonaises formant la collection d'un amateur, par E(rnest) L(eroux). (Sale, June 19–22, 1891, Hôtel Drouot.) Paris, E. Leroux, 1891, large 8vo.

Catalogue, Goncourt. Objets d'art japonaise et chinois, peintures, estampes, composant la Collection des Goncourts (Vente à l'Hôtel Drouot du 8 au 13 mars 1897). Paris, 1897, large 4to, with heliogravures of objets d'art (pp. 397 *et seq.*, Artists' Signatures).

Catalogue, Gookin Collection. Loan Exhibition of Japanese Colour-prints. Catalogue by F. W. Gookin. Chicago, 1908.

Catalogue de l'Exposition rétrospective de l'Art Japonais, par L. Gonse. Paris, 1883, large 8vo, illustrated.

Chassiron. Le Japon, la Chine et l'Inde. Paris, 1894, with illustrations after Hokusai.

Chesneau, E. L'Art Japonais. Paris, 1869, 8vo.

Chesneau, E. Le Japon à Paris. In the Gazette des Beaux Arts, ii. pér. 18 (1878), pp. 385 and 841 *et seq.*, with illustrations.

Deshayes, E. Considérations sur l'histoire de l'Estampe japonaise. In l'Art, July 1, 1893. Paris, fol.

Dickins, F. V. Fugaku hiyaku kai; or, A Hundred Views of Fuji (Fusiyama), by Hokusai. Prefaces with translations from the Japanese, and descriptions of the plates by F. V. Dickins. London, 1880, 3 vols. of illustrations and 1 vol. of text, 8vo.

Documents décoratifs japonais tirés des Estampes et Livres anciens de la Collection C. Gillot. Paris, 1894 *et seq.*, large 8vo. In 8 series, each of 8 parts at 1 franc 50 cents.

Dresser. Japan, its Art and Art Manufacturers. London, 1882.

Duret, Théodore. L'Art Japonais; Hokusai. In the Gazette des Beaux Arts, 1882, ii. pp. 118 *et seq.*, 300 *et seq.*, with illustration. Also printed separately, and reprinted in the author's Critique d'Avant-garde. Paris, 1885, 8vo.

Duret, Théodore. Livres et Albums illustrés du Japon, réunis et catalogués par Théodore Duret, 8vo. Paris, 1900.

Duret, Théodore, see also Catalogue.

Exhibition of Japanese Colour-Prints. Dresden, Royal Print Room. July–September 1897. Dresden, 8vo, two illustrations.

Fenollosa, Ernest F. Review of the chapter on Painting in Gonse's "L'Art Japonais." Yokohama, 35 pp., 8vo, and later at Boston, 1885, pp. 54, 8vo.

Fenollosa, Ernest F. The Pictorial Art of Japan (Review of Anderson's "Pictorial Art of Japan"). In Blackwood's Edinburgh Magazine, vol. 141 (1887), pp. 281–290.

Fenollosa, E. F. The Masters of Ukioye (*sic*). Catalogue of the Exhibition held in New York, January 1896, 8vo.

Fenollosa. See also Catalogue, Bigelow.

Geffroy, Gustave. La Vie Artistique, 1ère série. Paris, 1892, 16mo (pp. 85–135; xii., Maîtres Japonais: 1. Les Paysagistes. 2. Le Japon à l'Ecole des Beaux-Arts. 3. Utamaro. 4. Hokousai. 5. Hokousai à Londres. 6. A propos de la Vente Burty).

Gierke, Prof. Dr. H. Japanische Malereien aus dem Besitz des Prof. Dr. H. Gierke zu Breslau. Kunstgewerbemuseum, Berlin, 2nd special exhibition. Oct. 24–Dec. 15, 1882. Berlin, 1882, small 8vo.

Gierke, H. Japanische Malerei. In Watermann's Monatshefte. May 1883.

Gillot. See under Documents.

Goncourt, Edmond de. La Maison d'un Artiste. Paris, 1881, 2 vols. 8vo (vol. i. pp. 192–239, Les Albums japonais; vol. ii. pp. 350–359, Les Kakémonos).

Goncourt, Edmond de. Outamaro. Le Peintre des Maisons Vertes. Paris, 1891, 8vo.

Goncourt, Edmond de. Hokousai; ses albums traitant de la peinture et du dessein, avec ses préfaces. In the Gazette des Beaux Arts, iii. pér. vol. xiv. (1895), pp. 441 *et seq.*

Goncourt, Edmond de. Hokousai. Paris, 1896, 8vo, with a portrait of Hokusai at the age of eighty, by his daughter Oyei.

Goncourt, see also under Catalogue.

Gonse, Louis, L'Art japonais. Paris, 1883, 2 vols. large 4to. Profusely illustrated (vol. i., Painting and Wood-Engraving).

Gonse, Louis. L'Art japonais. Paris, 1883, 18mo, illustrated.

Gonse, Louis, see also under Catalogue.

Gookin. See under Catalogue.

Gowland, W., late of the Imperial Mint, Osaka. The Naturalistic Art of Japan. In Transactions and Proceedings of the Japan Society, i. 73–110. London, 1892.

Griffith, W. Elliot. The Corean Origin of Japanese Art. In The Century Magazine, December 1886.

Guide to the Chinese and Japanese Illustrated Books exhibited in the King's Library, British Museum. 1887, 8vo.

Guimet, Emile. Promenades japonaises, vol. ii. Tokio, Nikko. Paris, 1880, 4to, with drawings by Félix Régamey (pp. 175–192, dealing more especially with Kiosai).

Hayashi, T. Dessins, Estampes, Livres illustrés du Japon, réunis par T. Hayashi. Vente 2–6 juin 1902, 8vo. Paris, 1902.

Hirth, Frdr. Über fremde Einflüsse in der chinesischen Kunst. Munich and Leipzig, 1896, 8vo (pp. 45 *et seq.*).

Histoire de l'Art du Japan, fol. Paris, 1900. Commission impériale du Japon à l'Exposition Universelle de Paris, 1900.

Huebner, Baron de. Promenade autour du Monde, 1871. Paris, 1873, 8vo (ii. 118–127, Peinture).

Huish, Marcus B. Japan and its Art, London, 1889; 2nd edition, 1892, 8vo (pp. 242 *et seq.*, Xylography).

Japanese Wood-cutting and Wood-cut Printing (from Report of U.S. National Museum), 8vo. Washington, 1894.

Japanese Books and Albums of Prints in Colour in the National Art Library, South Kensington (compiled by Mr. Edward F. Strange). London, 1893, 8vo.

Japanese Colour-Prints. New York, W. H. Ketcham, 1895, 8vo.

Japon artistique et littéraire. See Le Blanc du Vernet.

Koehler, S. R. See Tokuno.

Kokkwa, Tokio, 1890 *et seq.*, fol. Reproductions of works of art, with explanatory text in Japanese and in English.

Le Blanc du Vernet. Le Japon artistique et litteraire. Paris, 1879, 16mo.

Le Blanc du Vernet. L'Art japonais. In L'Art, 1880 (i. p. 286; ii. pp. 132, 250; iii. p. 229).

Leighton, J. On Japanese Art. A Discourse. London, 1863, fol., illustrated.

Leroux, E. See under Catalogue.

Madsen, Karl. Japansk Malerkunst. Kopenhagen, 1885. Illustrated.

Matsumura, J. Nippon skokubutsumeii, or Nomenclature of Japanese Plants in Latin, Japanese, and Chinese. Supervised by R. Yatabe. Tokio, 1884. 8vo.

Migeon, Gaston. Chefs d'œuvre d'Art japonais. Paris, 1905. Illustrated.

Migeon, Gaston. Au Japon. Paris, 1908. English translation. London, 1908, 16mo, illustrated.

Morse, Edward S. Notes on Hokusai. In the American Art Review, vol. i. (1880), pp. 145 *et seq.*, illustrated.

Morse, Edward S. Japanese Homes and their Surroundings. New York, 1889, 8vo, illustrated.

Münsterberg, Oskar. Japanische Kunst und japanisches Land. Leipzig, 1896, 8vo, illustrated.

Muther, Richard. Geschichte der Malerei im xix. Jahrhundert (vol. ii. pp. 583 *et seq.*, chap. xxx., ii. Die Japaner). Munich, 1893, large 8vo, illustrated.

Nordenskiöld. See Rosny.

Okakura, Kakuzo. Ideals of the East, with special reference to the Arts of Japan. London, 1903.

Pagès, Léon. Bibliographie japonaise ou Catalogue des ouvrages relatifs au Japon qui ont été publiés depuis le xv. siècle jusqu'à nos jours. Paris, 1859.

Reed, Sir Edward J. Japan, its History, Traditions, and Religions. London, 1880, 2 vols. 8vo, illustrated (chap. iv., Drawing and Painting).

Régamey, Félix. Le Japon Pratique. Paris. Hetzel, N.D. (*c.* 1890). 8vo. With 100 drawings by the author (pp. 170–175, Les Images, Gravure, Impression).

Renan, Ary. L'Art Japonais. Paris, 1884.

Rosny, Léon de. Catalogue de la Bibliothèque Japonaise de Nordenskiöld à la Bibliothèque Royale de Stockholm. Paris, 1883, 8vo.

Satow, Ernest. On the Early History of Printing in Japan. In Transactions of the Asiatic Society of Japan, vol. x. (1881), pp. 48-83. Further notes on movable types in Korea, and early Japanese printed books. Ibid., p. 252.

Satow, Ernest, and Lt. A. G. S. Hawet. A Handbook for Travellers in Central and Northern Japan. 2nd edition, London, 1884, 8vo. Section on Pictorial Art, pp. 92–100, by W. A[nderson].

Strange, Edward F. Japanese Illustration. A History of the Arts of Wood-cutting and Colour-printing in Japan. London, 1897, 8vo, illustrated.

Strange, E. F. See Japanese Books.

Tajima. Select Relics of Japanese Art. Periodical, published in Japan, with text in Japanese and in English.

Tasset, Jacques. Etudes sur la Gravure Japonaise. In Mémoires de la Société Sinico-Japonaise, vol. x. (1891), pp. 51–87. Paris, 8vo.

Tei-San. Notes sur l'Art Japonais (Mercure de France, 1905–1906).

Tokuno, T. Japanese Wood-cutting and Wood-cut Printing; edited by S. R. Koehler, Washington (Smithsonian Institute), 1894. 8vo. Tokuno was the Head of the Department for Wood-engraving and Printing in the Japanese Ministry of Finance.

Transactions of the Asiatic Society of Japan. Yokohama, 1872 *et seq.* 8vo.

Wenckstern, Fr. von. A Bibliography of the Japanese Empire. Leyden and London, 1895. 8vo (pp. 165 *et seq.*, Pictorial Arts).

Wyzewa, T. de. La Peinture japonaise. Revue des deux Mondes, July 1, 1890. Reprinted in Les grands Peintres de l'Espagne, &c. Paris, 1891.

Yatabe. See Matsumura.

ALPHABETICAL LIST OF THE SIGNS WHICH COMPOSE THE NAMES OF THE MOST IMPORTANT JAPANESE ARTISTS

(The names of the artists from which these signs are taken appear in brackets. The cross-references denote that a sign has two different pronunciations.)

馬 ba (Hokuba)

文 bun (Bunchō)

珍 chin (Chinchō)

重 chō (Chinchō) / see shige

調 chō (Bunchō)

潮 chō (Shunchō)

岳 gaku (Gakutei)

川 gawa (Utagawa) / see kawa

羽 hane (Hanegawa)

春 haru (Harunobu) / see shun

廣 hiro (Kiyohiro)

菱 hishi (Hishikawa)

北 hoku (Hokusaï) / see kita

爲 i (Iitsu)

居 i (Torii)

石 ishi (Ishikawa)

一 itsu (Iitsu)

葛 katsu (Katsushika)

勝 katsu (Katsukawa)

川 kawa (Hishikawa) / see gawa

溪 kei (Keisai)

木 ki (Suzuki)

菊 kiku (Kikugawa)

北 kita (Kitao) / see hoku

清 kiyo (Kiyonobu)

湖 ko (Koriusai)

國 kuni (Morikuni)

満 man (Shumman) / see mitsu

麿 maro (Utamaro)

政 masa (Masanobu)

倍 masu (Kiyomasu)

満 mitsu (Kiyomitsu) / see man

守 mori (Morikuni)

師 moro (Moronóbu)

村 mura (Okumura)

長 naga (Shigenaga)

西 nishi (Nishimura)

宣 nobu (Moronobu)

信 nobu (Kiyonobu)

尾 o (Kitao)

奥 oku (Okumura)

樂 raku (Sharaku)

理 ri (Sōri)

龍 riu (Koriusai)

朗 rō (Shunrō)

貞 sada (Kunisada)

齋 sai (Koriusai)

扇 sen (Shunsen)

泉 sen (Yeisen)

寫 sha (Sharaku)

之 shi (Yeishi)

重 shige (Shigenaga)
see chō

飾 shika (Katsushika)

昌 shō (Yeishō)

章 shō (Shunshō)

春 shun (Shunshō)
see haru

俊 shun (Shumman)

宗 sō (Sōri)

鈴 suzu (Suzuki)

橘 tachibana (T. Morikuni)

戴 tai (Taito)

斗 to (Taito)

祐 suke (Sukenobu)

鳥 tori (Torii)

豊 toyo (Toyonobu)

歌 uta (Utagawa)

英 yei (Shunyei)

榮 yei (Yeishi)

美 yoshi (Masayoshi)

芳 yoshi (Kuniyoshi)

喜 yoshi (Nagayoshi)

山 zan (Yeizan)

INDEX

Printed by BALLANTYNE & COMPANY LIMITED
At the BALLANTYNE PRESS
LONDON

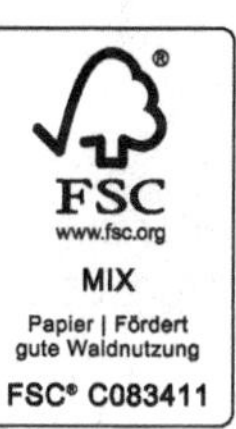

Zeitfracht Medien GmbH
Ferdinand-Jühlke-Straße 7
99095 Erfurt, Deutschland
produktsicherheit@kolibri360.de